Studies in

Ramesh K. Srivastava's Short Stories

Studies in

Ramesh K. Srivastava's Short Stories

A Collection of Critical Articles

Edited by

Barinder K. Sharma

AUTHORSPRESS

Worldwide Circulation through Authorspress Global Network
First Published in 2022
by
Authorspress
Q-2A Hauz Khas Enclave, New Delhi-110 016 (India)
Phone: (0) 9818049852
E-mail: authorspressgroup@gmail.com
Website: www.authorspressbooks.com

Studies in Ramesh K. Srivastava's Short Stories:
A Collection of Critical Articles
ISBN 978-93-91314-41-5

Printed in India at Kensington Press

Acknowledgements

Grateful acknowledgement is due to Dr Ramesh K. Srivastava and Prestige Books, New Delhi, for "Authors Note," retitled as "My Idea of a Short Story"; to Smita Das and *MIT International Journal of English Language and Literature* for "Theory and Practice of Ramesh K. Srivastava's Short Story"; to Dr Atma Ram and Bahri Publications, New Delhi, for "R. K. Srivastava: A Writer of Simple Ways"; to Neeta Maini and B. R. Publishing Corporation, New Delhi, for "Ramesh K. Srivastava as a Short Story Writer"; to Smita Das and *Writers Editors Critics: An International Biannual Refereed Journal of English Language and Literature* for "Human-Animal Relationship in Ramesh K. Srivastava's Short Stories" and "Suppression and Revolt of Women in Ramesh K. Srivastava's Short Stories"; to Dr Usha Bande and ABS Publications, Jalandhar, for "Loving Vignettes – Mother Figure in Ramesh K. Srivastava's Short Stories"; to Dr Leela Kanal and *International Journal of Multicultural Literature* for "East-West Encounter in Ramesh K. Srivastava's Short Stories"; to Swati Srivastava and Surabhi Publications, Jaipur for "Wit and Humour in the Works of Ramesh K. Srivastava"; to Dr Priyanka Agrawal, Dr Sadhana Agrawal and *New Man International Journal of Multidisciplinary Studies* for "Sufferings of Women in Ramesh K. Srivastava's Short Stories"; to Dr Manisha Sharma and *Indian Scholar: An International Multidisciplinary Research e-Journal* for "Irony, Humour and Satire in Ramesh K. Srivastava's 'Cooperative Colony'"; to Dr Barinder K. Sharma and *International Journal of Multicultural Literature* for "Symbolism in Ramesh K. Srivastava's *Cooperative Colony: Stories* and *Masks and Men: Stories";* to Dr Shipra G. Vashishtha and *International Journal of Multicultural Literature* for "Masks and Masqueraders in Ramesh K. Srivastava's Short Stories"; to Dr Barinder K. Sharma and *Poetcrit: An International Biannual Refereed Journal of Literary Criticism and Contemporary Poetry* for "Ramesh K. Srivastava's 'Century': A Study"; to Smita Das and *Illuminati: A Transnational Journal of Literature, Language and Culture Studies* for "Ramesh K. Srivastava's 'Games They

Play': A Study"; to Dr Lata Mishra and *Virtuoso: A Refereed Transnational Bi-Annual Journal of Language and Literature in English* for "Narrative as Discourse: A Study of Ramesh K. Srivastava's *Under the Lamp and Other Stories";* to Dr Shipra G. Vashishtha and *Writers Editors Critics: An International Biannual Refereed Journal of English Language and Literature* for "Ramesh K. Srivastava's 'Under the Lamp': A Study"; to Dr Leela Kanal and *Illuminati: A Transnational Journal of Literature, Language and Culture Studies* for "Conflict and Resolution: A Study of Srivastava's *A Christmas Gift and Other Stories";* to Dr Priyanka Agrawal, Dr Sadhana Agrawal and *Chronicle of Humanities and Culture Studies* for "Freedom of Women in K. S. Duggal's 'Butterfly' and Ramesh K. Srivastava's 'The Prodigal Returns'"; to Dr Gurdeep Tripathi and *International Journal of Multicultural Literature* for "Dream and Reality in Ramesh K. Srivastava's 'Road Not Taken'"; to Dr Gurdeep Tripathi and *Writers Editors Critics: An International Biannual Refereed Journal of English Language and Literature* for "Love and Exploitation in Ramesh K. Srivastava's *Road Not Taken and Other Stories*"; to Dr Y. Joy and *The Critical Endeavour* for "Ramesh K. Srivastava in Conversation with Y. Joy"; to Smita Das and *Illuminati: A Transnational Journal of Literature, Language and Cultural Studies* for "A Good Short Story is a Frozen Moment of Life Revealed through a Sequence of Words" now retitled as "Looking Behind his Short Stories: An Interview with Ramesh K. Srivastava."

Barinder K. Sharma

Preface

Ramesh K. Srivastava is a gifted writer of short stories. In his childhood, he took interest in listening to the stories from the *Ramayana* and the *Mahabharata, Panchatantra,* Akbar and Birbal. Though born in a village where good educational facilities beyond the Primary School did not exist, he showed his clear inclination towards reading something or the other. Even though his father had strictly forbidden him from reading fiction which, for him, was synonymous with lies, Srivastava did read Hindi fiction at the first available opportunity in B.A. Part I in 1955. As a voracious reader, he completed one Hindi novel a day for three months, which not only enriched his knowledge of Hindi language and literature, but bred in him a vague inner feeling that he too could write some creative pieces.

In September-October 1955, he lost one rupee which was of substantial value at that time. Afraid of being scolded by his elder cousin-cum-guardian as well as his father, he remained terribly upset for two days and could not have a good sleep. It was in this state that he ventured to write a short story "*Ek Rupaya*" [one rupee] in Hindi which was published in the local paper *Dainik Jagaran* of Jhansi (U.P.). The day the story got published, his friends and class fellows congratulated him, considering it as the evidence of a creative writer in infancy. Encouraged by the publication, Srivastava published twenty short stories in Hindi during his two-year B.A. degree course work in 1955-57.

Srivastava suspended his creative writing from 1957 onwards for other pressing activities. He took up a job in the Cooperative Society in Jhansi, passed his M.A. (English) examination from the University of Saugar, took up a job in Government Colleges, Gwalior, competed for a Fulbright Fellowship and was awarded one in 1969, studied for and was awarded a Ph.D. degree by the University of Utah, Salt Lake City, Utah (U.S.A.) in August 1972, and took up a job in Guru Nanak Dev University, Amritsar (Punjab) in September 1972.

Srivastava had published his last story in Hindi in June 1957. Since he had completed his education and had got a job in the university, he was now free from any compulsive academic requirements. During the long gap of 16 years, he had lost his command over Hindi but after his stay in the U.S. for over three years, he had developed good command over English. Hence from 1972 onwards he began to publish short stories in English in various popular magazines and newspapers, such as, *Caravan, Woman's Era, Eve's Weekly, Thought, The Tribune, the Indian Express* and *the Pioneer,* among others. When the number of published short stories had reached 20, they were anthologised in three volumes, namely, *Love and Animality: Stories* [1984], *Cooperative Colony: Stories* [1985] and *Masks and Men: Stories* [1986]. The anthologies received good reviews. K. V. Chacko, reviewing *Love and Animality: Stories,* wrote: "Srivastava is a gifted writer of stories who knows the tricks of his trade well – an endearing narrative, nearly impeccable language and appropriate technique to deliver an interesting theme into the reader's lap as a short story." Sulekha Sharma praised "Century" of *Cooperative Colony: Stories* "for the fine flow of language, spontaneous charm and controlled climax."

In 1984-85, Srivastava was awarded a Senior Fulbright Fellowship for advanced study on Henry David Thoreau at Boston, Massachusetts (U.S.A). By this time, he had also completed his first novel *Neema* which was to be serialised in *The Sunday Tribune* but could not be materialised because of the conspiracy of some of his jealous colleagues.

Srivastava's *Games They Play and Other Stories* is the 4th collection of short stories which was published in 1989. It had good reviews. Jaidev in *Indian Book Chronicle* considered its story "Games They Play" a "superb performance" and "a poignant classical tragedy." In 1993, his fifth collection of short stories came out as *Under the Lamp: Stories.* Since the Punjab had a reign of terrorism during 1980's and 1990's, some of his stories deal with this theme. Usha Bande in *Indian Book Chronicle* considered the story "Terrorism in the Kitchen" as depicting "the fractured psyche of the Punjab." Suresh C. Verma considered the story "a great satire on the waywardness of the people in stress-ridden Punjab."

Since Srivastava's act of writing short stories was taken by his university colleagues as his incompetence in writing critical books and articles, he accepted it as a challenge, suspended his creative writing and published a number of critical books and articles, such as, *Hemingway and his For Whom the Bell Tolls* [1980], *Perspectives on Bhabani Bhattacharya* [1982], *Perspectives on Anita Desai* [1984], *Six Indian Novelists in English* [1987], *Critical Studies in English and American Literature* [1993], *Symbolism in Indian Fiction in English* [1997], *The Novels of Kamala Markandaya: A Critical Study* [1998], *Ten Indian Writers in English* [2005], and *Wit and Humor in Indian English Literature* [2008].

Throughout the 1980's and 1990's, Srivastava had a series of problems and court cases in the university because of his jealous colleagues. In June 2000, he retired from Guru Nanak Dev University, Amritsar and joined as the Director, Institute of Languages, Bundelkhand University, Jhansi. He was awarded the University Grants Commission Emeritus Fellowship during 2003-2005. In 2008, he left Bundelkhand University and joined S.R. Group of Institutions, Ambabai, Jhansi (U.P.) where he continues to work even now.

In recognition of his scholarship and creative writing, Srivastava was chosen as the President of All-India English Teachers Conference held at Shri Shivaji Arts and Commerce College, Amravati (Maharastra) in December 2009. In 2011, Srivastava's second novel *Coils of the Serpent* was published.

In December 2012, the Association for English studies in India honored him by conferring the "AESI Senior Delegate Award 2012" at Sardar Patel University, Vallabh Vidyanagar (Gujarat). In 2014, his collection of essays was published in an anthology titled *Read, Write and Teach: Essays on Learning to Live Together*. In 2014, the Management of S. R. Group of Institutions, Ambabai, Jhansi honored him for his "Special contribution in Education and Institutional Development."

In 2015, his sixth collection of stories – *A Christmas Gift and Other Stories* – was published. Having twenty-eight short stories, it had some excellent reviews. Prabha Shankar Dwivedi compared the stories to Neo-classical writings which "instruct and delight, carrying the inbuilt piercing satirical intentions in order to motivate the reader for the corrective measures."

In 2016, Smita Das published a book-length study of the author titled *Ramesh K. Srivastava: Man and his Work – a Collection of Critical*

Articles. It has an exhaustive introduction to the writer's life and his works. The book is divided into four sections: Introductory, Short Stories, Novels and Interviews.

In 2017, the Researchers Association, Odisha, Cuttack, honored Srivastava for his contribution to English Language and Literature. The same year his autobiography *My Father's Bad Boy* was published. It is a mine of his lifelong activities and experiences out of which his novels and short stories have been churned out.

In 2018, Srivastava's seventh collection of short stories – *Road Not Taken and Other Stories* – was published. It has 20 short stories. The collection was received well. Binod Mishra called the book "a subtle example of artistic excellence blended with crtical insight." Smita Das opined that each story "is so well-constructed, so artistically chiseled and polished that it becomes a unique artistic piece capable of sending a powerful message to the society."

On 23rd April 2018, Srivastava was honored by Bundelkhand University, Jhansi, "in recognition of his scholarship and valuable contributions to English Language and Literature." Meanwhile, Dr Y. Joy received his Ph.D. degree on "The Short Stories of Ramesh K. Srivastava" from Mahatma Gandhi University, Kottayam (Kerala). Dr Priyanka Agrawal was also awarded a Ph.D. degree on the "Socio-Cultural Aspects in the Works of Ramesh K. Srivastava and K. S. Duggal" from Jiwaji University, Gwalior (M.P.).

In 2020, Dr Shipra G. Vashishtha of Bundelkhand University, Jhansi published a book titled *The Recognition of Ramesh K. Srivastava: A Collection of Book Reviews on his Creative Writing*. It is a collection of book reviews on his 11 works in the field of creative writing. In mid-2021, Srivastava sent a typescript of eighth collection of short stories titled *A Man of Gold and Other Stories* which has been published now.

The present collection of critical papers is being brought out to help such desirous teachers, researchers and students who wish to do intensive study of the works of the author. It is hoped that the anthology will be of immense help to teachers and researchers who wish to pursue some work on the author and his writings.

Barinder K. Sharma
Associate Professor of English
Baring Union Christian College,
BATALA (Punjab) 143 505

Contents

CHAPTER 1

My Idea of a Short Story

Ramesh K. Srivastava

A short story is an artistic portrayal of ever-unfolding mysteries of human existence. It is a tiny mirror that intensely reflects a focused fragment of vast moving kaleidoscope of life that each day, each moment passes by us in its new yet recognisable ever-changing patterns and combinations. It is a frozen moment of life, carrying in it the seeds of perennial truths. It reveals in a flash an image of hitherto unexplored aspect of life fleeing each moment before us. A good short story is like a supply of fresh air that makes the human life delightful, meaningful and no less healthy. It is not, as is occasionally made out to be, an artistic conglomeration of unusual characters, unfamiliar landscapes and witty dialogues to titillate and tickle one's fancy but a literary creation that shows to the reader a patch of greenery here or a bunch of flowers there which to the accustomed eyes had been a piece of uninviting desert land. It must also not be taken merely as a means of entertainment, a traveling companion or a puzzling literary experiment in which a moment is disproportionately stretched and each word of which sends the reader's brain reeling to history, geography and mythology of distant lands.

Whereas the short story would lose its place in serious literature if fashioned solely as a means of modem entertainment, it would also jeopardise its coveted popularity when made out as a complicated and puzzling literary creation. A highly complex and unintelligible story may tease and please an intelligent reader by his sense of discovering something not easily decipherable but confuses an average reader who, suffering from the feeling of belonging to a lower class, grudgingly shares the royal feast albeit not with the same ease and care freeness with which the high-perched Brahmins would do. Hence unconsciously or consciously, the writer is and must be influenced and his stories molded by the type of readers available for him. To wholly disregard them while carving and whittling a literary piece would be as inappropriate as to play the Western classical music to rickshaw-wallahs.

A fine short story is the joint-product of the heart and the head. It originates from an inspiring idea, an appealing incident, a dramatic-situation, a memorable character or an unforgettable experience. The seed of the story sprouts in the writer's head. It grows and swells to take the shape of a story carrying around it a mass of herbage, like a foetus in amniotic fluid, which protects as well as stunts, and which has to be cleared before its unfurled leaves and its extending branches could assert its separate entity. The fully-grown, well-trimmed plant of the story then stands majestically before the world, concealing the hand that had given it a loving care or oblivious of the seed that had given rise to the creation.

In their earliest forms, the Indian tales date back to the interpolated stories in the *Ramayana* and the *Mahabharata*, the fables in *Panchatantra*, the tales of *Betal*, and the myths and legends abounding in the *Puranas*, as also in ancient Indian literatures of various languages. These too embody enriched moments of life even if paraded in outlandish garbs. They contain the essence of life. The short prose narrative in its present form was pioneered and popularised by the Americans. The basic difference between the short stories as they existed in the past and those we have today is both in their execution and in the intention of their creator. The main thrust of the earliest stories, both Indian and European, was usually religious, moral and reformative but rarely literary. In the modern times, the short stories, some of which could be myths and legends rewritten, have some literary value even if with the undercurrents of moralistic and reformative concerns.

With the shrinking boundaries of the world and with the increasing complexity of modern times, the nature of the short story has also changed considerably. It is no longer a tale relating to the exploits and adventures of gods and goddesses, fairies and witches, kings and queens, and birds and animals told by a grandmother to lull her children to sleep or to sweeten the bitterness of life; instead, it is a powerful and effective means of portraying prismatic reality of our time. Seen from different angles, the short story assumes varied forms, evolving out of different viewpoints, structures and narrative techniques.

Whatever the type of the story, a prerequisite to its being appreciated is that it must be readable. With this end in view, the story must be short, interesting and in a tone that creates a harmonious relationship between the writer and the reader. An appetite, like the one needed to enjoy a hearty meal, has to be created in the reader to see something new in what appears to be the oft-trodden ground, and then to sustain it with legitimate artistic means, such as suspense, humor and irony. An element of wonder originating from such a discovery or from the change of fortunes associated with fairy tales can also have a similar function.

A short story, for Poe, is a classic in miniature with precision-made parts and singleness of effect, the latter being above everything else in the world to which every character, incident, sentence and every word must contribute. The singleness of effect depends largely on the end of the story which, like that of a play, must have a resolution or a sting so as to leave an unambiguous impact on the reader.

The length of the short story is to be determined not by the number of pages or by the duration in which it is read but by its capacity to hold the reader's interest. To talk of the length of the story in terms of pages is to talk of a certain number of people who might make a good company. At times an interesting story read in a desolate place can give the reader better company than would so a bunch of gloomy-faced people in a crowded railway compartment. The story should not be too long to permit unavoidable interruptions and to encroach upon the areas of the novella or the novel. It would have a full impact only if it is short enough to be viewed in totality like the painting of an entire human figure rather than a microscopic scrutiny of his face, his torso or his legs at different times. Indeed, a good impact is like a powerful slap with all fingers and palm striking together which would not be so were they to strike separately. The questions of impact and of length become more relevant for short stories meant for popular magazines, usually devoured by the traveling or relaxing people who invariably prefer short and interesting ones. The story too brief, on the other hand, may have the effect of a cracker's explosion that unnerves one for a moment and then is forgotten. In fact each organic part of the story, as of a human being, is beautiful not in itself but in relation with others. All parts must be so closely woven that nothing can be added, nothing taken away. Hence the story, like a good sculpture, is not a lifeless assemblage but a receptacle of the artist's vision and soul.

The greatness of the short story writer consists not in creating a memorable menagerie but in painting a realistic picture of life. In order to draw the image of a person, reconstruct an episode, create a scene of terror, highlight the irony of a situation or to paint a personified passion, a writer must select appropriate tools. A beggar in the street is a despicable thing one avoids but a beggar in the story can be a memorable pathetic character, melting all the resistance of the reader till softer feelings gush forth from us. Of course, there are no rules to suggest how all this is to be done perfectly; which characters and incidents to choose and which to reject; what to write and how much to be left to the reader's imagination. Such questions are better left to the artist.

The question of probability and improbability in a fictional work remains a matter of serious concern for critics who would like every word or action to be tested on a Richter scale of their imagination, disregarding the fact that a writer does not buy his material sifted and cleansed of improbable elements from some laboratory but selects it in its crude form directly or vicariously from the life itself. Some elements of improbability liable to be found in such material should not cause undue alarm. One has to pick up any standard newspaper to see that quite a few incidents reported in it are far from probable; for an incident or a character becomes worthy of being reported only when, by being unusual, it touches the fringes of improbability. What one has to avoid are impossibilities – occurrences of unnatural feats and miracles. To superimpose divine exploits on mortals is to encroach in the area of fantasy and fairyland which might be a staple diet for Indian movies and television serials but must be kept out of the short story.

As incidents ought to be probable, characters must be from real life. Some characters are so inimitable that they haunt the memory long after the short story is over. To me the characters many times come with the same intensity as do incidents and situations. Once a character comes before my eyes, small things altogether unconnected crowd my imagination and gravitate meaningfully to the aid of its portrayal. Little by little, a character is formed or transformed till he becomes a perfect presentable creature. I have often looked around in astonishment how diversified the world really is without having two people exactly alike in personality or mental make-up. It has too some beings with the human part missing who, like Shantanu's six sons, would better have been drowned into the Ganges without causing any loss to the society. A couple of such wicked people have troubled me personally for a long time, tried to disturb my tranquility and block the flow of my pen, but I have persevered. Some mysterious power urges me to go on. A folk saying heard in my childhood remains meaningfully embedded in my memory: the dogs bark but the elephant goes on.

Creative imagination does not trudge along a predetermined track, nor can it be shackled by administrative controls. The short story writer is a man of imagination, of moods, and is the sole arbiter of when to write and on what. No subject matter can restrict the writer's vision. He writes of people largely from personal experience, not from mere imagination. A writer can many times be like an experienced village *vaidya* who holds a wrist, feels the pulse and diagnoses the disease in an instant what many physicians with a series of tests on ultra-modern machines fail to find out. The writer knows exactly which character in a given situation will behave in a particular way. One does not have to devote pages upon pages of psychological analysis of a character; a word, a phrase, even a glint in the eye is enough to reveal his intentions. Just one grain can show whether the rice is cooked.

Dialogues in Indian fiction in English have occasionally been a problem, particularly when concerned with non-English-speaking people. Having been born and brought up in a village, I saw the elderly people conversing effortlessly in a native dialect which was pictorial, idiomatic and alive. It throbbed with life and wisdom. These dialogues remain my priceless possession even today. I have often endeavored to re-create them in English, avoiding the oddity which a literal translation often creates. In order to see that the dialogues are natural, I have leaned my ears in many a secret place, listened to women talking about almost nothing for hours together, to the children who delightfully exchange idiocies as pearls of profound wisdom.

The fact that English is not the language of most of my characters has provoked some criticism. The objectors often forget that English is merely a medium of communication for the writer and a touch of artificiality is inevitable when characters and situations happen to be purely Indian, but it is no more than a momentary confusion. Once the reader has adjusted his vision, his understanding and his reflexes, once he has mentally aligned himself with the medium, everything becomes natural. After all, the problem is no different when a literary work of one language is translated into the other. One has to remember that it is largely through English that India and its literature have come to be well-known and understood outside and inside the entire country.

In the matter of point of view, I prefer the first person to the third person narrative because the former generates feeling of intimacy between the writer and the reader. While writing a novel or a short story, I identify myself with the first person narrator whether it be an old maidservant or a rag-picking boy and narrate everything as it might have happened to me. Of course, to overcome certain difficult situations which cannot be covered easily in the first person narrative, I switch to the omniscient point of view. I have often felt amused when some readers erroneously associate the "I" of the story with me as a person and laboriously discover similarities between the two, asking me whether I had written everything from *my* personal experience! I wonder what would they say about my novel *Neema: A Village Girl* which is in the first person narrative and the narrator happens to be a village girl!

A good short story touches a serious issue of life, what Henry Seidel Canby has called, "specific gravity." The story must not be merely an extended joke with a few twists and turns added to cheat the reader; it must take up serious issues of life – of men and manners, of hopes and frustrations. However, the treatment of serious issues by no means justifies an uninteresting and tiresome short story; its essential trait lies in being interesting. For a short story is the food that cannot go down the gullet without being palatable even if comprising all healthy and nutritive elements. I do not write merely for academics and scholars whose praise for a literary composition, as for a crossword puzzle, increases or decreases in proportion to the brain-teasing complexity it has or lacks. To read a good story is like going on a pleasant journey in the company of delightful personages who share an experience, exchange pleasantries, scour the gloomy cobwebs and end up by letting in a rejuvenating gust of fresh air. But to read a dull even if ingenious short story is like walking uphill with leaded shoes and the completion of each page gives one a feeling of a man-made obstacle tiresomely surmounted.

For some people to have a vein of humor in a literary work is to transgress the limits of serious writing. They do not realise that comic mode is an important aspect of life, enjoyed by all, even if only a few have been endowed with a vein of it. Humour demands of its writer a relaxed mood, a perfect control on the language and an immense capacity of playing upon words. All this is easy enough in a native tongue but difficult in a foreign language. It is creditable that among Indian short story writers, R.K. Narayan and Khushwant Singh have been successful in introducing, even in English, plenty of wit and humor which make their stories quite interesting and eminently readable.

A judicious use of not only humour but irony, suspense and narrative strategy can make a short story eminently readable. But sensationalism as a device to make a story interesting is to be avoided. Violence, sex and murder titillate the reader and make him go on with the story. However, to use them perpetually as mere baits is to addict the reader. Sensationalism in a short story is like chilies and spices in food; a little may add flavor but excess of it is injurious to health. A surfeit of sensationalism in Indian movies has spoiled the taste and dulled the sensibility of younger generation. Nothing can be a greater disservice to humanity than to dull the sensitivity of the people which weakens their empathy and makes them indulge heartlessly in violence, crime and murder. But as long as sensationalism originates from observed experience rather than from contrived situations, it fulfills an artistic requirement.

My own method has been to write a short story on any subject that happened to inspire me intensely. That is why the subjects varying from story to story are as diverse as love and infatuation, crime and punishment, materialism and spiritualism, poverty and riches, illusion and reality, villages and cities, and so on. Nothing is barred, nothing excluded. Some subjects may require a full-blown treatment; others merely suggestive and symbolic. I look around, watch, and re-create my impressions into words. Hence it differs from story to story. I could begin the story with vague hints of a character, a situation or a plot which become solidified into an image and which, in a polished form, are passed on to the reader. If I see a conflagration in a spark and an ocean in a bowlful of water, my effort would be to convey the impression in a more explicit manner to the reader.

In my stories, I captured a particular moment from the past or the present, shaped it to my needs, fashioned it to my likings, decked it in appropriate colors and fused it with life so that the story competes with the very life itself. The scene of action may be in New York or in New Delhi, the characters may be from the village or the city, but stripped of their peculiarities, they all embody various facets of life. Beneath their obvious dissimilarities, the same heart throbs and the same blood circulates in their veins. At some point of my life, each of these short stories had become a throbbing three-dimensional image which could not be kept away and had to be given a creative outlet. For me, a short story is the concretised creative urge of the writer.

CHAPTER 2

Theory and Practice of Ramesh K. Srivastava's Short Story

Smita Das

Theory and practice of literary writings and fine arts may appear to be two sides of the same coin but are not always compatible. One who gives a systematic theory sometimes ends up in violating it. Most creative writers do not give a set of principles or theories of their writing, whether they be novels, short stories or poems, often disclaiming that they were written according to some plan. But the mere act of selecting one character, one plot, one theme out of a number of them involves some built-in mechanism of choices within a writer and which after a series of creative pieces – short stories or poems – crystallises into a set of preferences and principles which collectively turn out to be his theory of writing, though Srivastava himself cautions in his "Preface" to *Under the Lamp: Stories*: "Creative imagination does not trudge along a predetermined track, nor can it be shackled by administrative controls" (v). These tracks and controls could be of even writer's own making!

Three American fiction writers, namely, Edgar Allen Poe, Nathaniel Hawthorne and Henry James propounded systematic theories of fiction, including the short story. Though such theories of literature do exist in Sanskrit, not many Indian writers in English have given such a theory. Mulk Raj Anand, Raja Rao, Bhabani Bhattacharya and Anita Desai in their interviews, prefaces and forewords have given their aims and objectives of writing which give some idea of their theories of fiction.

The same thing can be said about Ramesh K. Srivastava. In addition to two novels *Neema* and *Coils of the Serpent,* he has to his credit six collections of short stories: *Love and Animality: Stories* (1984), *Cooperative Colony: Stories* (1985), *Masks and Men: Stories* ((1986),

Games They Play and Other Stories (1989), *Under the Lamp: Stories* (1993) and *A Christmas Gift and Other Stories* (2015). Even then he has not given any systematic theoretical framework for writing a short story. However, there are enough hints about his views on the short story through his Author's Notes, Prefaces and interviews. In the "Author's Note" to *Games They Play and Other Stories*, Srivastava defines the short story as "a frozen moment of life, carrying in it the seeds of perennial truths. It reveals in a flash an image of hitherto unexplored aspect of life fleeing each moment before us. . . . It is not, as is occasionally made out to be, an artistic conglomeration of unusual characters, unfamiliar landscapes and witty dialogues to titillate and tickle one's fancy but a literary creation that shows to the reader a patch of greenery here or a bunch of flowers there which to the accustomed eyes had been a piece of uninviting desert land" (*Games* 9). It is obvious that for Srivastava the short story is not a sort of museum to parade unusual and exotic characters and situations, but something portraying hitherto unexplored areas hinting at the universal truths of life.

Influenced by the theory of Edgar Allen Poe who considered the short story an interesting narration which could be read in half-an-hour, Srivastava feels that "the story must be short, interesting and in a tone that creates a harmonious relationship between the writer and the reader. An appetite, like the one needed to enjoy a hearty meal, has to be created in the reader to see something new in what appears to be the oft-trodden ground, and then to sustain it with legitimate artistic means, such as suspense, humour and irony" (*Games* 10). He is opposed to using the short story merely as a tool of entertainment and, at the same time, is quite conscious that it must also not become a brain-teaser to display the writer's pedantry and learning which makes the reader fume and fret in the process of reading when, to use Srivastava's words, each word of it "sends the reader's brain reeling to history, geography and mythology of distant lands" (*Games* 9). That is the reason why he gives importance to the reader and does not feel anything wrong if the stories are moulded to suit the taste of readers. He writes: "Hence unconsciously or consciously, the writer is and must be influenced and his stories moulded by the type of reader available for him. To wholly disregard them while carving and whittling a literary piece would be as inappropriate as to play the Western classical music to rickshaw-wallahs" (*Games* 9).

It is worth pointing out that the early successful short stories of Srivastava, such as, "A Drowning Man," "Hospitality," "The Human Thirst," "Maharshi Satyanand," "Century," "Friendship, Love and Marriage," "Confession" and "Lasting Victory," among others, were published in *Caravan*, *Woman's Era* and *Eve's Weekly* before being included in various anthologies. He refers to an incident to support his view. His short story "Hospitality" was open-ended. The editor of a popular magazine accepted the story for publication but insisted on having a rounded conclusion, giving the plea that the story was incomplete without it. After Srivastava had added a paragraph to give it a rounded conclusion, it was accepted and published. Keeping in mind such a rider, Srivastava began to write short stories with well-rounded endings. Reviewing one anthology of Srivastava's short stories, K. V. Chacko calls him "a gifted writer of short stories who knows the tricks of his trade well: an endearing narrative style, nearly impeccable language and appropriate technique to deliver into the reader's lap as a short story."

Taking a cue again from Edgar Allen Poe who in his "Review of Hawthorne's *Twice-Told Tales*" and "The Poetic Principle" had given an elaborate description of the process of writing a short story or a poem, Srivastava too writes about it. The process of writing a short story is very complex and no single factor can be considered responsible for the creation. He writes: "A fine short story is the joint-product of the heart, the head and the hand. It originates from an inspiring idea, an appealing incident, a dramatic situation, a memorable character or an unforgettable experience. The seed of the story sprouts in the writer's head. It grows and swells to take the shape of a story" (*Games* 9-10). In an interview with Atma Ram, Srivastava gives a detailed account of how his short story grows from a seed to a creation. He writes: "First, an idea takes the form of a seed that sprouts and grows to become a plant or a tree if given the right moisture, fertile soil and proper care. When I am struck by an idea, I see in what form it will have the best manifestation – an article, a short story or a novel. For a number of days I see its feasibility. While I walk, read, travel or lie down, the idea grows, takes many shapes and hues with various impressions and details gathering with it. The story continues to evolve as I start writing it down. Then follow revisions and rearrangements; the process continues even when I type out the final draft" (19).

Many of Srivastava's short stories are based on real incidents, characters and situations. They, however, serve merely as seeds out of which plants grow and take shapes about which even the author himself had no clear idea. His short story "The Living Doll" has two characters Kashi and Darua who worked at the writer's ancestral house in the village. "Under the Lamp" is centred on a blacksmith's widow Karmaibai who lived -- and continues to live even now – in the writer's neighbourhood in his village Banpur. "Century" is based on the real character of Jasbir Singh—an engineering student in an American university—as also on the feeling of alienation affecting the psyche of most Indian students in the USA. "Friendship, Love and Marriage" points out various attempts of many Indian students in the USA who come in contact with American girls. "Rescuers" is based on a real incident which took place in Amritsar but it was made universal by making all the three boys belonging to three different religions whereas Father Sault has been made a Christian. "Hospitality" tells of widespread corruption in the Punjab in which some people stoop so low as to offer their wives for earning money or for getting favours. "Terrorist in the Kitchen" gives a graphic picture of the fractured psyche of the terrified people in Punjab badly affected by the senseless violent activities of terrorists in the 1980's and 1990's. The cat and kittens in the story used to frequent the writer's residence in Amritsar and appear more humanistic than the terrorists.

Differentiating the present short story with that of the past, Srivastava feels that the modern short story is not so blatantly didactic or moralistic though it may have symbolic undertones in it. He writes: "The main thrust of the earliest stories, both Indian and European, was usually religious, moral and reformative but rarely literary. In the modern times, the short stories, some of which could be myths and legends rewritten, have some literary value even if with the undercurrents of moralistic and reformative concerns" (*Games* 10). The same point is emphasised in his interview with Y. Joy when Srivastava replies: "When a short story writer selects an incident, a character or a situation for presentation, he also thinks of how it would best appeal to the readers. If in the process of depicting a dark tunnel, he turns a hint of how to come out of it, there is nothing wrong as long as the hints do not turn into obtrusive solutions and a short story does not become a part of propaganda" (376). In this connection, he maintains that in the modern times, it is not an easy job to portray the reality of the world which is complex and multi-layered. Hence when the short story writer portrays the complex reality, it could mean different things for different persons. He maintains that "The short story is a powerful and effective means of portraying prismatic reality of our time. Seen from different angles, the short story assumes varied forms, evolving out of different viewpoints, structures and narrative techniques" (*Games* 10). "Games They Play" is highly symbolic in which cruelties and heartlessness of the ancient and modern rulers are compared. Smita Das feels that "symbolically such power games have been perennially universal" (110). For Anil K. Tewari, it is "the rendition of both macro and micro power discourses" (46).

For Edgar Allen Poe, "the unity of effect or impression is a point of the greatest importance" (173). Henry James too emphasises the need of "singleness of effect" (434). Of all the constituents of a short story, the singleness of impression or effect was so important to them that any other part could be sacrificed for it. As a matter of fact, like Poe, Srivastava maintains that "every character, incident, sentence and every word must contribute" to the total impression of the story. He goes on to say that "the singleness of effect depends largely on the end of the story which, like that of a play, must have a resolution or a sting so as to leave an unambiguous impact on the reader" (*Games* 10). He gives another example of this effect by comparing it to "a powerful slap with all fingers and palm striking together which would not be so were they to strike separately" (*Games* 11). In "Maharshi Satyanand," all the miraculous activities point to the holiness of the Maharshi till at the end he is found to be a cheat Ranga. In "Straw in the Eye," a student leader Rola remains lawless and violent before the teachers and the Principal of the college but learns a lesson of life when he is insulted by a sweeper. In "A Drowning Man," Shyam is shocked to find at the end of the story that the innocent virgin he was dreaming for marriage turns out to be as adept at playing sexual games in an Indian village as he was in the USA.

Even though various constituents of the story are important, it remains a fact that it is the short story in its totality which ultimately affects the reader. In "A Christmas Gift," the reader is touched when the maidservant's daughter Saloni gives to Suchitra madam a Christmas Gift of her own living baby instead of the painting of one she had promised to complete. Srivastava writes: "In fact each organic part of the story, as of a human being, is beautiful not in itself but in relation with others. All parts must be so closely woven that nothing can be added, nothing taken away" (*Games* 11). The story "Games They Play" encompasses a vast period of pre and post-independent India in which the rulers play the same dirty games as they did in the past at the cost of poor human beings. Here characterisation, description, dialogues and atmosphere contribute together to paint a pathetic picture of the people destroyed due to the whims of the rulers. Another story "Century" portrays authentically the inner struggle and dilemma of an alienated Indian student who ultimately opts for moral principles. Here the characters, atmosphere, narration, dialogues and incidents – all contribute to the success of the story.

That raises the question of probability and improbability in a short story. Srivastava writes with a tinge of irony about "critics who would like every word or action to be tested on a Richter scale of their imagination, disregarding the fact that a writer does not buy his material sifted and cleansed of improbable elements from some laboratory but selects it in its crude form directly or vicariously from the life itself" (*Under* vi). If the above statement is carefully scrutinised, Srivastava is not completely averse to a very small degree of improbability only up to that point when the reader does not shake his head in disbelief. After all it is the addition of strangement to a common incident or action which makes it worthy of a short story. The actions of protagonists in "The Living Doll," "A Drowning Man," "Century," "Friendship, Love and Marriage" and many more could appear to be slightly in departure from average actions, but they cannot be considered improbable. Srivastava goes on to add: "What one has to avoid are impossibilities – occurrence of unnatural feats and miracles" (*Under* vii). Such things have carefully been kept out of his short stories.

In the same way, Srivastava believes that characters too must be from real life: "One writes of people from personal experience, not from mere imagination." In order to make them appear quite real, "one does not have to devote pages upon pages of psychological analysis of a character; a word, a phrase, even a glint in the eye is enough to reveal his intentions" (*Under* vii). Most of Srivastava's characters are from real life. His story "Savagery" depicts real characters of the Rajputs pitted against the tribal in which the latter take revenge in their own way. One of the tribals was Srivastava's class fellow in the village primary school. "Ganga Ma" is based on a newspaper report in which a child died after being given a dip on the occasion of Makar Sankranti in the cold water which incidentally was flowing from a leakage in an underground pipe though it was mistaken as a divine miracle. As has been pointed out earlier in this essay, some of the characters have been taken from his village, his educational institutions and from among those whom he had met or had heard of earlier in various places of his stay – Jhansi, Gwalior, Amritsar and many cities in the U.S.A.

Questions have often been raised about the place of humour in a short story. Some people consider humour as an impediment in the serious work of art. Neeta Maini writes: Srivastava has "blessedly an abundance of humour which makes his short stories so lively, interesting and enjoyable" (194). Srivastava argues in its favour by writing in his "Preface": "The treatment of the serious issues by no means justifies an uninteresting and tiresome short story; its essential trait lies in being interesting. For a short story is the food that cannot go down the gullet without being palatable even if comprising all healthy and nutritive elements" (*Under* vi). He believes that the "comic mode is an important aspect of life, enjoyed by all, even if only a few have been endowed with a vein of it" (*Games* 11). R. K. Narayan and Khushwant Singh have been successful in introducing an abundance of wit and humour, making their literary work quite interesting. In an interview with Mehta, Srivastava writes that humour, irony and satire are important parts of life and hence they too must find adequate place in a short story: "Besides, a good work must be readable before it conveys anything. I am told that humour and irony make my writings fairly interesting and readable. Satire obviously is to demolish those institutions, individuals, customs and traditions which have outlived their use" (171).

Swati Srivastava feels that Srivastava has done "a commendable job in not only introducing comic vein in his novel and short stories in English but in making them eminently entertaining, easily readable and wonderfully delightful without sacrificing their literary value" (106). Most of Srivastava's short stories were written for and published in popular magazines like *Caravan*, *Woman's Era* and *Eve's Weekly* in which the reader's interest is the uppermost. While reading stories like "Friendship, Love and Marriage" and "Cooperative Colony," readers have been known to laugh vigorously. The stories also depict characters such as the Education Minister in "Cooperative

Colony" and American girl Loveleen in "Friendship, Love and Marriage" whose monumental ignorance provokes abundance of humour. Discussing the short story "Cooperative Colony," Manisha Sharma writes: "With the help of irony, humour and satire, Srivastava has indeed castrated the entire society of various professions since people in the name of cooperation show their utter selfishness and inhumanity" (199).

In the process of writing, Srivastava's style also evolves in accordance with the need of the story. If the need for expression of intense feelings and emotions arises, Srivastava's prose becomes lyrical. For example, "Century" poetically depicts the alienation of the protagonist in the USA. "The Human Thirst" mirrors the frustrations of a romantic college teacher in a poetic language. Neema's and Jeewan Jyoti's frustrations find graphically portrayed in a ceaseless flow of lyrical language.

Indians writing creatively in English have always been questioned about their competence in the use of English. Srivastava had begun to write short stories for magazines and journals and hence his writings were reader-centric. It was natural that he wrote in a simple language which could easily be understood and appreciated by the readers. However, when he wrote his novels, the language has often been found to be elevated and dignified. Mr. Mehta in interviewing Srivastava found "academic" flavour in his writing and Srivastava's reply was: "You had earlier pointed out that the style is the man. I am an academic by profession and hence despite my efforts to the contrary, an academic flavor is bound to creep in my writings. I also do not wish to deny the fact that occasionally the academic flavor is injected consciously, too, so as to make the work literary – for permanence and posterity" (179). It is the language of the writer which determines his position among men of letters. It can be pointed out here without any reservation that Srivastava's language has so much of pliability and resilience that it can rise to all occasions.

Dialogues have always posed a problem for Indians writing in English, particularly when there are non-English speaking characters. Srivastava writes about it in his "Preface": "Having been born and brought up in a village, I saw the elderly people conversing effortlessly in a native dialect which was pictorial, idiomatic and alive. It throbbed with life and wisdom. These dialogues remain my priceless possession even today. I have often endeavoured to re-create them in English, avoiding the oddity which a literal translation often carries" (*Under* vi-vii). Srivastava's short stories and novels dealing with rural life have in them the native language, including its idioms and sayings, beautifully transcreated into English. Prof. Pashupati Jha calls his descriptions of rural part "superb" and goes on: "To add raw power of authenticity, Prof. Srivastava, at many places, has Indianised English.... Such expressions add vigour to Indian English creative expressions" (244).

In the concluding paragraph of the "Author's Note," Srivastava summarises his views on the subject matter: "In my stories, I captured a particular moment from the past or the present, shaped it to my needs, fashioned it to my likings, decked it in appropriate colours and fused it with life so that the story competes with the very life itself. The scene of action may be in New York or in New Delhi, the characters may be from the village or the city, but stripped of their peculiarities, they all embody various facets of life." (*Games* 12). In his "Preface," Srivastava considers the short story "a tiny mirror that intensely reflects a focused fragment of the vast moving kaleidoscope of life that each day, each moment passes by us in its new yet recognisable ever-changing patterns and combinations" (*Under* v).

With the help of his interviews and replies given to inquisitive readers and after scrupulously analysing his short stories, it can be pointed out that Srivastava practices what he advocates. His short stories with all their organic constituents are well-grounded in reality. To a very large extent, Srivastava's views on the short story have originated from his own experience of writing and naturally he has observed them well in his short stories.

Works Cited

Chacko, K. V. Book Review of Srivastava's *Love and Animality: Stories. Hitavada,* Nagpur (9 September 1984).

Das, Smita. "Ramesh K. Srivastava's 'Games They Play,'" *Illuminati: A Transnational Journal of Literature, Language and Culture Studies.* Vol. IV (2013-14), 105-110.

James, Henry. Quoted by Leon Edel (Ed.). *The Ghostly Tales of Henry James.* New Brunswick: Rutgers' University Press, 1948.

Jha, Pashupati. "Truly a Professor's Novel: Ramesh Srivastava's *Coils of the Serpent.*" *The Indian Journal of English Studies.* Vol. XLIX (2012): 241-246.

Joy, Y. "Ramesh K. Srivastava in Conversation with Y. Joy." *The Critical Endeavour.* 19 (January 2013), 375-392.

Maini, Neeta. "Ramesh K. Srivastava." *Studies in Contemporary Indian English Short Story: A Collection of Critical Essays,* Ed. A. N. Dwivedi. Delhi: B. R. Publishing Corporation, 1991. 185-197.

Mehta, M. L. "Interview with Ramesh K. Srivastava." *The Critical Endeavour.* 8 (December 2002): 167-179.

Poe, Edgar Allen. "*Twice-Told Tales* by Nathaniel Hawthorne: A Review." *American Literature Survey.* Vol. II (Ed.). Milton R. Stern. New York: The Viking Press, 1969.

Ram, Atma. "Ramesh K. Srivastava." *Interviews with Indians Writing in English.* Ed. Atma Ram. Calcutta: Writers' Workshop, 1992. 14-24.

Sharma, Manisha. "Irony, Humour and Satire in Ramesh K. Srivastava's 'Cooperative Colony.'" *Indian Scholar: An International Multidisciplinary Research e-Journal,* Vol. I, Issue 2 (December 2014), 195-199.

Srivastava, Ramesh K. "Author's Note," *Games They Play and Other Stories.* New Delhi: Prestige Books, 1989. 9-12.

……."Preface" to *Under the Lamp: Stories.* Jalandhar: ABS Publications, 1993. v-x.

Srivastava, Swati. "Wit and Humour in the Works of Ramesh K. Srivastava." *Stars Behind the Clouds; Unexplored Indian Writers in English.* Ed. Syed Mashkoor Ali. Jaipur: Surabhi Publications. 2004. 89-106.

Tewari, Anil Kumar. "Psychodynamics of Power Discourse in Srivastava's *Games They Play.*" *Punjab Journal of English Studies.* Vol. VII (1992), 45-53.

CHAPTER 3

Ramesh K. Srivastava: A Writer of Simple Ways

Atma Ram

The contemporary fiction writer is keen to describe and interpret life in terms of new images or metaphors. His stories are characterised by a deep sense of realism, an understanding of human situations. This is particularly discernible in case of teachers of English who are also creative and critical writers – Shiv K. Kumar, Madhusudan Prasad, Ramesh K. Srivastava, D. R. Sharma, Chaman Nahal, Jaidev, Manoj Das, Murli Das Melwani and Sunita Jain – to name a few. Some of them had an encounter with the West through their education or teaching assignment. Their interaction and experiences abroad enabled them to widen their horizon and see their own culture and life-pattern in a clearer and better perspective.

I came across Dr Srivastava when he had come to Shimla in connection with some assignments. A thin, lean academician, heading towards the University Guest House, often leaving the poor coolie carrying his luggage behind, is the first picture I have of him. Later, his creative and critical writings, as also his keenness to help others attracted me towards him. Ever ready to contribute a perceptive paper to a seminar, he helped us further to have get-togethers at Dharamsala.

He is now Professor and Chairman, Department of English, Guru Nanak Dev University, Amritsar. Besides being a conscientious and devoted teacher, he is a prolific writer in English; he has published, to-date, six books of critical nature, three collections of short stories, and a novel *Neema.* The fourth collection – *Games They Play and Other Stories* – is almost ready for release. His critical studies include "Determinism in Hemingway," *Hemingway and his For Whom the Bell Tolls, Perspectives on Bhabani Bhattacharya, Six Indian Novelists in*

English, Perspectives on Anita Desai, and *Thoreau's Walden.* His three anthologies of short stories are: *Love and Animality: Stories, Cooperative Colony: Stories,* and *Masks and Men: Stories.*

Ramesh K. Srivastava began his literary career in 1955 with the publication of his short story, "*Ek Rupaya*" in the Hindi daily *Dainik Jagaran* (Jhansi). Thereafter, he published about twenty stories in Hindi till he had to suspend his creative work in order to go in for M.A. English. After earning his doctorate from the University of Utah (USA) in 1972, he returned to fiction, but now in English.

Like Thomas Hardy, he was impressed by the elemental simplicity of the village folk, as he confessed to the *Contemporary Authors:* "Having been born and brought up in a village where people live and continue to live in elemental simplicity, where the entire village is considered one family, where the joys and sorrows of one are shared by all, I developed a strong liking for their simple ways of life and became shy, even suspect of excessive courtesies, polished behaviour and hypocritical nature."

All these provide a sure clue to the nature and scope of his fiction. He considers a short story "a frozen moment of life revealed through a sequence of words. It must be short, readable and meaningful." The creative activity, as he once confessed to the present writer, gives him immense joy: "I enjoy writing short stories, articles and novels. It is a form of creative outlet I want to share with others."

Srivastava takes up anything and everything as the theme of his fiction – from a farmer ploughing his field to a hawker balancing a brass plate or a cobbler mending shoes. However, his prominent motifs are love and sensuality, East-West cultural relationship, and problems as well as patterns of urban and rural modes of living in India. He embodies these themes with considerable competence and artistic skill.

The technique employed by him is usually according to the subject matter. For example, the first-person narrative should not confuse the reader – it is only a strategy used to heighten the impact. Says the author: "The 'I' of the short story does not refer to me at all; it refers to the narrator and his personality."

As the author is a conscientious artist writing primarily for the popular magazines, he is rather conservative with regard to technique. He often presents a narration of events in time sequence.

The simple narrative, whether shorter fiction or the novel *Neema,* flows like a song or a waterfall, taking various turns and shapes, as the situation warrants – poetical, dramatic, ironical, humorous and descriptive. He is particularly successful in his dialogues. At times, the creative process helps him achieve this: "First, the idea takes the form of a seed that sprouts and then grows to become a plant or tree if given the right moisture, fertile soil and proper care."

At times, the external voice or judgment makes the writer change or elaborate his endings. The taste and temperament of readers in case of popular magazines also makes a difference. But Srivastava is at his best when he looks inward for inspiration, unmindful of the readers or critics. He does not have the pattern too bare or imposed on a work of literary art. He scrupulously avoids authorial comments and lets the narrative flow freely. Sometimes the comment is incorporated in the description itself.

A discerning fiction writer and fiction critic, Ramesh K. Srivastava provides a new dimension to the contemporary shorter fiction in English. In his hands, short story becomes a down-to-earth, simple yet effective narrative marked for its clarity and directness, connotative nuances and Indian impressionism. The writer's vast and varied experience, meticulous "revisions" and "corrections" pass through the crucible of his imagination. What comes out is the fiction characterised by pace, passion and intensity, the shorter fiction which achieves its avowed objective – what Edgar Allen Poe calls "the unity of impact or impression" [1989].

*Published in Indian Express [Chandigarh] on March 4, 1989.

CHAPTER 4

Themes and Techniques in Ramesh K. Srivastava's Short Stories

Neeta Maini

The short story, no doubt, has a small canvas, good for miniatures, excellent for filigree work, but, unlike the novel, somewhat cramped and congested for painting life in all its complexities. However, it scores a point over the novel by singleness of aim and totality of effect in relating a single experience of life. Edgar Allan Poe, considered to be the father of the short story in general and the American short story in particular, in his review of Hawthorne's *Twice-Told Tales* pointed out that "the unity of effect or impression is a point of the greatest importance" (173). He went on to say that a skilful literary artist constructs a tale not by fashioning his thoughts to accommodate his incidents but "having conceived, with deliberate care, a certain unique or single *effect* to be wrought out, he then invents such incidents – he then combines such events as may best aid him in establishing this preconceived effect" (174). While writing to H.G. Wells about *The Turn of the Screw,* Henry James also referred to the necessity of singleness of effect. Unlike the American short story, the Indo-Anglian short story can boast of no such skilled writers and theorists to patronise exclusively this *genre* and is considered merely as a by-product of the novel writing. M.K. Naik rightly diagnoses that the Indian short story in English does not have "the variety and fecundity of the post-Independence novel" (247). Since the short-story writing has been done mostly by the novelists, it has those very characteristics that their novels have. In some cases, the novelists put in their best in the novel, treating the short story in a casual way. The short stories of R.K. Narayan, Mulk Raj Anand, Raja Rao, Ruth Prawer Jhabvala and Anita Desai are marked by the attitude and response fully characteristic of their novels. The same eccentric Malgudian characters characterise Narayan's novels and short stories.

Some of Raja Rao's short stories read like scattered episodes from *Kanthapura.*

Viewed in this perspective, Ramesh K. Srivastava, who has to his credit one novel *Neema* (1986) and three volumes of short stories – *Love and Animality: Stories* (1984), *Cooperative Colony: Stories* (1985), and *Masks and Men: Stories* (1986), has exploited the *genre* not as a by-product of novel writing but as an independent *genre* to depict varied experiences of life. The short stories have a wide range and variety both in the subject-matter and technique. While some short stories are packed with action, others catch a mood or feeling. Some have an omniscient narrator; others are in the first person. For some, a single episode forms a bare-bone structure, simple and manageable; for others, the main episode provides merely the basis for an impressive complex structure with well-lighted or mysterious chambers and labyrinthine passages, testifying to the skill of the artist. In subject-matter, too, the stories deal with rural and urban problems, traditional and modern values, poverty and affluence, East-West encounter, social and political aspects of life. Highlighting various facets of life, the stories present a kaleidoscopic view of life, revealing too the gulf that lies between appearance and reality, what appears to be and is. Shyam with a physician's job at the University of Hawaii in "A Drowning Man" ventures to wed an unfamiliar, raw, rural girl setting a high price on her virginal purity and chastity only to be shocked at the time of consummation that she, too, like her western counterparts, had indulged in pre-marital sexual games. Having observed life so closely, the author seems to say with Sudama in "Masks and Men": "1 have seen so many persons, and most of them are hypocrites" (*Masks* 87).

Though each of Srivastava's short story paints a different segment of life and has correspondingly different characters, one character – mostly the first-person narrator – emerges gradually silhouetted against a hazy background of other people. It hardly matters whether his name is Shyam, Kanti, Sharma or Verma, or his profession happens to be medicine, teaching, studies or administration. Having deep moral and humane concern, he may err here or slip there, but he strives hard to ensure that the evil is punished and justice done to all. With his mental acuity, he makes Parkash and his wife – the adulterators – arrested in "Hospitality." It is the sharpness of mind, his rationalistic attitude and his refusal to believe in superstitious that he unmasks Maharshi Satyanand's real identity as Ranga, the dacoit. He is not altogether an ideal hero – and it is good that he is not or else he might have slipped into a tailored monster of virtue – but has certain blemishes in his character which make him so earthy and human. His major weakness is for sex which, added with wine, makes him initially a victim of Parkash and his wife in "Hospitality." In "The Human Thirst," even being a father of a married daughter, he looks for sensual relations with his young students Alpana and Banmala.

In "A Drowning Man," "Friendship, Love and Marriage" and "Century:" he goes to the U.S.A. and does not hesitate in having romantic and sensual quests with American girls. But confronted with a situation when sex and humanity contend for prominence, it is humanity that wins. He is opposed to sex divorced from humanity. In "Century," Mohan claims:

> Humanitarian considerations have been the heaviest fetters on me. I do not exploit a person I do not know and I cannot exploit a person I know. The mere sight of a girl arouses within me feelings of amorousness. I envision loving and sleeping with her... The net is tightened, but when we become friends and the moment of fulfillment comes, I feel somewhat the twitches of conscience. My resolve weakens. Humanity awakens within me, and I withdraw myself, weak and repentant. The original motive of exploitation shies away and I remain rooted where I was at the beginning (*Cooperative* 69).

In this story, the protagonist prepares himself for a sexual escapade with his student Marcy but does not have a heart to exploit her against her will, whereas Jasbir, his counterpart in the story, had already exploited her, made her pregnant and abandoned her after making a false promise of marriage. In "The Human Thirst," too, he comes back to the fold of his home and his wife after his unsuccessful amorous adventure with Alpana.

Love and sensuality constitute a dominant theme in Srivastava's short stories, particularly those in *Love and Animality: Stories.* In each story, the author portrays love and sex life of the protagonist in its varied aspects. Kashi, a physically powerful but mentally retarded person in "The Living Doll," certainly possesses some traits of love and animality. He can push a wooden cart or bend a tree with his bare hands but cannot stay peacefully without his Japanese doll. His love for the doll reveals the delicate springs of his being and retains his sanity, but when he is denied this symbol of love, his enormous physical strength, like that of a sleeping giant, becomes transformed into animality so much that he mistakes his sister-in-law for his doll and kills her. Kashi and Darua in the story echo Lennie and George in Steinbeck's *Of Mice and Men.* In "Love and Animality," Sharma never treats his semi-literate and irritating wife inhumanly, whereas Chadha treats his educated and intelligent wife inhumanly, by indulging in immoderate sex and physical thrashings. Out of such contrastive studies emerge the values that the writer upholds: love against animality, chastity against impurity, sanctity of marriage against promiscuity.

East-West cultural relationship which has attracted almost all the Indo-Anglian writers is another important theme of Srivastava's short stories. Meenakshi Mukherjee rightly observes:

> The majority of Indo-Anglian writers today (with one or two notable exceptions), it will be observed, have had at least a part of their education abroad. Because of their intimate experience of a culture other than their own, they are made aware of their Indianness as well as of the difference in the two systems of values: one rather acquired, the other inherited and often taken for granted (66).

Raja Rao in *The Serpent and the Rope,* Kamala Markandaya in *Possession,* Khushwant Singh in *A Bride for the Sahib and Other Stories,* Bhabani Bhattacharya in *A Dream in Hawaii,* and Anita Desai in *Bye-Bye, Blackbird* used the theme extensively. Each of these novelists had stayed abroad, some of them continue to do so even now, and their exposure to two cultures finds a place in their novels. Ramesh K. Srivastava too had had an intimate experience of the western culture during his studies in the U.S.A. from 1969 to 1972 and, as a result, his stories have east-west encounter as one of the recurring motifs. However, unlike in Kipling where the East and the West are poles apart and never meet, in Srivastava's stories they do so as in "Tigers of the Steering Wheel" in the marriage of Marilyn, an American young girl, and Palwinder, an Indian truck driver. The craziness of the one is well-matched by the rashness of the other. In "A Drowning Man," East and West seem initially to be poles apart with contrasting backgrounds, situations, characters, attitudes to life, ways and manners, but ironically enough at the end the differences are wiped out, and it becomes hard to see any difference between the two—one being as good or as bad as the other. Shyam has in the beginning a viewpoint which is so different from what he is forced to have at the end. He feels:

> There is in Indian women so much of shyness, timidity and maidenly reserve that make them inscrutably captivating in comparison with their Western counterparts. These were precisely the qualities I was looking for

> in my wife and how thrilled I was to find that she had them in plenty (*Love* 20).

But his initial euphoria in having found in Sarala the kind of wife he wanted is changed into depression and shocking disappointment when the reality dawns on him that his wife whom he had considered "simple, quiet, innocent... a flawless product of Indian culture" (21) was not really so and she had enjoyed sexual games with the village boys, even though she showed her shyness in exposing her face or in baring her body in privacy. Ironically, what may be considered good and acceptable in one culture may not be so in the other, and many times one leaves real objects at home in order to chase shadows abroad. In the end, one finds no difference between Sarala and her American counterparts – Amelia, Cathy and Jamie – who had enjoyed pre-marital sex. As a matter of fact, the author seems to hint that the American girls with their promiscuity are better because they are honest in their view of life, be it wrong or right, moral or immoral, in contrast to Indian girls who make a great deal of hue and cry about moral values in trivial matters but gloat over serious violations.

Srivastava's experience in the West and his inherited Indian values seem to have a very deep impression on the character used in the sense of 'quality' of his short stories. Some of his protagonists are a curious mixture of the two cultures – "a hybrid product of two different cultures and habits, picking things from both and judging one by the standards or even taboos of the other (21). In "A Drowning Man," Shyam himself indulges in sexual adventures with young American girls, but wants his wife to be chaste, pure and intact. Chaturvedi, in "Friendship, Love and Marriage," feels lacerated if Americans make fun of India but enjoys befooling them by painting a highly exaggerated and funny picture of India to tease their crazy imagination. On the one hand, he is much concerned with India and what it stands for; on the other, he disregards the Indian sanctity of marriage by flirting with the American girl Loveleen. But once he comes to know that he has got her into trouble, he feels twitches of conscience and even thinks of making amends by divorcing his wife for her sake. The reason is simple. He would not like to give the impression that he had deceived her when at the back of his mind the feeling is always there that as an Indian, he is also an ambassador of his country India. However, at the end of the story, Chaturvedi is thoroughly disillusioned to find in Loveleen a great cheat who had never loved him but was after the luxurious life she would have had as a wife of a Maharaja. The moment the illusion is shattered, she abandons him. In "Century," Srivastava shows how Indians spoil their image in the West. Jasbir is obsessed with the idea of completing his century of love affairs with American girls even if it means betraying them by making false promises of marriage. He had done so to Marcy and when she had become pregnant she was deserted. But it is Mohan who repairs the image of Indians by sparing her at a point he could have used her.

The stories also reveal two facets of India – urban and rural life. Simple living, unassuming nature, mutual cooperation but at the same time belief in superstitions and credulity are what normally one associates with the rural life, whereas ostentatious living, condescending attitude, self-centeredness, pretension and hypocrisy are what characterise the urban people. Srivastava's stories reveal some of these traits. His aim appears to expose and satirise so as to correct some of these vices. It is not that he opposes every credulous act of the rural people. To do so would be to falsify the village life where it still exists. Hence, occasionally his ambivalent attitude. In "The Living Doll," the absence of a child's cry at the time of his birth is an unusual phenomenon that portends a misfortune not only for the family but for the whole village and it turns out to be true in the case of Kashi. But in "Ganga Ma," Srivastava clearly satirises the ill-founded credulity of the village people who consider it a sin not to take a holy dip in Prayag or any other holy river on Makar Sankranti and lets a child die when an underground pipe-burst is mistaken for a divine fountain of Ganga Ma! In "Maharshi Satyanand," he satirises the credulity of the Indian people by exposing the venerated Maharshi to be no other than the dacoit Ranga.

In contrast, Srivastava shows corruption and hypocrisy of urban dwellers. The life in cities is so hard that the artists like Sudama and Madhurima have difficulty in making both ends meet. Garib Das in "Cooperative Colony" begs day and night to have a small amount in order to be eligible for a house in the Cooperative Colony where the residents are supposed to be helpful and cooperative but ironically enough it is they who mistake him for a thief, torture him and loot his money without even giving his dead body a decent cremation! By juxtaposing the natures of urban and rural people, Srivastava seems to suggest that there may still be hope for the Indian village where a road to prosperity could be constructed in the teeth of opposition of the Sarpanch but cities confront a bleak future.

The urban areas have problems of the educated youth, too. Six feet tall, muscular, Rohtas Lal, known as Rola, is a big nuisance for his teachers in "Straw in the Eye." He cannot be handled so well by meek and gentle teachers as by the rash and rude sweeper. In "Lasting Victory," Gurmel, another student boss, is ready to molest his female teacher; however, the courage, cleverness, patience and sympathy of the teacher make him repentant of his misdeeds. In "New Generation," a mod girl may not mind mixing with boys but fights against exploitation by them. Jyotsna makes Yadavendra accept Deepika as his wife whom he had betrayed after her pregnancy.

While most of his themes relate to the contemporary scene, Srivastava's approach in the matter of technique is traditional. No stream-of-consciousness, no interior monologue, no disturbed chronologies, no frequent flashbacks and no impressionistic or expressionistic technique find a place in his stories. One does not have to go far to seek reasons for it. He wrote most of the stories for popular magazines for which readability is the best test.[1] Artistic stories in English, like art movies, have yet to find suitable magazines and readers in India. Hence, Srivastava must have taken care to see that his short stories are quite interesting and eminently readable. What is needed, he realised, is that the stories be read first and for that they must reach the readers. K.V. Chacko calls Srivastava "a gifted writer of stories who knows the tricks of his trade well: an endearing narrative style, nearly impeccable language and. appropriate technique to deliver an interesting theme into the reader's lap as a short story." Srivastava's writing is resilient like the skin of a porpoise and moves with the currents of the story. It is at various stages poetical, dramatic and descriptive. Karnail Singh feels that "the form of his stories is not an end *per se*. It is the content that determines it," and that "the tone and timbre of stories modulate accordingly as the context demands." Keeping these factors in mind, he employs the form which could be "conventional, lyrical, dramatic, and the tone satirical, ironic-cum-humorous, morose or even erotic." There is in his writing a ceaseless flow of emotions and illustrating images. Here is an example from "The Human Thirst":

> Every July brought the much-awaited rain-carrying clouds to quench, as it were, my thirst and yet it always rained elsewhere. Or if it drizzled for me, far from quenching my thirst, it created some moistness, enough only to sprout some seeds of hope which dried up in the absence of nourishment (*Love* 68).

In these lines, the vivid images "rain-carrying clouds," "drizzling" and "sprouting of seeds" are symbolic of the sexual fulfillment the college teacher hankers after. The allusions to the straying cow and the comments of Phool Vati over it are suggestive of the teacher's straying away from his wife. The moment he begins his amorous advances to Banmala in his study, his wife's shrill voice disturbs him: "The cow has gone out again today. I am so annoyed by this wretched cow. I give it the best feed, green grass and oil cakes and it is such a stupid, ungrateful, faithless, greedy cow that it prefers to get a beating for I don't know what it gets at other places" (*Love* 75). All the epithets hurled at the cow are applicable symbolically to her husband, who, like the cow, goes astray and comes back after receiving a beating.

The creation of a dramatic situation in a short story is a test of the writer's acuity and adroitness. The notable dramatic situations in Srivastava's stories are the climactic scenes in "A Drowning Man," "The Living Doll," "The Confession" and "Cooperative Colony." Regarding the endings and climaxes of Srivastava's stories, critics have contrasting views. For K.V. Chacko, the endings of Srivastava's stories' are "dramatic enough to have their impact on the reader's mind for days to come" whereas for Sulekha Sharma "his basic technique is to build up suspense, but he fails at the climax." No doubt, some of his endings are stereotyped, as in "Maharshi Satyanand" and "Hospitality," where the culprits are tamely caught and punished at the end as it happens in typical Indian movies.[2] However, in some short stories, the climax is very convincing and artistic. The last scene in "The Living Doll" is laid in the dark room of Kashi's house where he, in a fit of anger, molests and kills his sister-in-law, mistaking her as his doll. The scene is weird but convincing because of Kashi's physical prowess, mental retardation, his dizzy state of mind from hemp and no less significant for the fact that the first line of the story carries the seed of conclusion: "Kashi portended a misfortune for the poor family when he did not cry at the time of his birth" (*Love* 9).

Irony understandably appears to be Srivastava's *forte*. In a country where a spade can be called anything but a spade, where politics has gone into the blood of its people, where truth and honesty have found no places of pride, one can have only irony as a mode of communication so that he says one thing to mean another without facing the risk of being hauled up for wielding his pen rather freely.

As with R.K. Narayan, irony is a mode of perception with Srivastava. In his novels and short stories, Narayan reveals the contradictions between appearance and reality, individual and society, good and evil. Srivastava, too, is well-aware of the ironies inherent in life. But unlike Narayan who reconciles to the contradictions with *calm* amusement, Srivastava does not; he not only takes the mask off the culprit's face but punches him in anger. The stories "Hospitality," "Masks and Men," "Maharshi Satyanand" and "Ganga Ma" end up with the culprits either exposed in the eye of the public or sent to jail. Since justice is not always given in life and the culprits are not invariably punished, there are moments when an honest and meek individual – Garib Das in "Cooperative Colony" or Parbhua in "Seeds of Democracy" tries to stand up against social injustices and is crushed mercilessly. Srivastava shows his concern and arouses that of others by painting the pathetic pictures of such individuals.

Ironic mode has another advantage: it imparts his narrative a distinct shape. Most of Srivastava's short stories end up in ironic reversal of fortunes. In other words, the situation in the end is quite reverse to the situation in the beginning, as in "Friendship, Love and Marriage." In the beginning, Chaturvedi befools his American girl-friend Loveleen and her mother Patsy, but as the story advances it is Chaturvedi who is befooled by them. It is here that his irony becomes quite an effective device. In "A Drowning Man," details are accumulated to show the sensuality of the American girls just to reveal at the end that Sarala's chastity in the story too is not what it was thought to be. It seems that all the details in the story were brought to enhance the effect at the end.

Humour is a trait which is so rare among Indo-Anglian writers. For, humour is an inborn gift and depends not only on temperament, but also on the writer's observation, wit and his command over the language. Srivastava has blessedly an abundance of humour which makes his short stories so lively, interesting and enjoyable. Whether describing a situation, or portraying a character, or contrasting between the educated and the illiterate, the ignorant and the knowledgeable, he, like R.K. Narayan, draws the reader's attention to the incongruities of life. To ignore them would be to block an important aspect of human life which makes the human being the only laughing creature in the whole creation. The semi-literate wife Phool Vati in her innocence and ignorance becomes a humorous character because due to her faulty pronunciations in conversation, the word 'TV' comes out as 'TB,' 'ideal' becomes 'idle,' and 'flower-like' is articulated as 'floor-like.' For Jasbir in "Century," the beauty of an American girl is "terrible" instead of "terrific." In "Friendship, Love and Marriage," Loveleen shows off her knowledge of India by considering it as a part of Bombay! Srivastava's stories are replete with such amusing instances, and depict his practical sense of day-to-day humour. Many times his humour originates from exaggeration of some traits of a person by employing comic and funny comparisons. The Minister for Education and Cooperation in "Cooperative Colony" addresses the residents in English by reading out his speech written in Hindi script. Srivastava caricatures him by describing his teeth like "half-sunk milestones – bent and twisted, yellowing due to dirt and water – interspersed with long gaps on a grayish, curved, bumpy road" and his thick lips "like double bumpers of a dilapidated truck" (*Cooperative* 25). Srivastava is at his best when in his novel *Neema,* he caricatures Sunnoo whose ignorance is monumental:

> A number of answers given by him during the previous years had become classical examples of jokes. He had found no difference between Akbar and *akhwar* (newspaper), cauliflower and cabbage, longitude and latitude. For him Mahatma Gandhi was the Prime Minister of India and Constantinople the President of U.S.A. Simla was the hottest place in the country while Bombay was a fine hill station. The Punjab was known for its five mountains and Rajasthan for its rivers and greenery. The windmills were for the village what the table fan is for an individual: to generate breeze on windless days. He could never understand what difference it would make if ABC was or was not equal to BCA or CBA! Equally puzzling for him were divisions and multiplications of various letters of the alphabet with different powers. The tricky questions of arithmetic were no less disastrous. What on earth could be wrong, he wondered, and why did people laugh when he very clearly pointed out that two *sarees* would take two hours to dry if a single took one hour! (*Neema* 23-24)

Here his comic powers are comparable to R.K. Narayan's. Srivastava's comic imagination often captures the occasion and refreshes the readers. The comic vein is part and parcel of his art and is unlikely to be missed by any reader. And the fact is that without wit and humour, fun and pun, his stories would have looked bland and uninteresting. Many times the sense of humour when infused into the protagonist's character provides a solution to the baffling and vexing problem. The narrator in "Love and Animality" is annoyed and occasionally embarrassed in the presence of his wife, yet what saves him from becoming unpleasant and bitter is his habit of taking her foibles and follies in the stride with a sense of humour. It is this trait, more than others, that makes his short stories readable and interesting.

If the test of a short story is the singleness of effect, Srivastava's short stories concentrate on a selected aspect of life, employing all the elements and devices to have the intended impact. The stories may not be earth-shaking in their resolutions, nor could they claim to have epic dimensions in scope and intensity, but they do capture an unforgettable moment of life that remains delightfully embedded in the reader's memory. The moment lives on [1991].

Note

1. This writer was told by Srivastava that whenever he brought complexity in characterisation, philosophical reflections or open-endedness in a short story, either it was sent back for directed revision, outrightly rejected or its parts were heavily bowdlerised.
2. Srivastava disclosed an interesting fact about the ending of "Hospitality." The short story as originally submitted to *Caravan* had ended by giving ample hints about what the hospitality was meant for but the editor of the magazine sent the story back, praising it for its interesting plot, but regretting that the story had ended midway before reaching the conclusion. The author 'concluded' the story by adding the last page and it was published.

Works Cited

Chacko, K. V. Review of *Love and Animality: Stories. Hitavada* (September 9, 1984).

Mukherjee, Meenakshi. *The Twice-Born Fiction.* New Delhi: Arnold-Heinemann Publishers, 1974.

Naik, M. K. *A History of Indian English Literature.* New Delhi: Sahitya Akademi, 1982.

Poe, Edgar Allen. "*Twice-Told Tales* by Nathaniel Hawthorne: A Review," *American Literature Survey,* Vol. II, edited by Milton R. Stern. New York: the Viking Press, 1969.

Sharma, Sulekha. Review of *Cooperative Colony: Stories. The Tribune* (January 4, 1986).

Singh, Karnail. "Other Experiences – Review of Ramesh K. Srivastava's *Cooperative Colony: Stories.*" *Indian Book Chronicle,* Vol. XIII. No. 12 (December 1987).

Srivastava, Ramesh K. *Cooperative Colony: Stories.* Calcutta: Writers Workshop, 1985.

.... *Love and Animality: Stories.* Calcutta: Writers Workshop, 1984.

.... *Masks and Men: Stories.* Calcutta: Writers Workshop, 1986.

.... *Neema* (a novel). Calcutta: Writers Workshop, 1986.

CHAPTER 5

Human-Animal Relationship in Ramesh K. Srivastava's Short Stories

Smita Das

Human-animal relationship can be traced a long way back to thousands of years. Having social, cultural and ecological relationships, animals provided human beings not only with companionship and service as pets and as working animals but also food supply and animal products, such as, clothing and implements for human use. The importance of animals in the lives of human beings is quite significant in providing objects of human activities, such as, hunting, fishing, agriculture and other uses. Besides, societies have enshrined animals in their arts, literature and media. Paintings of animals have been found in the prehistoric caves.

Since the beginning of time, man and beast have had interesting connections. Animals have been used for many purposes in the past, but the greatest attribute can be considered their love and loyalty to the human beings. Clinton R. Sanders showed the importance of sociological perspective in studying human-animal interaction and its social implications, mentioning that "human interaction with non-human animals is a central feature of contemporary social life" (Sanders 2). The present paper aims at pointing out this interconnection in the short stories of Ramesh K. Srivastava.

In his autobiography, Srivastava gives details of his relationship with animals. In his early childhood, he learnt numbers by counting the cattle heads – cows, buffaloes and their young ones every morning. He also rode over buffaloes even though people made fun of him. While his elders milked cows and buffaloes, he observed them carefully even as he held their young ones to facilitate the elders' work. As an adolescent, he had stealthy rides on barebacked horses. During his fifties when his children had left for jobs elsewhere, cats and kittens "played an important part in our life and remain permanently embedded in our memory." Besides, "they gave us a lot of love" and the Srivastavas felt "happy in their company" (*Autobiography* 314). His love for animals, particularly for cats, finds reflected in his novel *Neema* and in several of his short stories.

The cat in Srivastava's "Terrorists in the Kitchen" is initially considered "a piece of embodied nuisance, a walking ill-omen" (*Under* 74), according to prevalent belief, but the cat and its kitten in the story became friendly with Nirbhaya Dayal and his wife Sonkali. In the midst of terrorism in Punjab, the mother and her kittens provided them "a constant source of relief in what was largely a grim world" (*Under* 76), more so in the absence of their children in Amritsar. The couple felt extremely happy in watching the antics of the feline world. Referring to his wife, Nirbhaya Dayal found that "the absence of young cats made her depressed and her face glowed on their return" (*Under* 81). Finally, when their house was attacked by the terrorists and the world appeared to be coming to an end for them, the cat accidentally spilled the packet of chilli powder which Sonkali threw "into the terrorist's eyes while Nirbhaya simultaneously hit with the pestle momentarily-dazed terrorist on the head" (*Under* 83). The ill ominous cat, instead of bringing ill luck, had saved the lives of the couple. In the same way, the cat saved the life of Neema who had kept her pussy cat lovingly for three years during her troublesome stay in her husband's house. During this period, she confessed, "I would often talk to my cat, unburden my fears and miseries, and she would softly purr and mew as if she understood everything. She has been as good as a child to me" and further realised that "the cat had saved my life by drinking" the poisoned milk (*Neema* 197). In both the cases, the cats saved the lives of their benefactors, but whereas no harm came to the cat from the terrorist, it lost its life by drinking the poisoned milk.

In the story "Truant Creatures," Shailaja's love for her cow Kaveri exceeded her love for studies, as is obvious in her regular absconding from school. However, her love for the cow became a nuisance for Shailaja's father Nek Pal, who was unable to sell it despite the complaints of several village people against it, because Shailaja and Kaveri "had become inseparable friends" (*Road* 44). Docile and obedient at home with Shailaja but fierce outside for others, the cow Kaveri not only "created demon-like scary, hoarse, guttural sounds as if donning the duty of a watchdog" (*Road* 45) but also showed its gratitude to Shailaja by licking her hand in the morning as if saying "Bye bye" for the day. Both Shailaja and Kaveri possessed the common quality of defending the weak from the strong ones. One day, when Madhur Raj, her class fellow, intentionally hit Kaveri with a cricket ball, Shailaja tweaked his ears. When Madhur Raj ironically taunted her about her preference for animals against human beings, she found some animals "better than human beings" (*Road* 48). Once, when Nek Pal and his wife had to go out of station for a day for the marriage negotiations, he feared his daughter's molestation in his absence, but Shailaja was confident of defending herself. In the absence of Nek Pal and his wife, Madhur Raj and his friend Ketan Lal decided to take revenge on her. They entered the house in the night, bolted it from inside, tied Shailaja's hands and feet and attempted to rape her by pinning her down on the bed. Finding the neighbors unable to help her even on her panicky calls because of the door bolted from inside, she frantically shouted for Kaveri who came running fast, "barged into the room and, inserting its horns like that of a fork-lift vehicle, threw Madhur behind its back" (*Road* 50). It also pushed away Ketan. When Madhur Raj fired a fatal shot into the cow's head, it gored his stomach with its horns but not before saving the life and honor of the girl.

Dogs have usually been considered faithful to their masters. Several instances can be given from everyday life in which dogs have been considered faithful pets who do not hesitate in sacrificing their own lives for their masters. William Shakespeare, however, seemed to have altogether a different attitude towards dogs. Even though in Shakespeare's play *Othello*, the most frequently used image is that of the dog, according to Emma Phipson, he "in no one instance mentioned with appreciation the moral qualities of the dog." To bark, to bite and to be always greedy seem to be its only function. She adds that Shakespeare "must have been singularly unfortunate in his experience of the canine race for his allusions are almost all of an unfavorable nature" (Phipson 40). Srivastava, on the contrary, seems to have a pleasant experience as in his story "Folk Musical Drama," he gives a touching portrayal of the dog Goldie. Jyoti Kiran was a beautiful dancing girl. Thakur Satya Narayan Singh, a zamindar, who was considered the uncrowned king of the village, was so much mesmerised by Jyoti Kiran's beauty and performance on the stage that he decided to have sex with her. When the manager of the *nautanki* company Jitendra Prasad told him that such a thing was not possible, the Thakur drugged Jitendra Prasad and Damodar Lal with heavy dosages of liquor and then bribed them with money. Consequently, they looked the other way to facilitate the Thakur's work. Reaching Jyoti Kiran who was sleeping with her daughter Nikki, he forcibly raped her and in the process of keeping her daughter Nikki from crying, he accidentally killed her. When her dog Goldie came to know that the Thakur had killed Nikki – its playmate – "Goldie sat near her, cooing slowly with tears falling down its eyes" (*Road* 210). Probably realising the feelings of Jyoti Kiran as also the fact that it was chained heavily so it could not have come to the rescue of the mistress and its playmate, it disappeared from the scene, went to the Thakur's place and killed him. In the process of killing, its mouth, feet and paws were smeared with blood and remnants of raw flesh. Jyoti Kiran cleaned up its appearance, realising that after her daughter's death, Goldie was "the only companion" she had (*Road* 211), and it had taken the place of her daughter.

George Eliot had felt that "Animals are such agreeable friends – they ask no questions, they pass no criticisms" (Eliot 228). Srivastava graphically portrays extremely friendly nature of animals in the short story "The Beauty and the Beast." Here the animals are humanised while Shishupal, the manager of the Universal Circus, is quite beastly. Teeshee, a small ten-year old orphaned girl was brought to the circus for a job. From the very first day, Shishu Pal looked at her as if she were "a goat or a chicken to be cut, cooked and eaten" (*IJML* 151) and later on, pressed his teeth around her bubbly breasts. When she was taken to the animals to familiarise herself with them, she found "no difference" initially among the animals and the manager. However, when she began to feed the circus animals, they appeared to be affectionate towards her. The animals felt "as if she were applying balm to their bodies. Her touches seemed to smother their beastly traits and brought out their kinder forms" (*IJML* 152). The elephant Gajraj "raised its trunk and kept its tip on her head as if in benediction" (*IJML* 152). As the time passed, Teeshee "felt really happy in the company of animals. They appeared so beautiful and so humanised" (*IJML* 154). She spent her own money and fed fruits to parrots, monkeys and elephants. Consequently, they became so much loving towards her that the tiger licked her fingers before grabbing the pieces of meat from her hands. The elephant Gajraj invited her with his trunk and made her sit on his back. When Teeshee, in her occasional frustrations, felt like committing suicide, the elephant, by waving its head sideways, forbade her from doing so. When she said to him that she had no friends, Gajraj "touched her head with his trunk and then brought it between his forelegs" (*IJML* 154) as if indicating that he could be taken as her friend. Teeshee told the elephant, "Gajraj, I find you much more human than the beast who goes around masquerading as a human being" (*IJML* 154). This statement is akin to what James Herriot says, "If having a soul means being able to feel love and loyalty and gratitude, then animals are better off than a lot of humans" (Herriot 87). In the last feat of the circus, Shishu Pal lay down on the ground and Gajraj kept both his forefeet on the head of the Manager without any pressure, but as Teeshee said, "Crush it," Gajraj put all his pressure on the head "broke and flattened it with a terrible sound while the blood was splashed all around" (*IJML* 156). This must have been done by Gajraj in order to help Teeshee who was perennially exploited by the Manager. In this story, the roles of Shishu Pal on one hand and that of Gajraj and other animals on the other, have been reversed so that the animals, by being lovingly treated by Teeshee, became humanised whereas Shishu Pal turned out to be more and more beastly.

The story "Serpentine Woman" portrays how a Koriwala snake of the family of Russell's viper took revenge on Shesh Raj, who had killed his close friend Jagran, a snake catcher and the husband of Rajani. Once when Rajani had gone to visit her father's house and her husband Jagran had called his friend Shesh Raj to stay with him, the latter was attracted by the beauty of Rajani and desired to marry her. With this purpose in view, he got her husband Jagran killed by putting a poisonous snake among the fangless ones. After the death of her husband, Rajani made both ends meet by cleaning grains and lentils at the landlord's shop. She also knew the work of catching poisonous snakes which always fetched good prices. Once she had caught a Koriwala snake of the family of Russell's viper and wanted to sell after it grew up a little for her household expenses. Though extremely poisonous, "the snake remained friendly with Rajani and her daughter Teju" (*Road* 243). The Koriwala snake "had sensed human speech or intentions that he [Shesh Raj] wanted to steal and sell it stealthily for money" (*Road* 246). Shesh Raj, after killing her husband, not only forced her to have sex with him but also pilfered her money. When he thrashed her before her daughter Teju and confessed killing her husband through a poisonous snake, Rajani became so angry that she got him killed through a poisonous snake.

Teju told her mother "The Koriwala snake gave him an appropriate punishment for his actions. You shouldn't cry for him" (*Road* 246). Unlike the help provided by the dog in "The Folk Musical Drama," and the elephant Gajaraj in "The Beauty and the Beast," which were intentional, the revenge by the Koriwala snake appears to be not altogether unintentional.

Whereas the foregoing illustrations point out to the humanised animals, particularly as they help in completing the unfulfilled tasks of their masters and by securing them justice and revenge, there are animal images which associate human and animal worlds by short comparisons, analogies, similes, metaphors and symbols. Srivastava used the animal imagery in abundance both in his novels and in his short stories. Smita Das writes: "Some of the images which Srivastava uses for depiction of characters are from animals, birds, insects and other such creatures. While these images could largely be for the purpose of illustration of an aspect of a character, they may also indicate an undercurrent of the novelist's attitude towards them as if trying to suggest that the characters had some traits of these animals" (Das 206). Thus Jawahar, Gopal and Sunnoo are as monkeys, Neema as a lizard, Parvati as a hungry dog, Sunnoo as a donkey, Nagina as a serpent, Jyoti Kiran as a fish, widow Rajani as a headless chicken, Nirbhaya Dayal as a tortoise, Sonkali as a cat, Teeshee as a goat or a chicken, and the Circus Manager Shishu Pal as an animal.

It has often been observed that similarities and coincidences, comparisons and contrasts somehow appeal to the people whether they be in life or in literature. Ramesh K. Srivastava has done a commendable job in the above both cases – in portrayal of animals and in imagery – by juxtaposing the two worlds of human beings and animals together. The detailed activities of the cow, the elephant, the dog, the cat and the snake in the above short stories have been shown contrastingly in their unbeastly, humanised activities which provide a pleasantly fascinating aspect of animals so much in contrast to the dehumanised human beings.

Works Cited

Das, Smita. "Imagery in Ramesh K. Srivastava's *Neema*" in *Ramesh K. Srivastava: Man and his Work* (Ed.). Smita Das. New Delhi: Authors Press, 2016, 197-210.

Eliot, George. *Scenes of Clerical Life*. London: Macmillan, 1906.

Herriot, James. *All Creatures Great and Small*. New York: St. Martin's Griffin, 1972.

Phipson, Emma. "*The Animal-lore of Shakespeare's Time.*" London: Kegan Paul, Trent & Co, 1883.

Sanders, C.R. "The Sociology of Nonhuman Animals" in C.D. Bryant and D.L. Peck (Eds.). *21st Century Sociology: A Reference Handbook. Specialty and Interdisciplinary Studies* (vol. 2). Thousand Oaks, CA: Sage Publications. 2007. 2-7.

Srivastava, Ramesh K. *My Father's Bad Boy: An Autobiography.* New Delhi: Authors Press, 2017.

………. *Neema.* Calcutta: Writers Workshop, 1986.

………. *Road Not Taken and Other Stories.* New Delhi: Authors Press, 2018.

……. "The Beauty and the Beast," *International Journal on Multicultural Literature,* Vol. 7, No.2 (July 2017), 150-156.

………. *Under the Lamp: Stories.* Jalandhar: ABS Publications, 1993.

CHAPTER 6

Loving Vignettes: Mother Figure in Ramesh K. Srivastava's Short Stories

Usha Bande

Ramesh K. Srivastava has made for himself a comfortable niche in the field of Indo-English fiction with his novel *Neema* and five collections of short stories, namely: *Love and Animality, Cooperative Colony, Masks and Men, Games They Play,* and *Under the Lamp.* The thirty-six stories contained in these volumes are written on a variety of subjects, but they all focus on the socio-cultural milieu the writer moves in, thus providing "an artistic portrayal of ever-unfolding mysteries of human existence" (*Under* 'Preface' v). The characters and situations are common, everyday ones which a reader may encounter anywhere in India – an ordinary middle-class man (or woman) with the humour or irony of his life, a truck-driver, a beggar's daughter, a rag-picker, a foreign-returned professor. Amid them sometimes looms the portrayal of the mother – loving, traditional, superstitious and yet strong! The mother may or may not be central to the thematic concern of a story, but she certainly makes an impact on the reader. My aim in the paper is to study mothers and mother-figures as they appear in Srivastava's short stories.

In his interview with Rama Vaidyanathan on Indo-English fiction, Nissim Ezekiel, though not very sanguine about the genre, remarks that on the positive side, Indo-English literature provides "glimpses of Indian life, Indian values and attitudes which form the stuff of any good literature. It must reflect the social environment" (Vaidyanathan 17). Srivastava succeeds in projecting the mother in her social environment. He gives a couple of realistic characters of mothers whom we can recognise, be she a labour-mother sitting on the road-side, caressing the child or a helpless mother staking her prized honor for the welfare of her child; one tends to admire her, love her, or pity her.

One such admirable yet pitiable mother is portrayed in "Under the Lamp," a short story revolving round a social scourge but giving, at the same time, an unforgettable character in Karmaibai. As the story opens, we meet her "behind the iron bars... a woman of thirty one, widowed," accused yet calm. She has lost the will to live; not that she is led by some existential crisis within her but because she has no faith in human goodness or in human justice. She has seen "so much darkness under the lamp, so many criminals masquerading as Samaritans under the very lamp which lights the path for others that the vision of a cool death seems so satisfying" to her (*Under* 105).

As a woman, Karmaibai is strong. She has lived with pride and self-respect as Fauladi's wife, she has faced the ups and downs of fate after his death, she has stood up to live for her son Siddha. She explains it thus, "after the death of my husband, I had never felt myself as strong as I did on that day [when her father-in-law taught her their family trade]. Now I felt that small tendrils even if fragile had begun to lend support to me, building up a kind of renewed faith and confidence within me" (109). The same self-supporting Karmaibai becomes weak when it comes to her son's welfare; she makes "small compromises" for the sake of her son, lets Bichitra Singh have his will, ignores malicious talks of neighbouring women and harbours a rosy vision of future when her son will be a big man to protect her. Not that she has killed her conscience; it rakes her often but her defense is "Siddha, you are all I have. It is for you that I suffer" (113). But Karmaibai, in her one-sided view of the well-being of her son, ignores the social factor. The slanderous remarks of the people about her chastity create a psychological turmoil inside the child.

Grown-up Siddha becomes wayward, leaves school and openly opposes his mother. One can imagine the shattering effect it has on her. The climax is reached when Siddha is killed and the "gentle" so far subdued mother becomes a fierce tigress and kills the source of her misery – Bichitra Singh. She accepts her arrest with resignation, "as long as Siddha was alive there was a ray of hope within me; it is all dark now and there is nothing for me to live" (121). One could almost say with MuIk Raj Anand's Janaki, "No one knows what a woman suffers. How much she has to bear, silently and without protest the abuse and the condemnation" (Anand 22). The focus of the story is not on the mother, but on a social situation in which the "haves" exploit the "have-nots;" and if the "have-not" be a woman, she has nowhere to hide. In the process, the mother in Karmaibai surfaces with all her gentleness, naivety and fierceness. One can read between the lines the corroding effect a mother's smothering love can have on the tender psyche of the child.

Another story in which a child becomes as much a victim of mother's misplaced love as Siddha is "Ganga Ma." Here, the main theme revolves round superstitions and the curse of blind faith. The author is more concerned with tradition and modernity, and superstition versus reason than with painting the mother. The image of the mother, in the bargain, loses much of its strength and charm. Cbhutkee, the village woman, is so much obsessed with taking a dip in the holy water of the Ganga on Makar Sankranti day that she disregards all sense, forces her son despite his fever to plunge into the icy water in freezing cold and becomes the cause of his death. It would be futile to indict Chhutkee, uneducated, headstrong and superstitious though she is, because whatever she does, is done with a naive faith that Ganga Ma would help her and her son Sunkoo. Instead, one should counter the hypocrisy, blind beliefs and ignorance. One should be rational enough to ward off the irrational fears evoked by priests for selfish purposes. Kanika does that and earns the love and respect of her aunt who had insulted her earlier. While Kanika and Buddhan appear strong in their rational approach, the mother appears weak. She is rather a block meant to fulfil the thematic concern. The author does not even allow her remorse. She looks less than human, though we would not call her inhuman.

On the contrary, a tender picture of a mother's capacity to love, not only a human child but even a kitten, is found in "'Terrorists in the Kitchen." Sonkali. Nirbhay Dayal's wife, considers the black cat as ill-ominous, though the couple – Sonkall and Nirbhay Dayal – enjoy the frolicking kittens and the loving cat-mother, and become fond of the lively creatures. The cat-family becomes a part of their lonely life. They tenderly call them 'terrorists in the kitchen' because of their destructive activities. Behind Sonkali's anger and apparent aversion for the mother cat and the kitten, one could feel her "warm concern, love and affection" (*Under* 81) for the feline mother and her kittens. Even when she scolds them, there is no contempt but a self-righteous anger as if directed toward a naughty child. The picture of the mother-cat playing with the kitten and training them in the art of survival, adds another dimension to mother-love. We miss here, however, the metaphysical touch of Raja Rao who sees in the cat the image of the mother (Rao 1971).

A short but sweet glimpse of mother's love is given in "Spilled Milk" in the portrayal of Mishri Mausi. She is sweet like her name, and is tenderness personified. Moreover, the author seems to suggest, obliquely though, that it is not necessary to be a woman to have tenderness and self-sacrificing spirit. Chhajjoo is almost maternal toward little Pinki and a reader can feel his affection for her. Further, Sister Margret in "Rebirth" though young, is another mother-figure who cures the shattered Kiran, both physically and mentally. Her affection instills life in her and restores her faith in living. Sister Margaret even unites Kiran with her mother-in-law. The mother-in-law is portrayed both as the traditional tyrant figure as well as the loving mother-figure. In "A Beggar's Daughter" we encounter a mother whose self-sacrifice and healthy vision of life becomes a boon. That Poornima should become an IPS officer signifies the 'from rags to riches' story on the one hand, and on the other, it speaks highly of the mother, her ambition, humility and sacrifice. In this connection, one may quote Dorothy Spencer, who thinks that the sacrificing mother in Indo-English fiction is intended to be "realistic portrayal." Discussing Prem Chand's works, she remarks that woman "in her capacity of mother... is capable of great self-denial and self- sacrifice" (Spencer 16). The mother considers her daughter Poornima as a son and vows to educate her. This awareness is much more than we could associate with her social status and class, but it helps the author to deal with his theme.

"Games They Play" shows the love children have for the mother. Nathunia's love for her children is expressed with descriptive touches, "a sudden spurt of affection, like an exploding firework, gushed from the depth of her heart" (*Games* 81) her false anger too reveals her tenderness toward them. As a mother, Nathunia is capable of teaching the children and of educating them. She seems to be a great story teller and has the ability to satisfy their curiosity. That the children love and adore her is clear from the children's concern for Suraj and Chanda. They cannot understand the concept of a "cursing mother" since their own mother is so soft and affectionate.

The author gives us only a few vignettes of the mother. He employs the technique of evoking a mood or an atmosphere by carefully piling up details of the social milieu and affords us an entry into the world they people. As Dr Atma Ram, in his introductory notes on "Contemporary Indian Short Story" observes, Srivastava's "stance may appear negative and anti-establishment on the surface but down deep he stands for a constructive order and positive values in life" (Ram 17). Mother being one of the upholders of the "constructive order and positive values of life" has been described with loving touches wherever she appears. Srivastava does not deify her nor does he defile her as some of the Indo-English authors seem to be doing; he simply paints her as she appears in her innumerable garbs in her social, familial and cultural functions.

Works Cited

Anand, Mulk Raj. *The Big Heart.* Bombay: Kutub Popular, 1945.

Ram, Atma and R. K. Dhawan, "Contemporary Indian Short Story" in Ramesh K. Srivastava's *Games They Play and Other Stories.* New Delhi: Prestige Books, 1989. 13-15.

Rao, Raja. *The Cat and Shakespeare.* Delhi: Hind Pocket Books, 1971.

Spencer, Dorothy. *Indian Fiction in English.* Philadelphia: University of Pennsylvania Press, 1960.

Srivastava, Ramesh K. *Games They Play and Other Stories.* New Delhi: Prestige Books,1989.

..........*Under the Lamp: Stories.* Jalandhar: ABS Publications, 1993.

Vaidyanathan, Rama. "Nissim Ezekiel on Indo-Anglian Fiction: An Interview," *Journal of Literature and Aesthetics,* 2 (April-July, 1982): 17-19.

CHAPTER 7

East-West Encounter in Ramesh K. Srivastava's Short Stories

Leela Kanal

A writer's mind is like a spider's web which catches and stores the tiniest of activities happening around him. The richness and depth of his writings depend on his wide experience and fertile imagination. Ramesh K. Srivastava chronicles in detail in his autobiography *My Father's Bad Boy* how his life was influenced in three broad areas: his rural upbringing, his urban education and employment, and his stay in the U.S. As a result of these influences, his novels *Neema* and *Coils of the Serpent* as well as his seven collections of short stories have abundance of portrayal of rural, urban and foreign life. Here my attempt is to critically examine only his portrayal of the western life and the interaction of Indians in it.

The portrayal of East-West encounter has been fairly common among Indian writers in English, particularly those who spent some time in the West. Naturally, they must have come across some people, places, scenes and manners which are in certain ways both similar and dissimilar from those in India. Raja Rao's *The Serpent and the Rope,* Kamala Markandays's *Possession,* Bhabani Bhattacharya's *A Dream in Hawaii,* Arun Joshi's *The Foreigner* and Ramesh K. Srivastava's short stories have dealt with this theme. Meenakshi Mukherjee defines it as "the conflicts and reconciliations of two cultures" (Mukherjee 54). Such interaction takes place in relation to love, sex, marriage, manners, cultural values and ways of communication. Smita Das feels that in Srivastava's short stories "the portrayal of the western people, their manners, their habits, their food and their attitudes come alive which have been so well contrasted with those of Indians" (Das 45).

In Srivastava's two novels *Neema* and *Coils of the Serpent,* there is no portrayal of the cultural clash, interaction and reconciliation of the East and the West because the characters and incidents relate to Indian villages and cities. However, there are a number of short stories in which the theme of East-West encounter has been dealt with in detail. In the story "A Drowning Man," Shyam is a physician who stays in the U.S., freely enjoys the company of American girls, dates them frequently, has sex with them but these very factors when viewed in a narrow perspective make him wish to marry an Indian girl who, being untouched by Western influence, would remain an innocent virgin. It is this typical attitude of Indian men who exploit American girls without any twitches of conscience but prefer to have virgin Indian girls for their wives.

In the story, different aspects of Indian and American culture have been given. Shyam finds shyness and timidity, simplicity and innocence in his wife Sarala who comes out as "a flawless product of the Indian culture" (*Under* 10) even though he himself happens to be "a hybrid product of two different cutures" (10-11). In contrast, American girls like Amelia, Jamie, Cathy and Susie satisfied him because of their "openness, boldness, officiousness, aggressiveness and even shamelessness" (*Under* 11). Karnail Singh feels that "Srivastava's mind shuttles freely across the boundaries of Indian and American cultures. The Indian puritan ethos comes into conflict with the American permissive code of morality and causes tension in the mind of the protagonist" (*Recognition* 29). Even though Srivastava criticizes Indian boys for their hypocrisy, he does not spare Americans. Since he lived all his life in India, he analyses it minutely and says, "hypocrisy is usually another name of our culture" (*Under* 17). Contrasting American and Indian girls, Shyam feels: "There is an advantage in marrying an American girl. You *live* with her whereas you *spend* your life with an Indian girl" (17). The climax of the story comes when Shyam's expectations of a virgin Indian girl are dashed to the ground on finding that despite her shyness and timidity before even her husband, Sarala was innocently having frequent sex in the maize fields of her village. The revelation makes Shyam feel "like a weather-beaten man, now drowning in an unfathomable ocean" (*Under* 23). Here Srivastava dispassionately depicts the positive and negative traits of both American and Indian cultures. Undoubtedly, no one is free from hypocrisy. Both cultures have their advantages and drawbacks. It would be a lopsided view to portray anyone country all-white or all-black as Indian and American cultures have often been exaggeratingly portrayed in newspapers and movies.

Srivastava's "Century" is a story of two Indians – Mohan and Jasbir who go to the U.S. for their studies. The story gives a detailed account of their adventures and problems in the U.S. Mohan experiences a burdening feeling of loneliness because of his conversational deficiency in English, its exotic food and different faces. Consequently, he often withdrew to his room. For him, American weekends were so vastly different from those in India. There were other Indians, including Jasbir, who enjoyed their life in the U.S. They went to drive-in movies, dances or strip-tease shows with girls while he remained alone and hence when someone spoke to him in Hindi, Mohan felt that "the sound of one's native language in a foreign country is like lovely, soothing rain on parched land, bringing hopes of greenery, fruition and good times ahead" (*Christmas* 54). Mohan considers America as a good place for higher studies which one cannot do in India, whereas Jasbir thinks that "America is a land to enjoy" (*Christmas* 54) and that studies can be pursued even in India. For him, U.S. "is a paradise so far as I'm concerned. I don't miss a single chance to trap girls, and soon I will be completing a century" (*Christmas* 56).

Mohan's alienation becomes quite acute on weekends in the U.S. in the absence of communication with others: "On week-ends, the telephones of others rang off and on, but mine went dead. No one called me. I yearned anxiously to hear it ring even once. But no one dialed my phone even by mistake" (*Christmas* 59). However, after he finds his student Marcy's company, he feels that her presence "kindled ecstatic feelings I had never experienced in life. It was like floating in the air or gliding on water" (63). Mohan's failure to have sexual union with Marcy arises partly because of his humanity and partly because he was told in India: "Every Indian is an ambassador of his country in a foreign place and his achievements and lapses will uplift or tar the nation's image" (*Christmas* 67). While Jasbir boasts of completing a century of sexual acts with American girls, Mohan misses an equal number. In Karnail Singh's view "The East and the West seem to have met on the bed on which Marcy and Mohan sleep all the night, not like Adam and Eve before their fall, but like two sensuous beings who are drawn between the pulls of pleasure and reality" (Singh 308). In the morning when all three of them – Mohan, Jasbir and Marcy – accidentally meet before the dormitory, Marcy calls Jasbir a "bastard" whereas to Mohan, she had said earlier, "You' are the nicest person I've ever known" (*Christmas* 67). At the end of the story, Jasbir goes significantly to the west and Mohan to the east, symbolising their faiths in different cultures.

His story "Friendship, Love and Marriage" has two main characters: Maharaja Kumar Chaturvedi, an Indian man, and Loveleen – an American girl. In the U.S., Chaturvedi, through "Friendly Introductory Service," contacts Loveleen initially only for friendship but it develops into love and comes to the point of marriage. However, when the misunderstanding of Loveleen and her mother Patsy about the word "Maharaja" in his name clears up that it was Chaturvedi's first name and that he was not a king, all the highly proclaimed idealistic claims to relationship from both sides are dashed to the ground. The story has beautifully portrayed the positive and negative points in the cultures of both the U.S. and India. In M. L. Mehta's view, the story exposes "the hypocrisy and hollowness of human relationship, the sanctity of which is desecrated by the mercantile mentality and commercial attitudes of an acquisitive society" (Mehta 81). American educational system is claimed to be the best in the world, but it is shocking that Loveleen has very poor knowledge of geography, though she claims to be getting all A's in the subject in High School. She considers India "a part of Bombay" (*Christmas* 99). Chaturvedi contrasts the roads in both the countries: "Indian roads looked like a national cemetery; American, a dead geography" (100) because Indian roads are often named after past national celebrities and American on their geographical locations. When Loveleen and her mother think that India has no cars and no electricity, Chaturvedi in a light mood tells them that the students go to college on elephants and camels and park them in attached stables. Instead of electric fans, they convert the severed ears of elephants as hand fans after attaching handles to them. The marriages are fixed by parents for their children which to Loveleen appears "like blind dates" (*Christmas* 101). The advertisement for Indian marriages in newspapers and the payment of dowry appear to Loveleen "a sort of legalised prostitution" (109).

Loveleen talks of high ideals of American girls who marry a person because of their love, not money, nor position and that she would gladly agree to marry Maharaja even if he "were a cobbler in your country . . . just because of love" for him (*Christmas* 112). However, all the idealistic claims of Loveleen and Patsy fail the moment they come to know that Chaturvedi was not a king. Consequently, they break off all contacts with him by changing their phone number within hours and making it unlisted. Afterwards, for Patsy, India becomes "a barbarian country" and Chaturvedi a "bastard" and an "absolutely ugly" person who walked like a camel and danced like a kangaroo (*Christmas* 114). This way Srivastava exposes the attitudes of both Indians and Americans.

Srivastava's "Road Not Taken" is about Kushagra Mathur's achievements and frustrations in India and in the U.S. Leela Kanal points out that the story "deals with the rise of mathematical genius, Kushagra Mathur, and his ultimate return to his life in rural India as a primary school teacher" (Kanal 130). Though belonging to a poor family in a village, Kushagra creates an academic history in his college, who, despite being in B.Sc Part I, solves a mathematical problem in three ways which his widely-renowned teacher Dr Eknath Ranade could do only in one way. It was his teacher's encouraging comment about Kushagra which had "placed him on an unusual road from where he was catapulted into the U.S." (*Road* 87). Later, in a series of tests, he solved the most difficult mathematical problems found in the syllabi of both B.Sc. and M.Sc. It was then that his teacher Dr Ranade contacted his own Professor Harold Johnson in the U.S. who came to India and took Kushagra with him. Given his circumstances, Kushagra could not have imagined to visit the U.S., "a place about which many students merely dream but cannot reach" (*Road* 85) for higher studies but with the help of Professor Johnson, his "dream" becomes a reality. He realised that whereas his father wanted him to be a Primary School teacher, he had taken "a different road – more ambitious, seemingly inaccessible" (*Road* 85) and that had made all the difference.

During his two years in the U.S., Kushagra had a lot of achievement to his credit. He had completed his Ph.D. and published many papers in international journals. He had helped Dr Johnson's daughter Jane in her Master's degree. Dr Johnson wanted Kushagra to get married to his daughter Jane but after his marriage instead with an Indian girl, Akriti Kulshreshtha, he surprisingly "noticed somewhat cooling down of her [Jane's] attitude towards him" (*Road* 103). Later, he found that his own research paper was published in the names of Harold Johnson and Jane Johnson. Kushagra was immensely shocked "by their acts of plagiarism" (103) because he had believed that there is unquestionable academic honesty in the American universities. But now his faith was shaken.

The problem of academic dishonesty of Dr Johnson and his daughter Jane, the ill-treatment of his sister Priya by her husband and the court case of Akriti Kulshreshtha for divorce disturbed his psychic balance and he had to be admitted to a nursing home which kept him as a hostage in the absence of payment of its dues of Rs five lakh. None had so much money to help him. It was Cynthia Winward, his American friend, who helped him in all possible ways. Becoming emotional, she promised "I'll NOT go back to the U.S. without bringing you out of this dungeon" (*Road* 101). After contacting some charitable organisations and with Dr Eknath Ranade's help, she collected adequate amount to get Kushagra released from the nursing home. After his release with Cynthia's help, he began to teach in the Primary School of his village and felt satisfied with the road he had taken under changed circumstances.

It is obvious that in the above stories, Srivastava has portrayed with reasonable objectivity both Indian and American cultures as also their bright and dark sides. No culture in the world can be categorised as completely flawless because it is the sum total of human activities and attitudes which are driven by the head and the heart and hence cannot be identical. Their variations lead to dissimilar activities. It goes to his credit that despite being Indian, Srivastava has not minced words in painting his own country, wherever needed, in dark colours. His short stories are a two-sided mirror that reflects both cultures in complete fidelity.

Works Cited

Das, Smita. "A Critical Introduction," *Ramesh K. Srivastava: Man and his Work: A Collection of Critical Essays,* ed. by Smita Das. New Delhi: Authors Press, 2016, 15-71.

Kanal, Leela. Book Review of Ramesh K. Srivastava's *Road Not Taken and Other Stories. Writers, Editors, Critics: An International Biannual Journal on English Languauge and Literature.* Vol. VIII, No. 1 (March 2018), 128-130.

Mehta, M. L. Book Review of *Masks and Men: Stories. Indian Book Chronicle.* Vol. XIV, No. 4 (April 1989), 80-81.

Mukherjee, Meenakshi. *The Twice-Born Fiction: Themes and Techniques of Indian Novel in English.* New Delhi: Arnold-Heinemann, 1972.

Singh, Karnail. "Other Experiences," Review of *Cooperative Colony: Stories. Indian Book Chronicle.* (December 1987), 306-308.

.... *Book Review The Recognition of Ramesh K. Srivastava: A Collection of Book Reviews on his Creative Writing ed. by Shipra G. Vashishtha.* New Delhi: Authors Press, 2020, 29-34.

Srivastava, Ramesh K. *A Christmas Gift and Other Stories.* New Delhi: Authors Press, 2015.

.... *Road Not Taken and Other Stories.* New Delhi: Authors Press, 2018.

.... *Under the Lamp: Stories.* Jalandhar: ABS Publications, 1993.

CHAPTER 8

Suppression and Revolt of Women in Ramesh K. Srivastava's Short Stories

Smita Das

Indian history and mythology abound in examples of suppression of women for several centuries. The forcible disrobing of Draupadi in the presence of her husbands and even elders in *The Mahabharata*, the kidnapping and enslavement of Sita and then her humiliating fire test in *The Ramayana*, the forcibly-imposed Sati system in which a woman was forced to burn herself along with the dead body of her husband, and the annexation of the State from the queen of Jhansi after the death of her husband are only a few cases of suppression. In a very few cases, they did revolt against their ill-treatment, but mostly they helplessly accepted it in the name of fate.

In Indian literature in English, several writers have taken up the theme of suppression of women in India. Mulk Raj Anand in *Gauri* depicts the docile character of Gauri as she is persistently persecuted till she picks up courage and fights against her tormentors. R.K. Narayan in *Dark Room* portrays the pathetic plight of Savitri. Anita Desai's Maya in *Cry, the Peacock* feels suppressed even if real or imaginary, but revolts against her husband and pushes him fatally from the parapet. Arundhati Roy in *The God of Small Things* graphically depicts the miserable plight of Ammu under her cruel father and subsequently by the society for loving an untouchable Velutha. Srivastava in his novel *Neema* writes of the suppression and torture of Neema by her impotent husband Jeewan Jyoti and no less by his mother Subhasini. She eventually revolts against her husband by flaunting before him her sexual act with her *devar* Rasik Lal. In his *Coils of the Serpent*, Srivastava shows how Shabana is tortured and repressed by Nawab Hashmi and excommunicated from the village. For various reasons, she could not raise her voice but her younger sister Nagina revengefully not only grabs the property but successfully eliminates her sister's victimizers.

In his autobiography, Srivastava gives minute details of the suppression of his mother by her husband, his elder and younger brothers, his sisters and their mother. Consequently, finding no way out, she had to fight resolutely "against discrimination and injustices within the family" (*Autobiography* 31). In several of his short stories, Srivastava has depicted the suppression of women in various forms. In his interview with Y. Joy, he said, "If at all I depicted women in several forms, I must have seen them in real life. Of course, they are usually modified with imagination" (Joy 325-326).

Srivastava's story "Under the Lamp" revolves around the sufferings of a young girl Karmaibai of blacksmith caste who because of her unusual beauty charmed and tempted others, including Bichitra Singh, the Sabhapati of Kaliana village. He not only broke her first marriage but attempted to sabotage the second one with Fauladi. After the death of her husband Fauladi, Bichitra Singh begins to be very kind to her by using "sympathetic words – words without spirit, hollow" (*Under* 107). She could understand that his real intention was to seduce and molest her. When she begins to work at her ancestral smithy, the first thing that she sharpened was the edge of a *gandasa* with "the belief that it would protect the family from all dangers" (108). Her father-in-law asked her to keep the "ancestral *gandasa* as a token of your resolve to struggle in this world and to fend for yourself" (*Under* 109). Shipra G. Vashishtha considers the *gandasa* "a non-human agent which is her source of strength and courage" (Vashishtha 49). Gaining confidence, she begins to work in the house of Bichitra Singh where she had to clean the cowdung and urine of buffaloes and cows which was never done by the people belonging to her blacksmith caste but she does it to be in the good books of the Sabhapati which was desirable for survival. In her daily visits to his house, Bichitra Singh begins to fulfill his sexual desires at will and Karmaibai has to knuckle under his whimsical demands for the wellbeing of her son Siddha, whom she wants to get educated.

When she complains to her father-in-law against Bichitra Singh's attempts at her molestation, he advises, "Avoid enmity with a crocodile if you are to live in a pond" (111). Her son Siddha happens to see them in a compromising position two times which alarms Bichitra Singh and as such he decides to eliminate him. Whenever Karmaibai refuses to yield to his wishes, he lashes her, beats her with iron rod, and burns parts of her body with lighted cigarette butts. Besides, through his own people, he makes her son Siddha an opium-eater and a thief. Once Bichitra Singh in a drunken state reveals how he had got Karmaibai's first engagement broken, how he had challenged her husband Fauladi to climb the highest branch of the mango tree which caused his death and that he had a hand in Siddha's death. Considering him "the chief architect of her woes," she becomes so furious against him that she beheads him with the *gandasa*. Usha Bande finds in Karmaibai "an unforgettable character" who, for the sake of her son, remains subdued but "becomes a fierce tigress and kills the source of her misery – Bichitra Singh" (Bande 143). Lata Mishra praises Karmaibai who "struggles to survive with dignity in a world that humiliates and subverts her every attempt for emancipation and progress" (Mishra 22).

The story "Lasting Victory" depicts the life of Vimala Tiwari, a lecturer in a predominantly men's college. Initially, she is portrayed as a suppressed woman who gradually resists, revolts and succeeds in her mission. The Principal of the college, a father-figure for her, attempts to ensnare her. When she goes to prepare tea for him and then into the storeroom for sugar, he holds her hand, but she pulls herself "forward with all the strength of desperation and he lost his hold over" her left hand (*Masks* 58). Failing in his attempt to molest her in his own house, he harasses her through Gurmel Singh, an impertinent student, who attempts to kidnap her at the point of a dagger, but Bhola protects her. Then he threatens to burn the college bus to embarrass her as a Students' Union Advisor, but she checkmates him by boarding it herself, and at the same time disallows the police to arrest him. This way she wins everyone's heart and attains a lasting victory with no ill feelings around.

In "Rescuers," Neeru tactfully resists the efforts of three young men in kidnapping her on a motor bike and saves herself from them by approaching Father Joseph Sault. She is awe-struck when she finds herself raped by her savior Father Sault. It was then that she realises that "the whole world was inhabited by wolves, some in their original, and some in sheep's skin" (*Masks* 80). When Father Sault blindfolds her eyes and asks her to hit the target with the knives on hearing the sound alone, she puts all her energy into the knives and hurls them one by one towards the voice of the Father which get deeply embedded in his neck.

The story "Silver Lining" describes the life of a girl Shravasti, who gets selected in the Civil Services examination (Preliminary) with the hope of serving the country by becoming an IAS or IPS officer. Her boyfriend Shahid persuades her to bring all her ornaments and money and to elope with him and his *bua* Farzana to Bombay. He had already assured her all help in making her a model or a movie actress. When the train stops at Mumbai CST, she finds her handbag containing money, clothes and gold jewelry missing. Both Shahid and his *bua* were also missing. On finding herself cheated, all her hopes were suddenly dashed to the ground. Crying helplessly, she is brought to a pickpocket's den by a girl named Marina. When she reaches the den, she is forcefully slapped by Balloo Dada and then physically thrashed by all other boys of the den to train her so as to ensure that she would not cry even if caught as a pickpocket and thrashed by the public. She could not forget that she had fallen into a trap because of the deception by Shahid Ahmad. In the den, a co-pickpocket Kittoo helps her in taking revenge by getting Shahid arrested on the charge of trafficking in women and supplying brown sugar. In the end, she happily realises that it was "the first silver lining I had noticed attached to an otherwise dark profession" (*Road* 34).

It is quite surprising that with his far-reaching imagination, Srivastava makes even a simple rope a lucky one by making it a means of revenge against the oppressor. The story "Lucky Rope" depicts the village of Chakarpur where the zamindar Raja Bhunaresh Singh had an unwritten rule that any adolescent girl or a newly married woman would have to be offered to him at the first available opportunity. Bhunaresh tells Bhanwari Bai to bring her newly-married daughter-in-law to him. When she fails to do so on the first day of her arrival, he thrashes her hard with the rope which appeared worse than the leather whip and warns her, "If you fail to bring her, I'll skin you alive before your husband and son" (64). Reaching home, she shows her injuries to Hulli, her daughter-in-law, and tells her, "This is all because of your lucky rope" (65). Unable to bear the sight of her mother-in-law's injuries, she agrees to sleep with Bhunaresh Singh and then succeeds in eliminating him by setting the entire room with Bhunaresh Singh on fire.

The story "Of No Use to Me" delineates how a woman gives a befitting reply to her greedy husband in a patriarchal society. In the beginning, Priyansh and Somya lead a happily married life. However, her happiness takes a u-turn when after a couple of tests it was found that she was incapable of being pregnant. Priyansh wishes to divorce her and remarry some other girl. Afterwards, all members of the family begin to create for her "the living hell in various forms" (221) on matters of the dowry and other excuses. Finally, Priyansh's mother tells Somya, "Because you cannot give us a child to continue our family line, you are of no use to me" (222). Finding herself helpless, Somya goes back to her father. After sometime when Priyansh tries to bring her back to his own house as if because of the change of his heart towards her, she reconciles to it. When Anandita, her friend, tells Somya that Priyansh had met with such a terrible accident that he had become impotent, Somya decides to take revenge. In response to Priyansh's pathetic cry in a helpless situation, "Now I am of no use to you" (227), she reminds him that when he had discarded her for her infertility, "Why should I not leave you because you are of no use to me?" (227).

In "Serpentine Woman," the protagonist Rajani makes preemptive strike against the male member Shesh Raj due to his exploitation and suppression of her and also due to his fatal conspiracy against her husband. After the death of her husband Jagaran, Rajani and her daughter Teju manage to survive by doing odd jobs, such as, cleansing grains and lentils in a grocery shop owned by Vijay Pal. As she also knew the art of catching serpents, she continues her husband's job of catching them, extracting their poison and then selling it in the market. Shesh Raj, the friend of Jagran, gets enamored of her beauty and wishes to marry the widow which Rajani declines because he was reluctant to keep her daughter Teju with him. Exploiting her helplessness, Shesh Raj not only rapes her periodically, but pilfers her money which she kept in a narrow niche of the mud wall of her house. He even thrashes her mercilessly and threatens to kill her and to run away with her daughter Teju to make her his wife in near future. When it becomes a regular habit of Shesh Raj to steal her money and to buy a pouch of country liquor, Rajani manages to take revenge against him through the Koriwala snake which stung him fatally.

These stories must not be taken merely as sociological documents portraying the class struggle between the oppressors and the oppressed. They are meticulously crafted pieces of literature which deserve to be considered on their literary merits as well. In his interview with Atma Ram, Srivastava defined a good short story as "a frozen moment of life revealed through a sequence of words. It must be short, readable and meaningful" (Ram 22). Most of Srivastava's short stories are short, simple and interesting but not devoid of hidden, unobtrusive symbolic meanings. Barinder K. Sharma finds "the dexterous use of symbols which add depth and richness to the literary creation" (211). His "Under the Lamp" is meticulously crafted short story which begins at the end when Karmaibai surrenders at the police station. She arouses so much interest in the beginning that the reader has no option but to go on to its end to find out the reason behind her action. The story "Rescuers" is a classically composed short dramatic tale with a message that the exploitation of women is not the monopoly of the people of one religion but on a given opportunity, people of all religions indulge in it. The story dramatically stuns the reader but with a sense of appreciation for the protagonist Neeru. Neeta Maini finds that Srivastava's "short stories have a wide range and variety both in the subject matter and technique" (Maini 186). There is such a perfect fusion of form and content in Srivastava's stories that an act of intense churning from various angles becomes a rewarding exercise.

Works Cited

Bande, Usha. "Loving Vignetgtes – Mother in R. K. Srivastava's Short Stories." *Mother Figures in Indian English Fiction,* Edited by Usha Bande. ABS Publications, 1997, pp. 142-147.

Joy, Y. "An Interview with Ramesh K. Srivastava." *Ramesh K Srivastava: Man and His Work.* Ed. Smita Das. Authorspress, 2016, pp. 320-337.

Maini, Neeta. "R. K. Srivastava," *Studies in Contemporary Indian English Short Story: A Collection of Critical Essays.* Ed. A. N. Dwivedi. B. R., Publishing Corporation, 1991. pp. 185-197.

Mishra, Lata. "Narrative as Discourse: A Study of Ramesh K. Srivastava's *Under the Lamp.*" *Virtuoso: A Refereed Transnational Bi-Annual Journal of Language and Literature in English*, vol. II, no.2, February, 2013. pp.17-24.

Sharma, Barinder K. "Symbolism in Ramesh K. Srivastava's *Neema.*" *Symbolism in Indian Fiction in English.* Ed. Ramesh K. Srivastava. ABS Publications, 1997, pp. 211-220.

Srivastava, Ramesh K. *Masks and Men: Stories.* Writers Workshop. 1986.

.... *My Father's Bad Boy: An Autobiography.* Authorspress, 2017.

.... *Road Not Taken and Other Stories.* Authorspress 2018.

.... *Under the Lamp: Stories.* ABS Publications, 1993.

Vashishtha, Shipra G. "Ramesh K. Srivastava's 'Under the Lamp': A Study," *Writers Editors Critics:* *v*ol. VII, no. 1. March 2017. pp.48-54.

CHAPTER 9

Wit and Humour in the Works of Ramesh K. Srivastava

Swati Srivastava

> "And what are you reading, Miss – ?"
> "Oh! It is only a novel!"... or, in short,
> only some work in which the most thorough
> knowledge of human nature, the happiest
> delineation of its varieties, the liveliest
> effusions of wit and humour are conveyed
> to the world in the best chosen language.
>
> Jane Austen, *Northanger Abbey.*

The purpose of introducing wit and humour in any literary work or activity has largely been to evoke some kind of laughter. Even though the term "wit" has gone through changes in meanings and associations over a period of several centuries, it has remained associated with creative imagination. In the nineteenth century, wit and humour became associated with the laughable. *New English Dictionary* defines them as "that quality of speech or writing which consists in the apt association of thought and expression, calculated to surprise and delight by its unexpectedness; later always with reference to the utterance of brilliant or sparkling things in an amusing way" (Quoted Thrall and Hibbard 510). Wit perceives similarities in things often seemingly dissimilar, and expresses it in an intelligent way, often by playing upon words, by contrasts or by paradoxes while humour deals with the foibles and incongruities of human nature. Carolyn Wells defines them: "Wit is intensive or incisive, while humour is expansive. Wit is rapid, humour is slow. Wit is sharp, humour is gentle . . . Wit is subjective while humour is objective . . . . Wit is art, humour is nature" (Wells 17). Many times they go together, are complementary, and decidedly make the literary works delightfully pleasant by lending sunlight to what otherwise would be the reigning darkness all around.

Professor Ramesh Kumar Srivastava has for many years been a university teacher, an erudite scholar and a versatile creative writer in English. In all these roles, he has been known to have liberally shown his inborn gift of wit and humour. His colleagues and his students in Guru Nanak Dev University, Amritsar (Punjab) where he taught in the Department of English for twenty-eight years, and his friends, admirers and readers all over India, including in and around Jhansi (U.P.) where he has settled down after retirement from the university service – all testify to his trait of indulging liberally in pleasant and witty conversation which makes his company quite delightful.

The basic reason behind the introduction of wit and humour is Srivastava's desire to make his works interesting and pleasantly readable, and to create fun and laughter which are often missing from the lives of tension-ridden modern urban and educated people. In his novel *Neema*, Srivastava writes about the quality of laughter and what it does to human beings:

> How sweet is spontaneous, impassioned, uninhibited laughter! It is like an unhampered fountain of pure water originating from a mountain, where the ugly, ominous shades of utilitarian or mischievous human beings have not fallen, which the dirty pollutants of deception and trickery have not contaminated, and which, like the water of the Ganga, carries with it minerals curing sick minds. Woe to the human race that this priceless commodity providentially given so freely by double handfuls to all creatures has not been properly used due to petty considerations
>
> (*Neema* 41-42).

When it comes to creative writing in English, India cannot boast of many writers who have shown comic vein in their writings, though a very large number of writers and poets in Indian regional languages provide rollicking laughter through their humorous poems in *Hasya Kavi Sammelan* (recitation of humorous poetry), in magazines and in their literary works. Among the contemporary Indo-Anglian authors, R. K. Narayan, Khushwant Singh and to some extent Arundhati Roy are three writers in whose works one can notice a powerful vein of humour and wit so as to make the readers laugh. Ramesh K. Srivastava is among the lesser known Indian writers in English whose novel *Neema* (1986) and his five collections of short stories – *Love and Animality: Stories* (1984), *Cooperative Colony: Stories* (1985), *Masks and Men: Stories* (1986), *Games They Play and Other Stories* (1989) and *Under the Lamp: Stories (*1993) display effusively his comic imagination.

In order to fully understand Srivastava's use of comic vein in his works, it would be desirable to see what his views are on the fictional work in general. Writing on the nature of a short story in "Author's Note" to his *Games They Play and Other Stories,* Srivastava defines a short story as "a frozen moment of life, carrying in it the seeds of perennial truths. It reveals in a flash an image of hitherto unexplored aspect of life fleeing each moment before us. A good short story is like a supply of fresh air that makes the human life delightful, meaningful and no less healthy" (*Games* 9). He believes that a short story is neither merely for entertainment, nor to tease the minds of only intelligent readers, but for all kinds of people for all times to come. He writes: "Whereas the short story would lose its place in serious literature if fashioned as a means of modern entertainment, it would also jeopardize its coveted popularity when made out as a complicated and puzzling literary creation. A highly complex and unintelligible story may tease and please an intelligent reader by his sense of discovering something not easily decipherable but confuses an average reader who, suffering from the feeling of belonging to a lower class, grudgingly shares the royal feast albeit not with the same ease and carefreeness with which the high-perched Brahmins would do" (*Games* 9). A writer, according to Srivastava, must be influenced and his works moulded by the kind of readers available to him. He warns: "To wholly disregard them while carving and whittling a literary piece would be as inappropriate as to play the Western classical music to rickshaw-wallah" (*Games*. 9). For Srivastava, the first requisite of a short story is that it must be "readable," thereby implying that it must be short and interesting. Besides, he believes that "an appetite, like the one needed to enjoy a hearty meal, has to be created in the reader to see something new in what appears to be the oft-trodden ground, and then to sustain it with legitimate artistic means, such as suspense, humour and irony" (*Games* 10). Srivastava goes on to clarify that in some literatures of the world, whereas a tragic subject was considered most appropriate for a great work of art, a comic subject, was considered frivolous and inappropriate, and hence relegated to a lesser importance. On the introduction of comic elements in a literary work, Srivastava is quite clear and writes:

> For some people to have a vein of humour in a literary work is to transgress the limits of serious writing. They do not realise that comic mode is an important aspect of life, enjoyed by all, even if only a few have been endowed with a vein of it. Humour demands of its writer a relaxed mood, a perfect control on the language and an immense capacity

> of playing upon words. All this is easy enough in a native tongue but difficult in a foreign language. It is creditable that among Indian short story writers, R. K. Narayan and Khushwant Singh have been successful in introducing, even in English, plenty of wit and humour which make their stories quite interesting and eminently readable (*Games* 10-11).

In an interview with Dr M. L. Mehta, Srivastava was asked as to why had the latter assigned a prominent place to humour, irony and satire in his fiction. His reply was:

> Since humour, irony and satire are part of everyday life, there is no reason why they should not be represented in a work of realistic art. Besides, a good work must be readable before it conveys anything. I am told that humour and irony make my writings fairly interesting and readable. Satire obviously is to demolish those institutions, individuals, customs and traditions which have outlived their use (Mehta 171).

Thus Srivastava makes it amply clear that his works must be readable and interesting, and that he practices what he preached.

Srivastava introduces wit and humour through various means – dialogues, descriptions, characterisation, similes, metaphors, puns, paradoxes, hyperbolic and ironical statements, epithets of disproportionate comparisons and contrasts, and so on. My attempt here would be to discuss Srivastava's use of wit and humour in all their varieties and manifestations with apt illustrations from all his works. Descriptions form an important source of his humour, some of which are full of exaggerated accounts, slanted vision, odd comparisons, mythological allusions, political references occasionally tinged with irony and satire. Here is the description of the village school in *Neema:*

> On one of its corners stood the old, weather-beaten, ramshackle building of the village High School, recalling its early youthful times or counting down its numbered days, or waiting, like the cursed Ahilya, for some minister's touch, or for a storm or earthquake to bring about the salvation. Chunks of plaster, like tattered rags, still clung to the walls revealing more than concealing its ribs. The tiled thatch, blackened by many years of sun, rain and dust, had sagged in the center like the nose of an old man suffering from anosmia. Half-dried trees, bent or broken with age, neglect and exploitation leaned heavily over the dilapidated boundary walls like terrified camel riders in a tempest-churned desert" (*Neema* 23).

Detailed descriptions of the funny activities of children contribute humour in both R. K. Narayan and Arundhati Roy. Srivastava also well describes the funny activities of children which make his works quite interesting. Gopal in *Neema* teases Sunnoo by calling the latter a girl because despite being a boy, he performs all those daily chores which were traditionally reserved for a rural girl. Gopal asks Sunnoo:

> "Are you a boy or a girl?"
> "A boy."
> "Jawahar told me that you're a girl."
> "I am a boy."
> "Do you bring water from the well on your head or not?"
> "I do."
> "And do you dance or not?"
> "I do."
> "And do you wash utensils or not?"
> "I do."
> "Then you are a girl."
> "No. I'm a boy." (*Neema* 18)

The playful activities of Chaman Lal in *Neema* create the same kind of comic atmosphere as do the activities of Balu, Babu and Swami in the novels of R. K. Narayan. After the class teacher Tirath Ram goes to sleep in the class, Chaman Lal plays the role of a morning cock that awakens the people. The entire description of his childish, funny activities is boisterously funny and provokes laughter:

> Chaman Lal went to his corner seat, and cupping his hands before his mouth croaked loud and clear like a cock proclaiming the dawn. The tips of his victim's mustachios vibrated. The cave closed. The stream damned. The cap flew off the head and Tirath Ram's eyes fluttered as he got up, perturbed, from his empyrean slumber. The tug at his tuft of hair gave him the notion of his hair being uprooted. The students thumped and yelled and nodded and laughed and tilted and twisted and tumbled as the teacher tried to get his hair free of the string. Each of his successive efforts accompanied by various grimaces and facial distortions sent the children into spontaneous bursts of laughter (*Neema* 26)

Here Srivastava not only presents a three-dimensional picture of the mischievous yet funny activity of Chaman Lal, but describes it in a mock-heroic manner reminiscent of Dryden, Pope and Swift. He calls Tirath Ram's mouth a "cave," his saliva a "stream," his classroom nap as "empyrean slumber," and so on. Such mischievous and playful activities are indulged in by Huck Finn in Twain's *Adventures of Huckleberry Finn* and by Swaminathan and his friends in R. K. Narayan's *Swami and Friends*. At another place, Neema, as an adolescent, plays a trick somewhat theatrically on Mulk Raj – a policeman – in order to sabotage the marriage proposal because of her reluctance to get married to him when she is being interviewed for the marriage:

> When the dreaded matrimonial interview had begun, I had walked in limping, and had shown a squint in the eyes. When Mulk Raj, a constable and my prospective bridegroom, had asked me in a squeaking voice like that emanating from an un-oiled door-hinge, "What's the climate of Honolulu?" "Very good," I had replied. "It is cold in winter, hot in summer and it rains a great deal in a rainy season." He had twisted his finger in his ear, and asked another, "What's that animal that supplies you milk, curd, butter and ghee?" and I had replied, "At present, my father; after marriage, my husband." "Can you climb a tree?" "Yes, those of gram and wheat" (*Neema* 37).

Being quite intelligent, Neema successfully sabotages the prospective marriage with a policeman by a number of mischievous activities and witty answers. Patiya – an old woman, and Gopal – a child, have some interesting conversation in which the latter believes that the wrinkles over the face of the old woman come from the devil who has scrawled all over her body:

> Meanwhile, Gopal came and asked her, "Is it true, Granny?"
>
> "What's true, my boy?" Patiya patted him. "That you are a little doll of a boy?"
>
> "That... that..." he faltered, suspiciously looking at me while talking to her, "that a devil has written on your face with a sharp needle?"
>
> "Quite true," Patiya replied, ignoring my protest. "I was like you long long ago with my cheeks swollen like a balloon. Then the devil came with a needle and he punctured and deflated me. Not satisfied with it, he took the sharp needle and scratched my face and hands and feet – all over my body."
>
> "Why didn't you run away?"
>
> "No one can. He catches everyone."
>
> "Even children?"
>
> "No. Not children. Nor young boys and girls."
>
> "What if he does?"
>
> "Do you see this stick?" Patiya told Gopal, showing her supporting staff. "If he ever dares to scratch the children or the young boys and girls, I'll beat him with this."
>
> "If he catches the old ones?"
>
> "Let him then. They deserve to be caught" (*Neema* 83).

Even though the conversation is natural, showing a child's innocent inquiries to satisfy his curiosity and an old woman's simple answers, they make the reading of the novel quite interesting and pleasant. Another example of such a conversation can be found when Bindu, Neema's stepdaughter, talks with other children about marriages. The discussion may not be quite informative or profound but is delightful to see how their minds work:

> "Why do people marry?"
>
> "So they don't have to cook."
>
> "Why don't they marry their mothers then?"
>
> "Because their fathers had married them. You cannot marry someone who is already married. Can you?"
>
> "No. Of course not."
>
> "Why is it that the girl has to go to the husband's house after the marriage? I wish the husband were required to go to the wife's house."
>
> "That would be silly," this was Bindu's voice. "For anyone who comes to live in the in-laws' house will have to wear a *saree* and have a veil! How would you like the husband in a *saree* with a veil? And how would he cook?" (*Neema* 101).

Such prattling of children makes the mature readers delighted as they nostalgically travel in their own past and revisit their own childhood.

On a number of occasions, Srivastava describes humorous situations arising out of sheer misunderstandings, monumental ignorance and idiocies, mispronunciation of English words or Hindi names, and so on. Such situations have often been depicted when an Indian is not good in English in the United States, an American is ignorant of Hindi and even about India, and when an Indian in India is not very good in English. In the short story "Friendship, Love and Marriage," Maharaja Kumar Chaturvedi is in the U.S. where he wishes to strike friendship with an American girl named Grace H. Smith but she fails to understand Mr. Chaturvedi's English in Indian accents. When he pronounces his name in English, she suspects him of speaking in a foreign language, but when he begins to spell out his name and utters "M A H," she takes it to be an abbreviation of Modern Animal House. He calls another American girl Loveleen who claims to have a good knowledge of geography, getting "A" grades in it, and says, "Now isn't India a part of Bombay?" (*Masks* 12). Realising that Loveleen has no knowledge of India at all, Chaturvedi befools her by telling that in place of cars, India has elephants and camels on which people ride to university or college; that for parking purpose, a sort of stable is attached to each university's building; that for "driving" elephants, one has to have a driving license; and that in place of electric fans, the ears of elephants are cut and converted "into beautiful hand-fans by attaching handles to them" (*Masks* 13). He goes on further in the same vein and paints a romantic vision before Loveleen that when she lands in India, "the people might mistake her for a goddess, carry her in a palanquin so that she may not have to put her foot on the ground," that Indians "live on the tops of trees. Every morning, they go and dig roots which mixed with some leaves and tree barks make the finest dish. On festivals, they fry frogs or snakes" (*Masks*, p. 15). Loveleen becomes so much excited by the romantic and exotic traits of India that she tells her mother, "one could sit on a throne, like Queen Elizabeth, and ask anyone to do anything, could see a cobra dance, eat mangoes or go in a palanquin to the Himalayan peaks." About servants, Chaturvedi tells her, "You could have twenty servants to pare your nails – one for each nail – one to put oil on your head, one to comb, one to turn your hair into braid, one to open the door, and one to close...." (*Masks* 16). It is interesting to see how people in such an advanced country like the U.S. could be so ignorant of basic knowledge of countries as large as India. The entire picture painted by Chaturvedi and easily swallowed by Loveleen becomes full of laughter and fun till one comes to a sense of disillusionment at the end of the story.

Sometimes comic vein carries with it strong traits of irony and satire. In the short story "Cooperative Colony," the Minister for Education and Cooperation has been made ironically quite uneducated, even ignorant. His speech has been written by a Sanskrit teacher who himself is understandably poor in the use of English. Furthermore, though the speech is in English, the script in which it has been written is Devanagari (Hindi) to enable the poorly-educated Education Minister to read it. Naturally, the speech is full of howlers and blunders, which provoke uproarious laughters in the audience but no less among the readers. While explaining the concept of Cooperative Colony and about the importance of a wide variety of inhabitants, the Minister speaks:

> "Brothers and Sisters, except one because my wife is sitting here (*laughter*)... This Cooperative Colony – this great experiment in cohabitation (*laughter*) is going to bring about a new transformer (*laughter*), that is, transformation in the country. You have a liar (*laughter*) or lawyer who will give you honest, free advice in legal matters. The physicist or physician (*laughter*), will give you free medical assistance. You have a Pandit to solemnise marriages and other ceremonies. There is one *pahalwan* who

> will train you in breastling (*laughter*), I mean, wrestling. You have a cheater to cheat (*laughter*), sorry, a teacher to teach your children. A policeman is there to guard you against thiefs (*laughter*), and a watchman to guard your colony for the whole night. We have, too, a businessman, a banker, a professor, a sweeper and people from all walks of life. The colony is the first of its kind in India. Gandhi ji wanted to bring Panchayat rule in the country, and I, by establishing many such colonies, want to bring a colonial rule (*laughter*). We have a shepherd for your sheep and a coward for your cows (*laughter*). There is an assembly hall with images of various gods and goddesses for people of all religions. where you can pro-pro-prostitute (*laughter*) I mean, prostrate. There are institutions for people of all sexes and ages – nursery for nurses (*laughter*), for infants infantry (*laughter*) and for adults adultery (*laughter*)" (*Cooperative* 26-27).

In another short story "Love and Animality," Manjula informs her husband Professor Sharma that Mr. Chadha has been arrested for "adultery" which creates a lot of suspense and tension though it becomes clear later on that the arrest was on the charge of "adulteration" and not "adultery." Similarly, when Mrs. Sharma tells her husband that Mrs. Chadha has got "T.B." he is naturally shocked but his worry is over when he finds that she had "T.V."(Television) and not "T.B."(Tuberculosis). (*Love* 95).

Srivastava is exceedingly good in the art of characterisation. He does not take only to the outer features of a character but goes deeply into its psyche as well. However, occasionally driven by a comic impulse, he makes a mockery of a character, lampoons and ridicules by portraying it completely in highly hyperbolic terms, exaggerating each trait of a character's personality till it evokes complete laughter. Sunnoo's character has always drawn Srivastava's sympathetic viewpoint but when he satirises the ignorance of a character, one begins to wonder what the aim of the novelist is. However, Srivastava's undercurrent of sympathy and good will behind his powerful lampooning and buffoonery saves the character and makes it clear that the novelist is not denigrating a poor, deformed, helpless Sunnoo but is using him merely to have a hearty laughter devoid of any ill will at all:

> A number of answers given by him [Sunnoo] during the previous years had become classical examples of jokes. He had found no difference between Akbar and *akhwar* (newspaper), cauliflower and cabbage, longitude and latitude. For him Mahatma Gandhi was the Prime Minister of India and Constantinople the President of U.S.A. Simla was the hottest place in the country while Bombay was a fine hill station. The Panjab was known for its five mountains and Rajasthan for its rivers and greenery.

> The windmills were for the village what the table fan is for an individual – to generate breeze on windless days (*Neema* 23-24).

Another instance of comic characterisation is that of Tirath Ram, a Sanskrit teacher whose personality has been drawn with ironical and satirical touches. If Srivastava makes a mockery of the class teacher, he must have seen such teachers in village schools. Tirath Ram – a hemp-eater – is fond of sleeping in the class. His manner of speaking and eating, his mustachios – all provoke abundant laughter. Srivastava writes:

> Giving his students an exercise in translation, Tirath Ram shunted his torso in the room, parked it in the chair, signaled his head down on the table and switched off his headlights. From his open mouth flowed saliva like a starved stream of water from a cave. The snoring sound, like that of a ship scraping the rocky bottom or of a heavy canvas torn apart, emanated rhythmically from his nostrils and made the tips of his mustachios lean, like the Tower of Pisa, only to be straightened again (*Neema* 25).

What particularly lends the comic tinge to the characterisation are some comic, metaphysical images. Tirath Ram's movements have been compared to a heavy vehicle, his mouth to a cave, his saliva to a stream, his snoring sounds to a ship scraping the rocky bottom, and his bending mustachios to the leaning Tower of Pisa.

The characterisation of Chanawala – a hawker selling sand-baked, sugar-coated or salted Bengal gram – is no less funny. He sells his grams, propagating "the efficacy and potency of the gram, as of a new powerful drug," in highly exaggerated and comic terms:

> They have the power
> To brave a coward;
> The king may win,
> With my gram and a pin.
> The lame may run
> The blind view the sun,
> And the priests have fun
> With many a nun;
> Make a donkey a horse
> With my gram, of course.
>
> For ill a balm, for crippled an arm,
> Crisp and crackling, my Bengali gram.
> (*Neema* 29-30)

Srivastava also creates humour by playing on words, by using puns, *double entendres* and verbal repartees, by injecting distortions in meanings and senses, and in appropriately given intelligent replies. When Neema goes to Chaman Lal, it is dark. The latter casually asks her well-being and she tells him that she has been fine. When Chaman Lal says, "You don't look that way, Neema," she becomes irritated, and sharply replies, "I am not any bulb that will *look* bright in the dark" (*Neema* 77). In "Road to Prosperity," Mahipal finds some grains of soil and sand in grams which otherwise were delicious, and Parsadi quips, "Mahip, you are here to construct the soil road, and you don't like a few grains of its soil in the grams!" to which Mahipal Das gives a proper, witty reply, "We've come to construct the road, not to eat it" (*Masks* 35). Some characters make use of *double entendres* – words with double meanings – and Srivastava's works have them in abundance. When Dhania in the short story "Confession" softly tells her Bhabhi, "The day is not far when in this house, too, I shall see a hanging pumpkin and a walking pumpkin" (*Masks* 45), she implies the latter's swelling breasts and after pregnancy her swelling belly. Dhania's words, "Kewal Singh's seed is of good quality," imply his fertilising semen, for she herself had become pregnant after having sex with him. Similarly, when Kewal Singh says, "Bhabhi ji, when are you going to let me taste your papayas?" (*Masks* 47), he means her breasts. In "Lasting Victory," Vimala prepares tea and asks the Principal of a college as to where sugar is, to which the latter wittily responds, "Vimmi, you are so sweet that you need to dip only one finger into a cup of tea to make it sweet" (*Masks* 57).

A number of good examples of Srivastava's wit can be seen in the dialogues in which each person tries to pull or push others down in order to get an upper hand. The best example of it can be seen in the short story "Cooperative Colony" in which the dialogues are not only witty, but full of puns, jokes, insults, humiliations, and wisecracks. The residents suspect a thief to be in the lavatory, now asleep. Some students ask Pandit ji to chant *mantras*, to which the angry Pandit retorts, "Tomorrow you go to the lavatory and if you don't have motion, you'll ask Pandit ji to chant *mantras* for you!" (*Cooperative* 29). Sher Singh, the police officer, calls the dog "*Sala*," and a man quips, "So the dog is related to the policeman. He called him *sala* – brother-in-law. That is why the policemen are called dogs" (*Cooperative* 33). When the son of Seth Popat Lal passes an ironical remark against the wrestler, the latter threatens the former, "I'll drink your blood" to which another person adds: "Mr. Wrestler! He has in his veins the blood of the fly-sucker Seth Popat Lal. If you drink his blood, you won't be able to digest it. Even mosquitoes die after stinging him." (*Cooperative* 35). In the same short story, the thief is found to be senseless, a person requests the physician to diagnose the illness of the thief and Doctor Kailash asks, "Who'll pay the consultation fee – you?" to which the man ironically replies, "You are Doctor Kill-us or Callous, aren't you?" (*Cooperative* 36-37). Srivastava's short story "Terrorists in the Kitchen" has many examples of wit in which the activities and movements of cats and kittens have been compared to the terrorists as well as residents of terror-affected Punjab. A cat takes its kittens to seven places for their survival, so must the terrorised residents of the Punjab. When Sonkali refers to the nectar in the cat's saliva which cures injuries and wounds, Nirbhaya Dayal laughs and says, "All that the government has to do is to terminate the services of the physicians and appoint cats in their places, each with a valid licking license." And his wife retorts, "And you have all the poison in your sharp tongue. The terrorists in the Punjab have simply to borrow your lethal tongue for the job they do with AK 47 rifles" (*Under* 75-76).

An important source of Srivastava's wit and humour in *Neema* is from his comic images – largely similes and metaphors – which are often used by bringing two similar, dissimilar or odd objects together for defining or clarifying things and the result is decidedly comic. These images are used largely to delineate a character, an incident, a facial feature, and so on. Jawahar sings a folk song which has numerous such images:

> "Your head is like a forest zone,
> Your face is like a millstone,
> Your eyes are bulbs no longer in use,
> Your ears are long of a donkey huge.
> .....
> "With teeth yellowed, forehead small,
> And a nose like a damaged wall;
> The peacock's legs, the camel's gait,
> The donkey's voice at any rate."
>
> (*Neema* 11)

There are other images too which have been used for Sunnoo to create humour. For example, the grotesque movement of his waist has been compared to "the shifting haunch of a camel" (*Neema* 10). Sunnoo's act of sulking away is like that of "a tortoise into a crevice" while Jawahar and Gopal were "dragged behind her like two bushy appendages" (*Neema* 12). Some of these images are used by

Pushpendra to make fun of his mother who always talks of the glory and decency of olden times. Pushpendra satirizes the olden times through exaggerated comic images: "At that time everything was great. Men used to be fat like buffaloes and tall as date trees. Their *choties* used to flutter over their heads like a horse's tail would over Kutub Minar" (*Neema* 41). Again, "In old times, mothers used to have sticks as big as a pole with which they used to beat their children as small as mice" (*Neema* 41). And again, "Sons used to behave in a sober way. They never laughed or showed their teeth even to a dentist. They brushed their teeth with their labium shutters down! Only once was there a case of a person opening his mouth before a dentist and that was when, being eighty, he had no teeth." (*Neema* 41) The children's sounds are compared to "squeaking and squealing sounds as if some chickens were being herded into a basket or as if a bull had strayed into an enclosure of piglets" (*Neema* 101) The Minister's "teeth looked like half-sunk milestones – bent and twisted, yellowing due to dirt and water – interspersed with long gaps on a grayish, curved, bumpy road" (*Cooperative* 25). One can use the words of Joseph Addison to characterise Srivastava's use of wit and humour:

> In all thy humours, whether grim or mellow,
> Thou'rt such a touchy, testy, pleasant fellow;
> Hast so much wit, and mirth, and spleen about thee.
> There is no living with thee nor without thee (Addison 47).

It is undoubtedly a matter of pride that Indian writing in English has found an important place in the literatures of the world in a fairly short time. Every couple of months, new names – some of them being international prize winners – are being added to it. At this juncture, it would be worthwhile to as well remember the silent contributions of lesser-known writers, particularly those who have not benefited from the sponsored publicity. Since not many Indo-Anglian writes have succeeded in introducing wit and humour in their works, Ramesh K. Srivastava has done a commendable job in not only introducing comic vein in his novel and short stories in English but in making them eminently entertaining, easily readable and wonderfully delightful without sacrificing their literary values.

Works Cited

Addison, Joseph. *The Spectator,* 68.

Mehta, M. L. "An Interview with Ramesh K. Srivastava." *The Critical Endeavour,* 8 (December 2002), 167-179.

Srivastava, Ramesh K. *Cooperative Colony: Stories.* Calcutta: Writers Workshop, 1985.

.... "Author's Note," in *Games They Play and Other Stories.* New Delhi: Prestige Books, 1989.

.... *Love and Animality: Stories.* Calcutta: Writers Workshop, 1984.

.... *Masks and Men: Stories.* Calcutta: Writers Workshop, 1986.

.... *Neema* (a novel). Calcutta: Writers Workshop, 1986,

.... *Under the Lamp: Stories.* Jalandhar: ABS Publications, 1993.

Wells, Carolyn. *An Outline of Humor.* New York: G. P. Putnam's Sons, 1923.

CHAPTER 10

Sufferings of Women in Ramesh K. Srivastava's Short Stories

Priyanka Agrawal and *Sadhana Agrawal*

Indian history and mythology abound in the stories of sufferings of women. Draupadi of the *Mahabharata* and Sita of the *Ramayana* symbolise such sufferers. Though thousands of years of reform in this direction have brought about a great deal of amelioration in the plight of women, a lot remains to be done. Such things are bound to be reflected in various literatures of the country, including Indian-English literature.

Ramesh K. Srivastava has written a large number of short stories concerning this problem. In his essay "My Idea of a Short Story," Srivastava had made it clear that the greatness of a short story writer consists "in painting a realistic picture of life" (*Read* 102). The realistic picture of women in this conservative, orthodox and tradition-bound country is often of suffering women in the society, even though the causes could be the erstwhile zamindari system, patriarchal society, joint-family system, traditions, superstitious and blind beliefs, among others.

Though the zamindari system was abolished in the country a couple of years after India's Independence, in certain backward places, away from the politically-awakened urban and rural areas, some pockets remained practically unaffected. In such places, remnants of the old system still prevail or, at most, it is replaced by the dictatorial village Panchayati system in which the Sabhapati wields unchecked power over the village people, particularly over the illiterate ones. In Srivastava's "Under the Lamp," Karmaibai is a widow of Fauladi, a blacksmith of Kaliana village. Her suppression and oppression began because of her unusual beauty and the "chief architect" of her woes was Bichitra Singh, an erstwhile Zamindar, who had become the Sabhapati of the village (*Under* 105). He broke Karmaibai's first matrimonial engagement and attempted to do the same with the second one but in vain. When she began to work at his house after her husband's death, he started having sex with her at will. The poor woman tolerated everything for her son Siddha's future. Considering the Sabhapati a ferocious crocodile and a revengeful cobra, her father-in-law had warned her against fighting with him unless he could be killed. Since Bichitra Singh also cultivated good relations with the Head Constable of the village police station, no one could dare to go against such a formidable person. When a better Head Constable came to the police station, Karmaibai showed him Bichitra Singh's cruelty to her in the form of "marks of lashes, sticks and iron rods" (119) on her back. After the passing away of her father-in-law, Bichitra Singh's crimes knew no bounds. He began to have sex with her at her own place and on her refusal, she was lashed, beaten and burnt with lighted cigarette butts. Later on, her son was also killed by him in connivance with the policemen.

For Usha Bande, the story is "on a social situation in which the 'haves' exploit the 'have-nots,' and if the 'have-nots' be a woman, she has nowhere to hide" (Bande 144). Lata Mishra feels that "the writer presents the oppression of women not only with greater self-involvement but also with a note of protest" (Mishra 22). Similarly in "Lucky Rope," Raja Bhunaresh Singh, called Raja Sahib, was a one-time zamindar of Chakarpur village who sexually exploited most of the newlyweds in the village, particularly Bhanwari Bai and her daughter-in-law Hulli. The former was frequently thrashed with a leather whip and a strong rope. One can imagine her exploitation when Bhanwari Bai had confessed that "she must have slept more with the Raja Sahib than with her own husband" (*Road* 60).

The joint-family system has been prevalent in the country for ages. While it undoubtedly has its advantages, certain ill-practices have also crept in the system and the mother-in-law has come to be regarded as an instrument of the suppression of daughter-in-law. In his novel *Neema,* Srivastava showed how Neema's mother-in-law had made the former's life hellish through her machinations and had even attempted to kill her. In "Rebirth," the sufferings of Kiran Arora happen to be because of her love marriage and consequently, she was harassed by her mother-in-law, particularly after the death of her husband. Even her husband's death was attributed to her "ominous presence in the house" (*Games* 20). Disallowing Kiran even to come inside the kitchen, her mother-in-law asked her only to scrub the utensils, to sweep the floor and to wash the clothes. She was also charged with devouring her husband and ruining the house. Anil Kumar Tewari calls the mother-in-law as one who "devotes the patriarchal power of her son over the other's daughter, her daughter-in-law" (Tewari 47).

India has been a religious country for ages and the evidence of it can be found in numerous temples, big and small, dotting the entire country. Over several centuries, the Hindu religion developed certain distortions and a large number of superstitions and blind beliefs began to take the place of genuine religious practices. Such malpractices gave rise to many false saints to whom exhibition of miracles became an easy device to dupe and to misguide the ignorant and the gullible. Hence many Asarams, Ram Rahims and Rampals came into existence who claimed to be next to gods. In Srivastava's "Maharshi Satyanand," Ranga, the dacoit, began to manage certain miracles with the help of stooges and people began to believe in him as an incarnation of god. In the story, Sheela's son Babloo was suffering from fever and a good physician's treatment was continuing but she believed "in the efficacy of the temple priest much more than in physician's" (*A Christmas* 13). Her excessive faith in priests came to the point of believing in superstitions and blind beliefs. Her expensive propitiation of gods and goddesses was called "killing cures" (14) by her husband. He felt revulsion "when her superstitious cures prevail over the doctor's treatment" (14). When she desired to join the Maharshi's ashram for good after renouncing the family, her husband, considering such saints as "holy imposters" (14), started investigations into the Maharshi's antecedents and found that he was Ranga, the dacoit, who carried the reward of fifty thousand rupees on his head for dacoities and murders. In "Ganga Ma," Chhutakee is so superstitious that she does not listen to any rational voice and it results in her son's death. In bitter freezing cold, she cannot avoid giving a holy dip to her ailing son which kills him. Neither her husband, nor her niece could put her on the right path. She mistakenly understood the underground pipe burst as the incarnation of the Ganga Ma. Kanika finally explained that she herself "believed in God, but there was difference between hypocrisy and faith, between coincidences and so-called miracles" (*A Christmas* 91). For Smita Das, both these stories "portray superstitions of both rural and urban people" (Das 42). Usha Bande considers it a case of "superstitions and curse of blind faith (Bande 145). Neeta Maini feels that here Srivastava "clearly satirises the ill-founded credulity of the village people who consider it a sin not to take a holy dip" in Prayag on Makar Sankranti (Maini 191).

In the urban areas, women who take up jobs have sometimes to suffer various kinds of exploitation from their employers or immediate bosses. This happens much more in those organisations where male members happen to be in vast majority. In "Lasting Victory," Vimala was a lady Lecturer in a predominantly men's college and her sufferings were because she refused to yield to the Principal's wishes. When he attempted to hold her, she escaped "like a cat suddenly freed from the jaws of a hound" (*A Christmas* 141). Having failed in his attempt to molest her, he operated by proxy in instigating Gurmel Singh, an impertinent student of the college, to harass her. At one stage, Gurmel unsuccessfully tried to molest her. As the President of the Students Association, he wanted to burn a bus in the college in order to bring an ill name to Vimala as the Students' Advisor but she checkmated his action by boarding the bus herself and asking him to burn it along with her.

Some of the sufferings of women are because of their inborn traits in their personalities for which none other than god or nature can be blamed. It is the ignorant and short-sighted people who find fault with the person due to their jaundiced attitude and prejudices. Shyamali in "An Ugly Duckling," suffers from god-given "coal-black complexion as if she had been designed by a devil" (*A Christmas* 195). If she suffers, it is because the society puts premium on fair complexion and downgrades those who have dark colour. Due to her black complexion, she has to bear injustices, physical thrashing and taunts at home from no other person than her own mother Meghana who considers Shyamali "an unending source of torture and tears" (199). Similarly, Garima in "A Short Work," suffers because she has the short height of four-and-half feet. When others made references to it, it "hit her heart like an arrow that remained painfully lodged in her heart and bred inferiority complex within her" (*A Christmas* 267). Though these are god-given traits of their personalities, the society, instead of consoling them for such traits, causes unending mental sufferings and tortures to them.

In the above stories, Ramesh K. Srivastava has graphically presented the sufferings of women in a rather artistic manner. The short stories have been structured in a form that grips the reader's attention, having all the parts – a appetizing beginning, an elaborate middle and a satisfying resolution as an end – all are well-synthesized into an organic whole. With the use of satire, irony and humour, he has highlighted the basic ills of the society which have been the cause of women's sufferings. Divorced from his art, the stories could have degenerated into didactic tracts. Srivastava paints a series of fascinating vignettes of the suffering women struggling courageously for survival in the patriarchal, male-dominated world.

Works Cited

Bande, Usha. "Loving Vignettes – Mother in R. K. Srivastava's Short Stories." *Mother-Figures in Indian English Fiction* (Ed.). Usha Bande. Jalandhar: ABS Publications, 1997, pp. 142-147.

Das, Smita. "A Critical Introduction," *Ramesh K. Srivastava: Man and his Work*: New Delhi: Authors Press, 2016, pp. 15-71.

Maini, Neeta. "R. K. Srivastava." *Studies in Contemporary Indian English Short Stories: A Collection of Critical Essays* (Ed.). A. N. Dwivedi. Delhi: B. R. Publishing Corporation, 1999, pp. 185-197.

Mishra, Lata. "Narrative as Discourse: A Study of Ramesh K. Srivastava's *Under the Lamp: Stories. Virtuoso: A Refereed Transnational Bi-Annual Journal of Language and Literature in English.* Vol. II, No. 2 (February 2013), pp. 17-24.

Srivastava, Ramesh K. *A Christmas Gift and Other Stories.* New Delhi: Authors Press, 2015.

.... *Games They Play and Other Stories.* New Delhi: Prestige Books, 1989.

.... "My Idea of a Short Story," *Read, Write and Teach: Essays on Learning to Live Together.* New Delhi: Authors Press, 2014, pp. 99-104.

.... *Road Not Taken and Other Stories.* New Delhi: Authors Press, 2018.

.... *Under the Lamp: Stories.* Jalandhar: ABS Publication, 1993, pp. 105-121.

Tewari, Anil Kumar. "Psychodynamics of Power Discourse in Srivastava's *Games They Play.*" *Punjab Journal of English Studies.* Vol. VII (1992), pp. 45-53.

CHAPTER 11

Irony, Humour and Satire in Ramesh K. Srivastava's "Cooperative Colony"

Manisha Sharma

Ramesh K. Srivastava's "Cooperative Colony" is an excellent short story full of irony, wit, humour and satire. Srivastava is a prolific writer who has to his credit five collections of short stories and two novels – *Neema* (1984) and *Coils of the Serpent* (2011). The story under discussion is an ironical commentary on the working of Cooperative movement in India. Karnail Singh points out that "the writer has a dig at the system which pretends to provide for the weaker sections of society by raising a colony; but in actual practice it precludes the weaker section from enjoying this facility, for the former has impoverished the latter beyond recovery" (Singh 306). H. L. Sharma calls it "a satirical portrayal of the government-sponsored cooperative projects which breed corruption, promote selfishness and opportunism, and harm the poor and the downtrodden in whose name a lot of money is siphoned off from the government exchequer" (Sharma 118-119).

Cooperative Colony was a residential colony consisting of about one hundred houses mostly for weaker sections of the society on a heavy subsidy from the state government. To facilitate its smooth functioning, many professionals like physician, lawyer, professor, businessman, banker, teacher, policeman, Pandit, wrestler, watchman, sweeper, cowherd and shepherd – people from all walks of life were also given accommodation so as to make this colony self-sufficient in all respects. The intention was to move towards a better India of tomorrow "where people of all castes, creeds and professions can live in the spirit of cooperation and mutual understanding" (*Cooperative* 27).

Unfortunately, such idealistic schemes of the government mostly end up in failure and this is what precisely happens with this project. After occupying the subsidised houses in the colony, most professionals fail to honour their commitment for rendering free service to other residents of the colony. The lawyer stopped giving free legal advice; physician gave no medical assistance; professor, the Pandit, teacher, policemen, watchman, banker – all changed and stopped giving free service or advice. Seth Popat Lal discontinued letting others use his phone free of charge, even for informing the police about the thief. Sher Singh, the Police Inspector, becomes arrogant and uses abusive terms. Professor Vidya Nath corrects grammar of speakers rather than doing anything. The watchman was not visible around and his whistle was reportedly lost. When Professor Vidya Nath corrects someone's English, the lawyer Tarak Ram advises him not to do so free of charge. Another person advises the lawyer not to give free advice to the professor. Adarsh Khanna points out that "the author attacks the self-seeking people of all professions . . . each one of them wearing a mask of goodness and nobility to hide his selfishness, greed, inhumanity and hard-heartedness" (Khanna 59).

This is put to test when an aspiring applicant for a residential accommodation in the colony fails to collect the requisite amount of one thousand rupees and was trying for a job of a night watchman as incidents of molestation were becoming frequent in the colony. During his act of protecting the physician's daughter, Garib Das was mistaken as a thief and was locked up in a public lavatory. Now people assemble before the lavatory to make him come out. The steel rod of his umbrella is mistaken for a gun and none dares to take a risk of his life in bringing the thief out. At the end, he turns out to be poor man appropriately named Garib Das who wanted to have a watchman's job for survival as well as for an accommodation in the Cooperative Colony but he dies, leaving behind Rs nine hundred and sixty two rupees which are looted posthumously by the residents of the colony.

The short story is a stinging satire on the greed and selfishness of the people who promise anything to claim benefits and then forget about their promises. Throughout the story, Srivastava has ridiculed such people by his powerful wit, irony, humour and satire. To begin with, he gives a caricature of the minister by playing upon words which make the education minister almost uneducated in pronouncing English words written in Devanagari (Hindi) script in such a way that they carry altogether different, distorted or even perverted meanings and implications. His speech is flooded with blunders and howlers. The colony was an experiment for inhabitation but the minister uses words wrongly – "cohabitation." He further employs "transformer" for transformation, "liar" for lawyer, "physicist" for physician, "breastling" for wrestling, "cheater" for teacher, "colonial rule" for widespread cooperative ventures, "coward" for cowherd and "prostitute" for prostrate. He goes on using horrifying expressions for institutions, such as, "nursery" for nurses, "infantry" for infants and "adultery" for adults. While such expressions constantly provoke laughter, they also show the incompetence of the minister as well as of those who prepared his speech.

Neeta Maini points out that "Srivastava has blessedly an abundance of humour which makes his short stories so lively, interesting and enjoyable" (Maini 194). In an interview with M. L. Mehta, Srivastava clarified his position on the use of irony, humour and satire: "Since humour, irony and satire are part of everyday life, there is no reason why they should not be presented in a work of realistic art. Besides, a good work must be readable before it conveys anything. I am told humour and irony make my writing fairly interesting. Satire obviously is to demolish those institutions, individuals, customs and traditions, which have outlived their use" (Mehta 17). Srivastava introduces humour and satire through characterisation and dialogues, similes and metaphors, puns and double-edged expressions.

There is in the story an abundance of comic images – both similes and metaphors – which, while presenting the picture of a person, makes the story interesting. Some of the comparisons in these images give exaggerated accounts, are often odd and disproportionate, having mythological allusions and political references as also using ironical and satirical shades in the expressions. The Minister for Education and Cooperation has "a big toothpaste brand smile;" his teeth bent, twisted and yellowing are "like half-sunk milestones;" his thick lips "like double bumpers of a dilapidated truck" and his act of cutting ribbon "as if it were Supnakha's nose" (*Cooperative* 25). For giving a speech, the Minister opened his "trunk-like mouth" and began to roar like a truck. After the speech, he sat down "like a buffalo that has just been milked."

Police Inspector Sher Singh had a pair of mustachios "like two tufts of black coloured coconut fibres." Some children had stones "like Hanuman and his monkey army;" an old man had a walking stick, and a teacher a green sapling – "his trademark." The wrestler had a mace "like that of Bhima." One lady had a pair of tongs while the other had a rolling pin which she had used frequently on her husband.

In the story, according to Swati Srivastava, "the dialogues are not only witty, but full of puns, jokes, insults, humiliations and wisecracks" (Srivastava 103). When the students request the Pandit to chant some *mantras* to make the thief come out of lavatory, he becomes angry and says, "Tomorrow when you go to the lavatory and if you don't have motion, you'll ask Panditji to chant *mantras* for you" (*Cooperative* 29). For some people, "I.P.C." could be the abbreviated form of "Illegal Police Custody" instead of Indian Penal Code. When a dog comes out of the lavatory, Police Inspector Sher Singh calls him "*sala*" and a person quips: "The dog is related to the policeman. He called him *sala* – brother-in-law. That is why the policemen are called dogs." One of the four boys slapped the Police Inspector who "fell down like Humpty-Dumpty" (*Cooperative* 33).

No one was willing to open the door of the lavatory in which the thief was supposedly hiding. Some people thought that "the most lily-livered man" Seth Popat Lal was moving forward to open the door, but they were surprised to find that he was going not to open but to bolt it from outside, fearing that the thief might not otherwise hurt him. When the Seth's son ridicules the courage of the wrestler in not proceeding to open the door of the lavatory, the latter threatens to drink the former's blood, but people warn him: "He has in his veins the blood of the fly-sucker Seth Popat Lal. . . . Even mosquitoes die after stinging him" (*Cooperative* 35). When the wrestler finally did jump and opened the door, the thief's gun was found to be the upper tip of his broken umbrella. The fellow instead of the thief turned out to be a poor person whose unconscious body was brought out of the lavatory, but whose heart was still throbbing. When people urged the physician to diagnose the person's illness, Dr Kailash declined to do so without his consultation fee, and people called his name "Kill-us or Callous" instead of Kailash by using the pun (*Cooperative* 37). The person died and he was confirmed to be a beggar. The physician's daughter corroborated that she was being protected by the person at midnight from a molester who had beaten him for saving her and had locked him up in the lavatory.

The newly arrived four students tried to collect some money for the beggar's cremation at the rate of twenty-five paise each, calculating that out of about 200 people, at least fifty rupees will be collected, but as they began to do so, the people left the place with various excuses. The students could collect only three rupees and seventy-five paise, and their comment was: "That is barely enough for a bottle of beer" (*Cooperative* 38) which shows that they were as callous and insensitive as others residents of the colony were. The Pandit refuses to perform obsequial rites free of charge because he had to go to the Seth's house for his son's nail-cutting ceremony.

The students searched the body of the beggar and found in an elongated cloth bag an amount of nine hundred and sixty two rupees. The moment the money was found, the policeman wanted the amount to be deposited in the police station. Pandit Ram Das was ready to perform the obsequies rites for the dead man's money which, he felt, should go to a Brahmin. When they wanted to give some money to the wrestler for showing bravery in opening the door of the lavatory, the latter said, he did not know who had pushed him there from the wall. As the students were holding the money, a crushing crowd fell on them and each one tried to grab whatever he could "like dogs pouncing upon a few pieces of bone" (*Cooperative* 40). The dead body of the poor fellow was abandoned at that very spot while everyone of them present there left the place.

Garib Das, according to the paper found with him, was a refugee from Lahore (Pakistan). His wife had died of illness. His daughter was raped and he had got no help from either the policeman or the lawyer. His son died a vagabond. After hearing of the good locality of Cooperative Colony, he had begged day and night but failed to collect the requisite amount of one thousand rupees to become eligible for an accommodation in the Coopertive Colony. He wrote: "If I die before I have a thousand rupees . . . my money should go to the welfare of the residents of the Cooperative Colony" (*Cooperative* 41).

The story, which was buzzing with fun and frolic, ends up anticlimactically on a tragic note with a complete reversal of the situation. Neeta Maini points out that most of Srivastava's stories "end up in ironic reversal of fortunes. In other words, the situation in the end is quite reverse to the situation in the beginning" (Maini 194).

The threatening thief turns out to be a potential resident of the Colony. His desire to have an accommodation in the Colony ends up with his dead body lying there. His last wish, according to the paper found on his body was to give his saved amount for the wellbeing of the members of the Colony but it was looted by them. The members of the Cooperative Colony, instead of helping him by giving his body a decent cremation even with the fellow's own money, harm him by abandoning it then and there unattended for the dogs. For H. L. Sharma, Garib Das symbolises "the pathetic condition of millions of poor Indians who make futile attempts of acquiring a house" (Sharma 19).

The story is a harsh commentary on the people of the world who have become absolutely devoid of human values. Even though the residents, particularly professionals, must have given solemn assurances of mutual help and cooperation to the authorities before being allotted an accommodation, no such atmosphere is visible in the colony. Instead of helping each other, they satirise, ridicule or make fun of each other, giving the impression as if, instead of Cooperative Colony, it were a non-cooperative or even an antagonistic colony. It is a world portrayed in its stark nakedness. The people are extremely selfish and hence inconsiderate to each other.

The four boys in the story symbolise the new generation. They arouse the initial hope of some help and consideration for others. However, in slapping the Police Inspector and in firing at the so-called thief, they symbolise lawlessness and violence which are becoming common in the new generation. Their collection of fund for cremation of the dead body of Garib Das probably goes for liquor of which they had given a hint. By grabbing the collected contribution and Garib Das's saved amount and, furthermore, by abandoning his dead body to dogs without its cremation, the younger generation proves to be much more inhuman and devoid of human feelings than is the older generation. This way all the people, old and young, present a very grim picture of the society.

As far as the language of Srivastava is concerned, he has a complete command over English. It is simple, easy to read and is even interspersed with colloquial expressions in order to create the Indian atmosphere. He uses Hindi words like *haram-zade*, *chapattis, kinaris* and *sala*. To quote Karnail Singh, "the chief characterstic of Dr Srivastava's prose style is its vividness and suppleness not wholly unrelated to an abounding energy of language that limps, walks and saunters at one moment but begins to run, soar and sweep the next" (*Singh* 308). Most similes and metaphors are from common life.

Whereas many stories of Srivastava are idealistic with happy endings and without loose ends, the present story ends up tragically. For Adarsh Khanna, the story presents "stark and grim realities behind the well-orchestrated façade of the glitter and shine of life" (Khanna 60). H. L. Sharma points out that in introducing a comic mode in stories through humour, fun and pun, Srivastava follows the footsteps of Narayan and Khushwant Singh "and succeeds well in using a lighter vein for imparting a serious message" (Sharma 120). When questioned by Y. Joy as to why did he not confine himself to a single tone, Srivastava's reply was that a writer usually confines to a single theme or tone but "to make it readable, interesting and enjoyable, introduction of minor digressions, anecdotes, wit, irony and humour may be desirable" (Joy 376). With the help of irony, humour and satire, Srivastava has indeed castrated the entire society of various professions since people in the name of cooperation show their utter selfishness and inhumanity.

Works Cited

Joy, Y. "Ramesh K. Srivastava in Conversation with Y. Joy." *The Critical Endeavour.* Vol. XIX (January 2013): 375-386.

Khanna, Adarsh. Book Review of Ramesh K. Srivastava's *Cooperative Colony: Stories* and *Masks and Men: Stories. Commonwealth Quarterly.* Vol. XIV. No. 39 (June-September 1989): 58-60.

Maini, Neeta. "R. K. Srivastava." *Studies in Contemporary Indian English Short Story,* Ed. A. N. Dwivedi. Delhi: B. R. Publishing Corporation, 1991. 185-197.

Mehta, M. L. "Interview with Ramesh K. Srivastava." *The Critical Endeavour.* Vol. VIII (December 2002): 167-179.

Sharma, H. L. Book Review of Ramesh K. Srivastava's *Cooperative Colony: Stories. Punjab Journal of English Studies* (1990): 118-120.

Singh, Karnail. "Other Experiences: Book Review of Ramesh K. Srivastava's *Cooperative Colony: Stories." Indian Book Chronicle* (December 1987): 306-308.

Srivastava, Ramesh K. "Cooperative Colony," *Cooperative Colony: Stories* by Ramesh K. Srivastava. Calcutta: Writers Workshop, 1985. 25-41.

Srivastava, Swati. "Wit and Humour in the Works of Ramesh K. Srivastava." *Star Behind the Clouds: Unexplored Indian Writers in English,* Ed. Syed Mashkoor Ali. Jaipur: Surabhi Publications, 2004, 89-106.

CHAPTER 12

Symbolism in Ramesh K. Srivastava's *Cooperative Colony: Stories* and *Masks and Men: Stories*

Barinder K. Sharma

Symbolism in a literary work is not something predetermined, sticking a spangle here and a star there; it is the result of the creative writer's mind operating on multi-levels simultaneously so that what comes out on surface level conceals hidden implications underneath. In the opinion of Thrall and Hibbard, "On the most literal level, a symbol is something which is itself and yet stands for or suggests or means something else" (Thrall 478). Ramesh K. Srivastava defines its nature: "Symbolism is the musk in the deer, the spark in the flint, the oil in *til* seeds, carrying invisibly its fragrance and fire, enriching the creation but discernible only to the astute observer and causing no violence to the incurious beholder" (*Ten* 90). He has imbued some of the characters and objects in his stories in such a way that they become pregnant with profound meanings and implications, and are transformed into symbols without in the least injuring the surface meaning of the story. Ernest Hemingway too had disapproved the superimposition on a literary piece "preplanned symbols like raisins sticking out in a raisin bread" (Quoted Baker 102). In the present paper, my intention is to find out Srivastava's use of symbols in his two works: *Cooperative Colony: Stories* and *Masks and Men: Stories.*

There are a number of stories which are good on surface level, but on deeper contemplation, one can find that some of the characters, objects or situations can be interpreted on symbolical level. In Srivastava's story "Savagery," Kanna and Bhola Singh respectively symbolise primitivism and civilisation. Kanna belongs to the nomadic tribe of Rawats who live on the outskirts of the village: "Far from civilisation and its tentacles, they maintained a virginal purity, undefiled by the artificialities and craftiness of civilised people" (*Cooperative* 45) without in the least bothering anyone. Kanna goes with a bow and arrows for "killing a fowl here, ransacking a beehive there" (*Cooperative* 44) for food and honey. These undoubtedly are primitive activities which are merely for survival without interfering in the lives of the civilised people. Bhola Singh, on the other hand, symbolises civilisation and its whimsical rules. He enjoys his father's power of being the Head of the village, lives within the village, bullying one person or the other. Not only Bhola but other Rajputs come in the same category. They terrorise the village people as well as the tribal. Sitting in the market, Bhola Singh arrogantly misbehaves with Kanna, abuses him and snatches the earthen pitcher containing honey. This is the encroachment of civilisation on primitivism. In order to coexist peacefully, Summa, father of Kanna, though the Head of the Rawat tribe, told Bhola Singh's father Roop Singh clearly, "Raja Sahib, I belong to a nomadic, savage tribe and am not bound by your *civilised* laws" (51). Despite this, Bhola Singh shows his superiority and arrogance over others. Kanna remains subdued in the village because it represents civilisation. However, in the flooded river, which is a symbol of primitivism, Kanna scores a victory over Bhola Singh. The reason is obvious. Srivastava writes: "The evils of civilisation had made him [Bhola Singh] inwardly hollow by sucking at his vitals" (52) whereas Kanna was "brought up in a place where nature in its extreme forms had been his constant companion" (*Cooperative* 47). Consequently, in the final duel, Bhola Singh is defeated and killed by Kanna. Here Srivastava seems to suggest that Kanna's victory in the final duel against Bhola Singh is ultimately the victory of primitivism over civilisation.

His story "Century," deals with two characters – Mohan and Jasbir – who symbolise respectively the East and the West. Both of them are Indian students studying in the U.S. While Mohan believes that the U.S. is a good place for higher education, Jasbir feels that one can study even in India and that the U.S. is good for enjoyment for which he traps American girls. Mohan was told in India that "Every Indian is an ambassador of his country in a foreign place and his activities and lapses will uplift or tar the nation's image" (*Cooperative* 70). Being a simple person, Mohan is ignorant of the art of befriending American girls, while Jasbir claims to be "a guru in the art of love-making" and employs "tricks to suit different persons and occasions" (*Cooperative* 55-56). Hence Mohan does not want to do anything which might spoil the country's image. Being shy, simple and hesitant, Mohan thinks only of "bird-watching" whereas Jasbir thinks of trapping "the bird first and then watch her afterwards inside and outside" (56-57). Mohan has a conscience and cannot exploit anyone because of "humanitarian considerations" (69) but Jasbir is thick-skinned and has no such qualms. Since Jasbir is a libertine, he does not "miss a single chance to trap girls" (59). Naturally, at the end of the story, Marcy, an American girl, calls Jasbir "bastard" for his exploitation of her after promising to marry her, while she kisses Mohan as a token of her gratitude to him for not having exploited her sexually.

A beautiful butterfly in Mohan's room is trapped in the window. It is a symbol of beauty in general and an American girl in particular. Whereas Mohan, symbolising humanity, attempts to rescue it, Jasbir, symbolising western utilitarian attitude, thinks of fixing butterflies on the walls and kills it with a pornographic book. Jasbir's act symbolises the breaking of trust of American girls by his sexual activities. He exploits American girls and takes pride in having slept with one hundred of them while Mohan misses an equal number. At the end of the story, when Jasbir with a girl drove "towards the west," Mohan went "to the opposite direction" (72) implying the East. Their acts are symbolical and point out that Jasbir believes in Western values whereas Mohan in those of the East. Sulekha Sharma points out that "Srivastava's inner world is the Indian sanctuary sheltered from Western winds" (Sharma 4). For Karnail Singh, Mohan appears to be "the mask of the writer" (Singh 307).

In "Ganga Ma," Chhutakee is a symbol of superstitious people, particularly women. She believes that the Goddess Ganga would be angry unless everyone in the family takes a holy dip in it on the occasion of Makar Sankranti. Buddhan, her husband, is somewhat sceptic and wonders whether it would be desirable to take a holy dip in such a cold weather, but Chhutakee insists, "Cold or no cold, we cannot commit the sin of not taking a holy dip in the Sangam" (*Cooperative* 82). Joshi-ji also advises her for it. He along with the priest symbolise unscrupulous elements in order to serve their selfish ends. Such people "extort some money or flour or rice from the people in the name of propitiating Shanishchar Devta" (89-90). When Joshi-ji is asked for his advice on the holy dip, he emphasises that they must have a dip by all means. Ram Dulari is another superstitious woman who believes that Ganga Ma has performed a miracle by appearing in the middle of the road, not realising that it was the rupture of an underground pipe-line. Kanika is a medical student and symbolises the weak voice of scientific and rational elements among the superstitious-ridden people of rural area. She calls the miracle of Ganga Ma "a fraud" (*Cooperative* 92). In order to expose the fraud, she decides to measure the depth of the pool created by the underground pipe burst, but the priests and other people protest against the action. Taken symbolically, the superstitions in India often override the rational thinking. After the death of fevering Sunkoo due to the holy dip in cold water, Kanika went to his parents and told them that "she believed in God, but there was a difference between hypocrisy and faith, between coincidences and so-called miracles" (99).

In Srivastava's "Friendship, Love and Marriage," Maharaja Kumar Chaturvedi, an Indian, and Loveleen, an American girl develop liking for each other. Lovelen mistakes his first name "Maharaja" for being a king but the moment reality dawns on her, their friendship falls apart. Maharaja Kumar had given her the image of Shiva, explaining her that he was "our god, symbolising goodness" (*Masks* 18). In their fast-developing friendship, the East and the West seem to approach closer in order to become one through matrimonial alliance. When Maharaja Kumar was driving and talking to Loveleen about the prospect of his marriage with her, he finds the traffic light red and brakes his car which symbolise a danger to their planned marriage, emphasising the fact that the East and the West are not going to be united. About the image of Shiva symbolising goodness, Loveleen says, "I don't care. I threw it away in the garbage can" (*Masks* 28). Loveleen had given him a "marble image of Venus" symbolising love, but it fell down and broke into "two pieces, one hitting him on his head" (29), implying the total failure of their love. The East and the West remain wide apart.

In "Masks and Men," Srivastava uses the metaphor of "masks" which becomes a symbol of hypocrisy among the people. Thrall and Hibbard clarify the difference between a symbol and a metaphor. According to them, a symbol "differs from metaphor in that a metaphor evokes an object in order to illustrate an idea or demonstrate a quality, whereas a symbol embodies the idea or the quality" (Thrall 478). Sudama and his wife Madhurima are honest painters who find hypocrites everywhere. Azad Gulati finds in the story the portrayal of duplicity among human beings. He writes that while "dealing primarily with men and masks, the stories present a kaleidoscopic view of life" (Gulati 1987). Madhurima and Sudama feel that most people are hypocrites and "wear masks. . . . It is hard to find one sincere, unmasked man" (*Masks* 87). By putting on the mask as a strategy, they expose their one-time friend Dhanik Lal whose sudden-aroused love for beautiful paintings was an excuse for seduction of Madhurima due to her beauty. M. L. Mehta feels that Srivastava's stories portray the Indian society "a masquerade and men masqueraders who hide their greed, lust, venom and lechery behind the masks of affability, respectability, public service and piety" (Mehta 80).

In "Rescuers," three young men – Harcharan Singh, Majid Khan and Ram Bharose – respectively symbolise Sikh, Muslim and Hindu religions. They attempt to pose themselves as rescuers of Neeru – a school-going girl who had problem in reaching her home in the absence of her rickshaw. Harcharan Singh assures her: "We are like brothers to you" (*Masks* 70). Even though all three of them belong to different religions, they are inwardly determined to have sex with her. Shipra G. Vashishtha says, "Srivastava universalises their hypocrisy by making them Hindu, Muslim and Sikh – three different religions" (Vashishtha 96). When they drop their masks and force her to accompany them, she escapes to Father Joseph Sault's car. He is a Christian, calls her his "daughter" and allays her fear by claiming to "believe in the religion of humanity" (*Masks 76)*. The next morning when Neeru finds herself raped by him, "She felt the whole world was inhabited by wolves, some in their original, some in sheep's skin" (*Masks* 80). Shipra G. Vashishtha finds that "the story lays bare the beastly nature of human beings who show compassion, pity and humanity merely as masks to exploit her subsequently" (Vashishtha 96).

The red traffic light on the road-crossing, as in "Friendship, Love and Marriage," is a symbol of danger for Neeru. It is there that the young men concretise their plans by deciding to sandwich her on the pillion of the motor bike between Majid and Harcharan Singh. The traffic light on the road crossing being out of order, it always remains red. Harcharan Singh calls it "Red-light district" (*Masks* 72). By planning to seduce and rape Neeru, he does attempt to make it so.

Fictionalising his real and felt experiences, Srivastava makes his stories effective through his use of satirical, ironical and symbolical language. M. L. Mehta writes, "Srivastava wields his pen like a surgeon's knife" (Mehta 81). Through the use of his powerful but unobtrusive symbols, Srivastava makes the reader realise that all that glitters on surface is not gold, and that one has to dive deep into his writing to find the hidden meanings and implications.

Works Cited

Baker, Carlos. *Hemingway: The Writer as Artist."* Princeton, New Jersey: Princeton University Press, 1963.

Gulati, Azad. "Masks People Wear Daily," Review of Ramesh K. Srivastava's *Masks and Men: Stories. The Tribune* (Chandigarh). 4 July 1987

Mehta, M.L. Review of Ramesh K. Srivastava's *Masks and men: Stories. Indian Book Chronicle,* Vol. XIV, No. 4, (April 1989), 80-81

Sharma, Sulekha. Review of Ramesh K. Srivastava's *Cooperative Colony: Stories. The Tribune* (Chandigarh). 4 January 1986.

Singh, Karnail. Review of Ramesh K. Srivastava's *Cooperative Colony: Stories, Indian Book Chronicle* (December 1987), 306-308

Srivastava, Ramesh K. *Cooperative Colony: Stories.* Calcutta: Writers Workshop, 1985.

.... *Masks and Men: Stories.* Calcutta: Writers Workshop, 1986.

.... "Symbolism in *Nectar in a Sieve," Ten Indian English Writers* by Ramesh K. Srivastava. Jalandhar: ABS Publications, 2005, 90-98.

Thrall, William Flint and Addison Hibbard, *A Handbook to Literature.* New York: The Odyssey Press, 1960.

Vashishtha, Shipra G. "Masks and Masqueraders in Ramesh K. Srivastava's Short Stories," *Indian Journal of Multicultural Literature.* Vol. VIII, No. 1 (January 2018), 92-98.

CHAPTER 13

Masks and Masqueraders in Ramesh K. Srivastava's Short Stories

Shipra G. Vashishtha

Ramesh K. Srivastava has frequently used the metaphor of "mask" in many of his short stories. One of his collections has appropriately been titled *Masks and Men.* My attempt here is to analyse the function of this image as well as others associated with it and how successfully they operate in his works. Smita Das defines imagery as "a set of mental pictures or images taken from a wide variety of objects for illustrating a subject" (Das 72). A writer's fertile imagination is ignited on seeing or thinking of a person or an object which brings before him an identical image or images from his real or vicarious experience which take the form of similes or metaphors. In most of Srivastava's works, one finds abundance of images which are rich in diversity and appropriate in presenting before the reader one or several pictures of an object described. In the present case, the hypocrisy of people in the society has led the writer to the creation of the image of mask, making it both illustrative and functional. While responding to a question of M. L. Mehta in an interview regarding the purpose of imagery in his novel *Neema,* Srivastava had said that the imagery was both ornamental and functional (Interview 172). Smita Das asserts that an important function of Srivastava's images in the novel *Neema* is "for characterisation whether these be for the depiction of outer features . . . or for inner portrayal of deep human feelings and complex emotions" (Das 73). It also applies to his short stories.

Through the image of mask and its other variations, Srivastava intends to portray that hypocrisy and duplicity have become so common that it is difficult to find one genuine person. Such persons are found in every sphere of human activity whether it be business, politics, education or human relationships. While reviewing

Srivastava's *Masks and Men: Stories,* Azad Gulati finds the portrayal of duplicity at different levels among human beings. He writes that while "dealing primarily with men and their masks, the stories present a kaleidoscopic view of life" (Gulati 1987).

In the short story "Masks and Men," Sudama and Madhurima are devoted artists who find the survival of their art difficult in this highly commercialised world. They find most people hypocrites, wearing invisible masks, parading themselves in deceptive colours. In order to find out people in their real colours, Sudama and his wife Madhurima also conceal their real identities by wearing real masks – the kind children often do – particularly on realisation that most people, being hypocrites, "wear masks. . . . It is hard to find one sincere, unmasked man" (*Masks* 87). By putting on the mask, Sudama exposes the real character of his one-time friend Dhanik Lal on finding that behind the sudden-awakened love of Dhanik Lal for paintings, his real intention was to seduce his wife Madhurima after seeing her beauty.

M. L. Mehta points out that Srivastava's stories portray the duplicity and hypocrisy of most people. He finds the Indian society "a masquerade and men masqueraders who hide their greed, lust, venom and lechery behind the mask of affability, respectability, public service and piety" (Review 80). Dhanik Lal puts on the mask of a connoisseur of art and begins his advances towards Madhurima by touching her fingers. When she tells Dhanik Lal that he, being a customer, was a king, he calls her "the queen, a beautiful one" (*Mask* 90). Exploiting her need of money, Dhanik Lal becomes ready to buy five paintings for two thousand rupees. In his new incarnation of a lover of art, Dhanik Lal "appears to her like some flesh-and-flood embodiment of generosity" (*Masks* 90), because she did not know that he had denied her husband a loan of even five hundred rupees against the mortgage of four of their paintings on the ground that they were not worth even one hundred rupees. Now charmed by Madhurima's beauty, he purchased five paintings and wrote a cheque of two thousand rupees. Meanwhile, Sudama comes on the scene. Since he had begun to put on a painted paper-mask because he had "not seen a single person without a mask" (*Masks* 92). In order to pull down the mask of his friend Dhanik Lal as the lover of art, Sudama drops his physical mask and tells his friend that he had even humiliated him by throwing his painting in a waste paper basket. After knowing the entire story, Madhurima burns Dhanik Lal's cheque of two thousand rupees. The burning of the cheque, for Karnail Singh, symbolically means "the condemnation of Mammon to infernal fire" (Singh 112).

The story "Friendship, Love and Marriage" refers to human relationships among both Indians and Americans. Srivastava wants to show that human nature is the same everywhere – in India or in the U.S.A.; it differs only in degrees. In the story both Maharaja Kumar Chaturvedi and Loveleen present themselves to each other in very attractive masks, hiding their real identities. The first name of Maharaja Kumar Chaturvedi falsely gives the impression that he is an Indian king which Patsy easily accepts due to the temptation of making her daughter Loveleen a Maharani by managing her marriage with him. Loveleen begins to dream that after becoming a Maharani, she would have hundreds of servants, palanquins, fabulous wealth, and all the royal paraphernalia which have long been associated with kings and queens. Hence, hiding her real self, Loveleen poses to be deeply in love with Chaturvedi. Her mother Patsy confirms Loveleen's sincere love for Chaturvedi by saying, "I would agree to your marrying Love even if you were a cobbler in your country" (*Masks* 26). The implied message is clear that Loveleen was marrying Chaturvedi not because he was a king but because of her genuine love for him. However, once they come to realise that Chaturvedi was not really a king, that the first name of Maharaja had given them a totally wrong impression, their masks of deep love for him drop off and they find India barbaric, Chaturvedi ugly, his act of kissing nauseating and his dance like that of a kangaroo. They not only break all relationships with him, refuse to take the telephonic call from him but get their telephone number de-listed to bar any future contact with him. A disenchanted Chaturvedi wonders: "Were all her claims of love and marriage false, pegged on to his misunderstood kingship?" (*Masks* 30). For M. L. Mehta, the story exposes "the hypocrisy and hollowness of human relationship, the sanctity of which is desecrated by the mercantile mentality and commercial attitude by an acquisitive society" (Review 81).

In India, religion is a very fertile area in which various cheats and crooks put on the cloaks of holy saints and swamis. In "Maharshi Satyanand," dacoit Ranga puts on the mask of a swami and cheats thousands of credulous devotees by manipulating miraculous activities and thereby becomes Maharshi Satyanand. His hired agents differentiate the Maharshi's acts of miracles from the street magicians by pointing out that the Maharshi does them "for the wellbeing of humanity" (*Cooperative* 12). Rather than plundering the people directly as a dacoit, Ranga puts on the holy garb of a swami and adopts the sophisticated methods by making illusory promises of the fulfillment of the devotees' wishes. Inspector Verma, who normally did not believe in such saints, is momentarily bewitched by the Maharshi's personality: "The mere sight of man from whose face oozed divinity created feelings of pleasant awe and gratitude" (*Cooperative* 13-14). On a careful investigation, he is found to be dacoit Ranga and is sent to jail. H. L. Sharma calls Maharshi Satyanand "a wolf in sheep's clothing, a dreaded dacoit who cheats the innocent god-fearing people but is adored as a god" (Sharma 118). For Prabha Shankar Dwivedi such "fake Swamis . . . project themselves to be the saviors of the suffering humanity and intend to equate themselves with the almighty" (Dwivedi 138).

The educational institutions in India, considered to be the cream of society, are not immune to this malaise. In certain cases where the teachers and administrators have powers, they exploit others by saying something pleasing on surface but intending to do something else underneath. Srivastava portrays the hypocrisy of our educationalists in the country through his story "Lasting Victory" in which the Principal of the college carries a mask and his words and expressions are often loaded with indecent implications. When Vimala Tiwari talks of knitting, he says, "Women are created for much better jobs" (*Masks* 55). Such expressions – *double entendres* – too are a kind of mask to conceal real intentions of the speakers behind two-pronged words. The Principal, when failing to seduce Vimala, exerts all sorts of pressures on her through the students in order to bring her round, but she struggles very hard – to use Mehta's words – in order "to win a lasting victory over the wolves masquerading as academicians" (Review 81) and succeeds in her attempts.

In "Rescuers," a school-going girl Neeru has a problem in reaching home in the absence of her rickshaw-wallah. Another rickshaw-wallah demands too much money and talks rudely with her. She considers him "a wolf in man's garb" (*Masks* 67), not realising that the person was honest and without mask. Three boys – Harcharan Singh, Majid Khan and Ram Bharose – pose themselves as rescuers. Harcharan Singh promises to help her by calling himself her brother: "Come on sister, have no fear. We are like brothers to you" (*Masks* 70). Inwardly, all of them are determined to have sex with her and openly discuss it among themselves, even though they feign to be good Samaritans to help her reach her place. Srivastava universalises their hypocrisy by making them Hindu, Muslim and Sikh – three different religions. When Neeru declines to accompany them, their pretenses are dropped. As Harcharan forces her to accompany him, she escapes with alacrity to Father Joseph Sault's car. The Father calls her his "daughter" repeatedly and asks her to have no fear. Taken in by his comforting words and his cloak of a Christian savior as sincere, she feels relieved in escaping from the exploiting boys. The bony and aged hands of the Father appear as "the best protection" to her (*Masks* 74), particularly when he convincingly professes to "believe in the religion of humanity" (*Masks* 76). The next morning when she realises that she was raped by Father Joseph Sault in the night, "She felt the whole world was inhabited by wolves, some in their original, some in sheep's skin" (*Masks* 80). The story lays bare the beastly nature of human beings who show compassion, pity and humanity merely as masks to exploit her subsequently. In the story Mehta praises Srivastava's use of "zoologico-ornithological imagery (wolves and hawks) to unmask the rescuers" (Review 81).

The masqueraders are not confined to urban areas alone; they inhabit rural areas as well. Two short stories "Confession" and "Seeds of Democracy" deal with dissemblers in rural areas who masquerade in different ways. In "Confession," both Lajvati and Kewal Singh show themselves to be different from what they are in reality. Lajvati has a mask of modesty, as her name suggests – a keeper of *Laj* – (modesty) but in reality, she is an adulteress who attempts to murder even her husband in order to satisfy her desire for sex with Kewal Singh so that she might have a child and the stigma of barrenness could be removed from her personality. For this very purpose, she had also attempted earlier to sacrifice a small girl Deepa but towards the end of her life, she is totally exposed. Kewal Singh is no less a dissembler who seduces Lajvati through Dhania and by using words with double meanings.

It is in the area of country's politics that the largest number of masqueraders abounds. In order to get elected, they present kaleidoscopic visions, make rosy promises, assure the people of creating heaven on earth but the moment they are elected, they become greatest exploiters. In "Seeds of Democracy," Lokendra Singh gets elected first as an M.L.A. and then as the Sarpanch by making false promises but becomes a merciless dictator and does everything contrary to the spirit of democracy and even humanity. Parbhua, a labor, is nearly ruined by him for contesting the Panchayat election against Lokendra Singh. On his dictates, the Panchayat takes wrong decisions against Parbhua in the name of justice. When Parbhua as a labour falls down from Kewal Singh's wall under construction, he declines to reveal his real injury and ironically tells Kewal Singh, "Whatever the members of the panchayat decide about the nature of my injuries, I'll accept the decision and repeat it accordingly" (*Masks* 107).

Since the stories seem to be fictional creations of real, felt experiences, the tone of Srivastava's stories is often satirical and ironical. M. L. Mehta writes that Srivastava's "irony is pervasive: power-drunk politicians, unscrupulous academicians, piously impious priests and sex-starved swindlers posing as friends – none escapes its darts.... Srivastava wields his pen like a surgeon's knife to restore the sick society to its health" (Review 81). Since direct, matter-of-fact, newspaper-type portrayal of such people has not been found to be very effective, Srivastava exposes them through his fictional creations. It is through the metaphor of mask and other related images that Srivastava successfully portrays the dichotomy between the world as it is and as it appears to be.

Works Cited

Das, Smita. "Imagery in Ramesh K. Srivastava's *Neema.*" *MIT International Journal of English Language and Literature.* Vol. I, No. 2 (August 2014), 72-77.

Dwivedi, Prabha Shankar. Book Review of Ramesh K. Srivastava's *A Christmas Gift and Other Stories. Littcrit: An Indian Response to Literature.* Vol. XLII, No. 1 (June 2016), 137-139.

Gulati, Azad. "Masks People Wear Daily" – Review of Ramesh K. Srivastava's *Masks and Men: Stories. The Tribune* (July 4, 1987).

Mehta, M. L. "An Interview with Ramesh K. Srivastava." *The Critical Endeavour.* Vol. VIII (December 2002), 167-179.

.... Book Review of Ramesh K. Srivastava's *Masks and Men: Stories. Indian Book Chronicle.* Vol. XIV, No. 4 (April 1989), 80-81.

Sharma, H. L. Review of Ramesh K. Srivastava's *Cooperative Colony: Stories. Punjab Journal of English Studies.* Vol. V (1990), 118-120.

Singh, Karnail. Review of Ramesh K. Srivastava's *Masks and Men: Stories. Punjab Journal of English Studies.* Vol. V (1990), 111-114.

Srivastava, Ramesh K. *Cooperative Colony: Stories.* Calcutta: Writers Workshop, 1985.

..........*Masks and Men: Stories.* Calcutta: Writers Workshop, 1986.

CHAPTER 14

Ramesh K. Srivastava's "Century": A Study

Barinder K. Sharma

Ramesh K. Srivastava is a well-known short story writer who has published seven collections of short stories, two novels *Neema* and *Coils of the Serpent* and thirteen critical books in English. Having lived both in India and in the U.S.A., he writes with equal facility about men and manners of both the countries. The present story was published first in *Caravan* – a popular English fortnightly magazine of New Delhi in December 1975 and after having been adjudged as one of the 10 best stories published in *Caravan* in forty years, it was republished in the same magazine in September 1979 in the *Fortieth Anniversary: Best of Forty Years Issue.*

In his essay "My Idea of a Story," Srivastava, believing in Poe's concept of the short story, feels that a short story "is a classic in miniature with precision-made parts and singleness of effect . . . to which every character, incident, sentence and every word must contribute" (*Read* 101). Srivastava's "Century" is a perfect example of his filigree work in which he has beautifully chiseled the pangs of the Indian protagonist's alienation in the U.S. the total effect of which is as clear as a powerful slap on the face.

Mohan, the protagonist of the story, went to the U.S. for higher studies. Even though he had already spent one year there, he continued to feel the absence of intimate friends with whom he could share his pains and pleasures. Consequently, he felt an overwhelming sense of alienation. Sidney Finkelstein defines alienation as "a psychological phenomenon, an internal conflict, a hostility felt toward something seemingly outside oneself which is linked to oneself, a barrier erected which is actually no defense but an impoverishment of oneself" (Finkelstein 137). Mohan's sense of loneliness was largely because of his absence of command over conversational English due to which he could not easily interact with American boys and girls. It was easier for him "to give a long lecture or to participate in a literary discussion, but difficult to indulge in simple, ordinary conversation where rules of grammar are conveniently forgotten" (*Cooperative* 55). The American food, faces and its places too were different from those in India and bred in him a sense of uneasiness and discomfort.

What mainly accentuated Mohan's loneliness was his absence of girlfriends. In India, two boys could be good friends and go anywhere but in the U.S., two boys going together are often taken as homosexuals whereas because of his in-built hesitation and timidity, he did not know how to befriend girls. He felt "terribly lonely" (55) because most people went out with girls on weekends, while he remained alone with television as his only companion. Without friends, the weekends in the U.S. could be "a veritable torture if you remain busy in your work" (55). Different from being in India where you have many things to do in the weekends, in the U.S. "you feel terribly lonely because you can find none of your friends at home, no one even picks up the phone, and you are confined to your room with a TV as your sole companion and the class assignment as the Sword of Democles" (55). In such a terrible sense of loneliness, when someone spoke in Indian language, he felt that "the sound of one's native language in a foreign country is like lovely soothing rain on parched land, bringing hopes of greenery, fruition and good times ahead" (56).

The presence of choicest beauties in the U.S. might have been a source of immense pleasure for others, but Mohan felt "they had made my daytime studies difficult, my sleepless nights prolonged, and my lonely weekends full of torture" (56). Sometimes, the torture of loneliness became so accentuated, he felt as if he "would go mad" (61) unless he talked to someone. He found that "on weekends, the telephones of others rang off and on, but mine went dead. None called me. I yearned anxiously to hear it even once. But no one dialed me once even by mistake" (62). Of course, the alienation comes to an end only when Marcy comes to him to discuss her theme and he had a good company for a night.

The story also presents a graphic portrayal of two contrasting Indians – Mohan and Jasbir, studying in the U.S. Mohan is a simple, shy and hesitant Indian who considered Indian students as representatives of their countries while Jasbir, being foil to Mohan, is a hedonist without conscience who sexually exploits the American girls by making false promises of marriage to them. He completes a century of cases in which he had slept with American girls. On the other hand, Mohan, being timid and with qualms of his conscience, misses an equal number.

Mohan is quite ignorant of tricks of befriending American girls whereas Jasbir comes out "as a guru in the art of love-making" who knew "tricks to suit different persons and occasions" (55-56). For Mohan, America is a place to study; for Jasbir, to enjoy. Mohan thinks only of "bird-watching" whereas Jasbir thinks of trapping "the bird first and then watch her afterwards inside and outside" (57). Being a libertine, Jasbir thinks only of enjoying American girls irrespective of consequences. He says, "I don't miss a single chance to trap girls, and soon I will be completing a century" (59).

Unlike Jasbir, Mohan has a sober cast of mind. Jasbir with his flawed English is so jubilant and resourceful that each time he would take a new girl out whereas Mohan remains "supine, cold, like a damp cracker" (58). Mohan has problems with conscience and cannot exploit any person because of "humanitarian considerations" (69), Jasbir has no such qualms. When Mohan comes to the point of exploiting girls, "the human being woke up within me at the sight of a fragile and defenseless creature" (70) and the idea of exploitation disappeared altogether. Since Jasbir had spoiled the image of Indians among American girls, instead of confirming the distorted image, Mohan wanted to correct it because when he had proceeded to the U.S. from India, he was told repeatedly: "Every Indian is an ambassador of his country in a foreign place and his activities and lapses will uplift or tar the nation's image" (70). When Marcy was drunk, she told Mohan how she was made pregnant by an Indian, obviously Jasbir, and had to go in for abortion. Karnail Singh feels that "The East and the West seem to have met on the bed on which Marcy and Mohan sleep all the night, not like Adam and Eve before their fall, but like two sensuous beings who are drawn between the pulls of pleasure and reality" (Singh 308). At the time of leaving Mohan's dormitory, Marcy called Jasbir "bastard" while warmly kissing Mohan, implying her appreciation of his attitude and behaviour. Jasbir takes pride in having slept with one hundred girls whereas Mohan feels he "had missed almost an equal number, and our centuries – posive and nagive, would coincide soon" (*Cooperative* 63).

Srivastava uses symbols in a very subtle way so that they remain completely unobtrusive. While Jasbir was in Mohan's room of the dormitory, a beautiful butterfly was trapped in the window. The butterfly is a symbol of a beautiful American girl. It was caught in the window and "fluttered frantically to come out" (60). While Mohan, symbolising humanity, makes all possible efforts to save it unharmed, Jasbir, symbolising utilitarian and exploitative attitude, kills it by throwing a pornographic book at it and it was "dead, crushed and mutilated" (61). The killing of a beautiful butterfly with a pornographic book symbolises destruction of the trust of innocent American girls due to his sexual acts. When Mohan attempts to free the butterfly, as he was to free Marcy later, Jasbir thinks of exploiting it by suggesting "you should catch it and fix it with pins" (61) as he had done and they had looked beautiful.

At the end of the story, when Jasbir drove away with a girl "towards the west" and Mohan "turned to the opposite direction" (72), implying the East, their activities point out Jasbir's interest in the western ways of life and those of Mohan in the eastern values. Probably that is what Sulekha Sharma means when she points out that "Srivastava's inner world is the Indian sanctuary sheltered from western winds" (Sharma 4). Karnail Singh considers Mohan "most probably the mask of the writer" (Singh 307).

The entire narrative is in the first person and flows so naturally that nowhere does it appear as if it has been written by an Indian which is a good comment on the use of Indian English. The story flows so naturally, so smoothly, so spontaneously that one cannot close the book without finishing it. Sulekha Sharma praises he story for "its fine flow of language, spontaneity, charm" (Sharma 4). The language is simple with words and phrases, similes and metaphors taken from everyday life. Jasbir uses many colloquial words from Hindi and Punjabi, like *"ki hal hai,"* *"changa ji"* and "*chhamak chhallos*" (*Cooperative* 56) among others. It goes to the credit of Srivastava that there are places when his simple languages rises to become rhythmic, full of provocative thoughts, such as, in the following lines:

> Humanitarian considerations have been the heaviest fetters on me. I do not exploit a person I do not know and I cannot exploit a person I know. The mere sight of a girl arouses within me feelings of amorousness. . . . The net is tightened, but when we become friends and the moment of

> fulfillment comes, I feel somewhat the twitches of conscience. My resolve weakens. Humanity awakens within me, and I withdraw myself, weak and repentant. The original motive of exploitation shies away and I remain rooted where I was at the beginning (69).

An interesting part of the story is that because of the first person narrative, Srivastava's colleagues, disregarding the writer's imaginative power, considered it a real, confessional story of his life in the U.S. As a befitting reply to them, he wrote his entire novel *Neema* – a story of a woman, in the first person narrative.

On the whole, the story is quite gripping. Even though there is abundance of elements of love and sex which "act as salt and pepper, adding to their interest and appeal to the masses" (Khanna 47), the story marches ahead towards its end uninterruptedly. Its characters, incidents and dialogues contribute to its creditable success as a story. Smita Das writes that for Srivastava, "a short story is not a sort of museum to parade unusual and exotic characters and situations, but something portraying hitherto unexplored areas hinting at the universal truths of life" (Das 28). It is a well-crafted story with no loose ends. For Dr Karnail Singh, it tends "to attain a classical standing" (Singh 308). Srivastava's "Century" is a priceless diamond carelessly trodden by ignorant pedestrians but jubilantly picked up for a crown by a discreet reader.

Works Cited

Das, Smita. "Introduction," *Ramesh K. Srivastava: Man and his Work*. New Delhi: Authors Press, 2016, 15-71.

Finkelstein, Sidney. *Existentialism and Alienation in American Literature.* New York: International Publishers, 1965.

Khanna, Adarsh. Review of Ramesh K. Srivastava's *Cooperative Colony: Stories. Commonwealth Quarterly,* Vol. XIV, No. 39 (June-September 1989), 58-60, rpt. *The Recognition of Ramesh K. Srivastava,* ed. By Shipra G. Vashishtha. New Delhi: Authors Press, 2030, 46-48.

Sharma, Sulekha. Review of Ramesh K. Srivastava's *Cooperative Colony: Stories. The Tribune* (Chandigarh). 4 January 1986, 4.

Singh, Karnail. Review of Ramesh K. Srivastava's *Cooperative Colony: Stories. Indian Book Chronicle* (December 1987), 306-308.

Srivastava, Ramesh K. *Cooperative Colony: Stories.* Calcutta: Writers Workshop, 1985.

………. "My Idea of a Story," *Read, Write and Teach: Essays on Learning to Live Together.* New Delhi: Authors Press, 2014, 99-104.

CHAPTER 15

Ramesh K. Srivastava's "Games They Play": A Study

Smita Das

Most Indian-English novelists have treated the short story writing as a by-product of the novel-writing, but such is not the case with Ramesh K. Srivastava. He has till now published two novels – *Neema* (1984) and *Coils of the Serpent* (2011) – and five collections of short stories, namely, *Love and Animality: Stories* (1984), *Cooperative Colony: Stories* (1985), *Masks and Men: Stories* (1986), *Games They Play and Other Stories* (1989) and *Under the Lamp: Stories* (1993). This way Srivastava has established himself both as a novelist and a short story writer. Neeta Maini feels that the writer has a wide range in both subject matter and technique; he presents "a kaleidoscopic view of life, revealing too the gulf that lies between appearance and reality, what appears to be and is" (186).

The story under discussion "Games They Play" is not about usual games and sports played by common people but refers ironically to those played by the men of power – royal dignitaries and hypocritical politicians as is suggested by the impersonal pronoun 'they.' To the religious-minded people, even gods and goddesses play games with human beings by giving rewards and punishments respectively to the virtuous and sinners through blessings or curses. The word 'games' also implies the constructive activities of children for benevolent purpose and destructive ones of the predators whose impious duty appears to harm others merely for their sadistic pleasures.

Set in the Matiari village of Madhya Pradesh, the story highlights the sufferings of the protagonist Nathunia. Though there is no mention of her age and physical appearance, she appears to be a young woman of twenty-five, happily married to a pincers-holder.

Mature and caring, Nathunia manages her family well. Her love and care for her children is revealed in her act of narrating the story of Suraj and Chanda (the sun and the moon) in daytime, even though considering such a thing to be ominous.

Srivastava gives a pictorial description of Matiari village and its people who live in primitive surroundings quite insulated from the modern world and its scientific, technological marvels. It is a tribal area with the near-absence of clothes among its inhabitants. They wear the ornaments of beads and conch shells, and live in their poorly thatched mud houses and grass-covered cottages. The villagers hunt animals with bows and arrows rather than with modern guns and bullets. Its people have not yet seen bridges and culverts over the rivulets. The picturesque description presents before the reader a vivid image of the rural world which is destroyed by wild animals and cruel human beings.

Since the village is totally unaffected by the urban life, superstitions and blind beliefs rule supreme. People being gullible and credulous readily accept them, considering everything to be divinely ordained and every minor incident preceding "a happy or tragic event as good or ill-ominous and indicative of a divine blessing or curse" (80). Nathunia initially declines telling a tale to her children in daytime because it tended "to portend ill-luck" (81). A man had lost his cow for telling a tale in daytime. Pooja had also heard that "to educate a girl is to bring ill-luck" (81). Even when the mounted soldiers come and make an announcement about the arrival of frenzied elephants, Nathunia feels guilty of "ill-ominously telling a tale to the children during daytime" (85) which was bound to result in dreadful consequences. Fear settles in her heart when she apprehends that the frenzied elephants might trample over her children.

For the villagers, hunting of animals is an act merely for their survival, not for pleasure and even then it becomes a dangerous game of life in which occasionally the roles are reversed; the hunted becomes the hunter and vice versa. In Hemingway's *The Old Man and the Sea,* Santiago considers it a sin to kill fish only for pleasure. Being a fisherman by profession, he fishes only to keep himself alive but without causing unnecessary pain, and apologises to the fish for wounding and causing pain to it. On the contrary, for kings and royal dignitaries, "the poor people and animals were mere playthings – mobile toys in flesh and blood – to be fondled or dashed against the ground" (80). Like the dumb animals, the poor have no voice to protest and remain docile, tongue-tied, taking everything to be a part of the divine plan. Even Suraj and Chanda played games in which the clever Chanda's trick of fooling had got him cool journeys whereas Suraj had to suffer in heat. The miscarriage of justice is universal whether the affected beings are human or divine.

The game of frenzied elephants was quite favorite of the Maharaja of Dewalpur. The sexually-aroused elephants, after being inebriated by gallons of liquor, bade farewell to their sanity and indulged in the game of mass destruction which made the Maharaja feel "immensely amused by their destructive activities" (85). In order to save the life of the Maharaja with a pair of red hot pincers, Nathunia's husband was "ripped into two from limb to limb almost as if the man were no more than a tooth stick one tears from end to end" (85). For the aged Pooja, the new rulers of the post-independent India were only as good or as bad as those in the pre-independence days. In the name of construction of the road, the mud-houses of the poor were being demolished. In contrast, Pooja and Kundan as children have a positive attitude and indulge in the playful activities of making a sand-house for Suraj. Their game is meant to correct the miscarriage of justice – to undo the wrongs done to Suraj by his mother.

Even the houseflies dart here and there as if playing their own games, but unlike the elephants, they are fearful and sensitive. They could be contrasted with elephants which are gigantic and dignified yet bring miseries to human beings by playing dangerous games. Of course, the elephants themselves are usually peace-loving creatures till provoked but here they become instruments in the hands of royal dignitaries. If at all they become destructive, it is when they act from fear of *ankush* (a goading device), in *mastee* (sexual frenzy) or in a completely drunken state.

Construction and destruction are two aspects of life quite obvious in the story. Suraj and Chanda seem to symbolise respectively constructive and destructive activities. While Suraj, being kind and considerate, saved some sweets for his mother from his own share, Chanda played a trick by stealing it and then substituting stones in its place which unwittingly angered his mother so much as to curse Suraj to travel perpetually in heat. It must have given Chanda the same malicious pleasure which the Maharaja of Dewalpur got in letting loose a couple of frenzied elephants in *mastee* to indulge in destructive activities. These elephants pulled down trees, smashed mud-houses, and killed Nathunia's husband – a pincers-holder. The second time, the elephants kill Nathunia and Kundan and destroy their house, including the sand-house. Nathunia's children, Pooja and Kundan, indulge in constructive activity by making a sand-house with the benevolent purpose of giving a cool shelter to Suraj.

The portrayal of children in the story is extremely natural and life-like. They provide a good contrast to the world of adults. Pooja and Kundan could be any sister and brother with their love for bedtime tales, for building sand-houses, as also for their innocence, simplicity and caring attitude for justice and fair play. When the five-year old Kundan asks for a tale from his mother Nathunia, she initially declines telling it in daytime because of it being ominous but she, "sweetly disarmed" by his mischievous answer, consents to tell a tale. Pooja's complaint against Nathunia's act of teaching oral sums becomes funny because the child finds confusion in her mother's earlier teaching of three and one making four, and later on, two and two making four!

The story of Suraj and Chanda in which the latter had caused unmerited curse for Suraj touches the sensitive hearts of the children. They blame their horrible mother for causing injustice to Suraj. Kundan decides to correct the wrongs done to Suraj by making a sand-house for him "to undo the wrong done by his mother" (82). Pooja agrees for it. As they go to the sandy brook, they find it a good area for all sorts of games and other activities of fun. Two children dig up a well by clawing and scooping up the sand. Another child furrows a sandy stretch with his clawed fingers as if for cultivation. Still others jump and frisk over shallow pools of water. After making a sand-house, Pooja and Kundan feel happy that "now Suraj will have at least one cool place to take rest" (83), otherwise it would have suffered in heat in the same way as a beggar woman had died of heatstroke.

It is so surprising yet so natural for children that they try to set right the wrongs done by the adults. This is what Wordsworth had meant by writing, "The Child is father of the Man" (l.7). Children, having fresh memories of their association with the divine, cherish moral values which are forgotten by the adults. While politicians and royal dignitaries indulge in destroying houses and in committing wrongs, children build them – at least symbolically. They don't even want to use acacia thorns which "might hurt other pedestrians" (83) and instead fix colored pebbles for fencing. Even while going back home, Pooja wants to make windows in the sand-house so that Suraj does not have to stay "in the dark, damp and airless house" (84). When the frenzied elephants wound her, she hysterically clamors for "some justice" for Suraj because Chanda was destroying the sand-house meant for his brother.

Two worlds of pre-independence and post-independence have been juxtaposed in the story. In the pre-independent period, India was ruled by kings and zamindars for whom the poor people and animals were mere playthings to be fondled or destroyed. In the post-independence period, the place of kings and royal dignitaries has been taken by modern day politicians and that of elephants by bulldozers and heavy earth-moving machines. Like the tyrannical kings of the past, the insensitive and heartless politicians demolish the mud-houses of the people in the name of construction. Pooja, now sixty, and her husband Surajmal had re-constructed their mud-house which was destroyed earlier by elephants. Now during the post-independent emergency, their re-constructed house is also destroyed. In their weakness caused by the surgical operation of vasectomy forcibly performed on them, they could do nothing even when their houses were being destroyed: "The re-enactment of the scene of man-made devastation after over fifty years appeared like the sadistic celebration of the demolition of her house by the frenzied elephants" (91). In both cases, it is the poor people who suffered.

In the matter of technique, Srivastava is somewhat traditional. He has not used steam-of-consciousness or flashback technique in this story. Since he writes mostly for popular magazines, he makes the stories interesting and readable. In an interview with Atma Ram, Srivastava had said that he does not believe in making his story "a highly experimental, complicated jigsaw puzzle in which comprehension and corresponding pleasure are doled out in bits and pieces" (18). The story must be eminently readable. K.V. Chacko calls Srivastava "a gifted writer of stories who knows the tricks of his trade well: an endearing narrative style, nearly impeccable language and appropriate technique to deliver an interesting theme into the reader's lap as a short story." It is the chronological method which has been adopted in "Games They Play." Since the story spans a period of over fifty years and deals with two generations of characters, it has been sub-divided into three parts, with the climax at the end where one comes to realisation that the poor people remain pawns into the hands of powers that be and that colonial rule or political freedom means nothing to them. The climax comes when the aged Pooja's reconstructed mud-house is destroyed by gigantic machines, while her husband Surajmal eventually finds a shelter in the sand as if the sand-house made earlier for Suraj had found an occupant after half-a-century in the dying person of the same name.

Irony is Srivastava's most favorite mode of narration both in his novels and short stories. Neeta Maini calls irony as "Srivastava's *forte*" (193). In a country where hypocrisy and double-facedness have become a way of life, telling bitter truths involves the risk of reprisals from powerful politicians. In such a situation, irony becomes the most appropriate mode of communication which implies saying one thing to mean another. Since the atrocities were being committed by kings and royal dignitaries in the past and now by the powerful politicians, their portrayal can best be in an ironic mode. Srivastava calls these powers as "they" and their acts of injustice and cruelty as "games." The kings and politicians drunken in power are identified with inebriated elephants and mechanical monsters. Tewari also feels that "the story teller metaphorically equates the rulers with frenzied elephants" (51). The able-bodied persons who were promised jobs by politicians are incapacitated through coercive vasectomy surgery. There is an ironic reversal of fortune in the story that whereas Pooja and Kundan wanted to do justice to Suraj by building a cool sand-house for him, it ends up in Pooja and her husband Surajmal facing death and burial in the same sand. The promised rosy utopia turns out to be a dark dystopia.

The success of a short story depends on the impact it has on the reader. Edgar Allan Poe wrote that "the unity of effect or impression is a point of the greatest importance" (173). Henry James also stressed the need of "singleness of effect" (434). Keeping such an effect in view, a writer selects appropriate material for it. Though Srivastava refers to the games of power which have been played by kings and modern day politicians respectively before and after India's political independence, symbolically such power games have been perennially universal. The colorful myths and historical accounts of most countries can symbolically be included in such games. Tewari refers to it as "the renditions of both macro and micro power discourses" (46). As one analyses this story minutely, layers upon layers of meanings and implications begin to be revealed. The games and their outcome in the tragic story touch the reader's heart and broaden his vision on realisation that they are a microcosm of cosmic power games.

Works Cited

Chacko, K. V. "Review of *Love and Animality: Stories*." *Hitvada* (September 9, 1984).

James, Henry. Quoted by Leon Edel (ed.), *The Ghostly Tales of Henry James*. New Brunswick: Rutgers' University Press, 1948.

Maini, Neeta. "Ramesh K. Srivastava as a Short Story Writer," *Studies in Contemporary Indian-English Short Story,* edited by A. N. Dwivedi. Delhi: B. R. Publishing Corporation, 1991. 185-197.

Poe, Edgar Allan. "*Twice-Told Tales* by Nathaniel Hawthorne: A Review," *American Literature Survey,* Vol. II, edited by Milton R. Stern. New York: The Viking Press,1969.

Ram, Atma, "Ramesh K. Srivastava," *Interviews with Indians Writing in English*, ed. by Atma Ram. Calcutta: Writers Workshop, 1992. 14-24.

Srivastava, Ramesh K. "Games They Play," *Games They Play and Other Stories*. New Delhi: Prestige Books, 1989. 80-92.

Tewari, Anil Kumar. "Psychodynamics of Power Discourse in Srivastava's *Games They Play*," *Punjab Journal of English Studies*. 7 (1992): 45-53.

Wordsworth, William. "My Heart Leaps Up."

CHAPTER 16

Narrative as Discourse: A Study of Ramesh K Srivastava's *Under The Lamp (Stories)*

Lata Mishra

Narrative theory or narratology can be traced back to the Russian formalist Vladimir Propp (1968) and French structuralist Claude Lévi-Strauss, Tzvetan Todorov (1977) traditions. In general, narrative is considered to be a sequence of events and in this case the theorists focus on the narrative itself regardless of the medium used. For Gérard Genette, Mieke Bal (1985), and Seymour Chatman (1978) narrative is a discourse. However poststructuralist present narrative as a complex artefact. Chatman in his *Narrative Discourse* differentiates between narrative form and narrative expression. He explains that a narrative conveys meaning of its own and, thus, has the form and substance of narrative expression as well as the form and substance of narrative content. Story is the substance of narrative expression while the set of possible events, actions constitute the narrative content.

Mieke Bal (1985) in her work *Narratology: Introduction to the Theory of Narrative* defines a text as "a finite, structured whole composed of language signs" (8). We may say that while the narrator links events rationally, on the basis of a cause/effect relationship or association, characters and settings create another structure within narrative on their own. Roland Barthes focus more on the workings of characters and settings (paradigmatic dimension). A paradigm in *Oxford Concise Dictionary of Literary Terms* is: "a set of linguistic or other units that can be substituted for each other in the same position within a sequence or structure" (182) whereas a syntagm is "a linguistic term designating any combination of units…which are arranged in a significant sequence" (255). The rational linking of events constitutes the syntagmatic dimension. This interaction results into one complex whole. Barthes in his *Structural Analysis* argues "the language of narrative is one of the idioms apt for consideration by the linguistics of discourse…" (Barthes, 84). In this way narrative is placed at the level of discourse.

Under The Lamp is the collection of twelve stories.

The Living Doll

The Living Doll is told by the omniscient narrator outside of the story. Using Genette's terminology, focalizer is Kashi. In the story Kashi in the process of growing up develops a fetish or paraphilia that involves being sexually attracted to a doll, psychologists call this 'Agalmatophilia'. Kashi is a nineteen year youth well-built but dull witted and hard of hearing. He does not cry on his birth and this is considered as an ill omen in north India. His mother dies soon after he comes into the world. At five years of age he is gifted a pretty Japanese doll by his doctor. The doll is the only female companion to him in a family of males, a father and an elder brother. Karni, a sixteen year old bride of Kashi's elder brother finds in Kashi an infatuated love. A love that is pure passion that starts and ends in no time. She is attracted physically to Kashi because of his well-built body and mild temperament. On the day of Holi, the two are alone at home when Karni tempts Kashi and the latter in moments of frenzy strangulates her. The focalisation in the story is internal and variable as Karni is the second focalizer. Kashi and Karni can be contrasted in the story. Karni is just at the threshold of youth, with de-energised and indifferent husband and no guardianship of family elders. Kashi lives in fancy world with a doll. The spur of the moment causes tragedy thus making the prophesy come true: "Kashi portended a misfortune for the poor family when he did not cry at the time of his birth" (1).

A Drowning Man

A Drowning Man is told by one of the characters in the story. Focalizer is 'I'. The narrator in the story is the writer himself. He narrates the story in conversational style. The reader is privy to all his thoughts and opinions, in this way the reader gets to know the protagonist faster, and relates to him more easily. The story opens as:

> Difficult even for me to believe, but here was I now married to a girl I had not seen. Our hired bus has left the bride's village an hour ago with me and my wife perched on the front seat. (10)

This is the story of a newly married couple. While the husband is an US immigrant, the wife Sarala is a simple (as her name suggests) village girl. All that this young doctor has aspired for is a virgin girl as his wife, though himself he has had many relations in USA. His dreams crash when it is revealed by his newly wedded innocent wife that she had been abused since childhood without herself even realising what village boys have done to her. The story in a very sensitive way demonstrates the results of keeping daughters uneducated and indoors by rural folk. By not sending them to schools lest they get polluted, the girls survive in darkness of ignorance. The sentence in the first paragraph contrasts with the one at the end of the story. The word *sanyasin* carries all the significance. Without herself experiencing any sexual pleasure the girl since her tender age has passively participated in games designed by males:

> Covering her face in a long drawn veil, Sarala, my wife sat there like a *sanyasin*, almost motionless (10).

> I felt like a weather-beaten man, drowning in an unfathomable ocean (23).

The man who has had experiences with several women is weather beaten as he feels bankrupt with the knowledge that he cannot enrich himself with the virginity of his wife.

Tigers of the Steering Wheel

Tigers of the Steering Wheel is told by narrator *in* the story. Focaliser is 'I'. It is a story with points of view of truck drivers of India. The drivers regard themselves to be tigers. They display their masculinity through driving aggressively or violently on the road. Driver in the story loses no opportunity to express dominance over others in public. In this way he expresses righteous indignation, fight for honour and challenges perceived threats to his manhood. However love conquers him and a researcher from *Boston Times* writing an article on 'The Main Causes of Disastrous Truck- Accidents in India' washes off all his insecurities and fears.

Hospitality

Hospitality is told by narrator in the story. Focalisers are Parkash and Dr. Kantiji. In 'third-person centre of consciousness', the 'reflector' is the focaliser, while the user of the third person is the narrator. The narrator in the story is Dr. Kantiji who visits Jullundur to investigate a case, but is deceived by his old friend Parkash who uses his wife to lure him, and extract confidential papers from his room in the night. On deeper level readers notice the doctor deceiving his wife and having sex with an almost stranger. Though he is in an inebriated state at the time of an incident but keeping in mind his expectations from his wife under similar circumstances, he does not seem innocent to the readers.

The Human Thrist

The Human Thirst is also written in first person and it begins as:

> In July every year, as the academic year begins, several fresh girls bloom in my classes and they revive old wounds of my lapses and failures- not in academic world where I have achieved a fair success but in matters of heart. (46).

As in the other stories of this collection, the narrator, a college professor with a married daughter and college-going son is disillusioned with the domestic life he lives in and secretly craves for the other women. In this process he poses threat not only to his domestic life but to life in its wider sense. The story also reveals that besides several restraints of gender, customs and traditions of our conservative society young girls today are also victims of exploitation, physical and mental torture, as the professor involves his students in his sexual escapades. A teenage girl from lower strata of society succeeds in showing him mirror while the one belonging to middle class transgresses from the established norms of Indian society.

Love and Animality

Love and Animality is told by the narrator in the story. Focaliser is Manjula. The story depicts the social conditioning of illiterate or semi-illiterate females in conservative patriarchal societies as ours where masculinity is assessed with the material comforts or the physical strength that a male can display. This happens to the extent that even wife beating is considered to be an act of masculinity by females themselves. Beating is compensated by gifts, and the act is romantic!

Terrorists in the Kitchen

Terrorists in the Kitchen is told by narrator in the story. Focaliser is 'I'. The omniscient narrator is at home in the characters' minds and can relate all that is going on inside them -- he knows about their various thoughts and memories. Through the words of the narrator, the reader is made aware of inner feelings and emotions of the characters but at the same time there is a kind of tacit agreement between the author and the narrator -- an understanding that the narrator will remain unobtrusive and not attempt to have his voice heard in a blatantly interfering way.

> Nirbhaya Dayal felt amused because behind her apparent indifference or even antagonism to the grown up cats lay her (Sonkali) warm concern, love and affection . . . But in Nirbhaya's presence, she maintained a stoic indifference and even threw the cats away as if to prove her attitude. (81).

This story too is the one of many that deals with the theme of deceit and mistrust seated in human beings, due to the circumstances they are forced to live in, but their innate goodness finally saves the aged couple from the life-threatening situation.

A Blessed Curse

A Blessed Curse is told by the narrator outside the story. Focaliser is Tulsa. Menaka and Tulsa grow together. Tulsa is an orphan living as a friend and maid to Menaka. While Menaka is educated and familiar with the outer world, Tulsa is uneducated and confined within walls. Menaka carries her beauty in a mature and graceful manner in the world. She forewarns Tulsa against the various corruptions but the latter has to be rescued by her when Tulsa is almost at the verge of being trafficked by her lover.

Two Odd Wheels

Two Odd Wheels is told by narrator outside of the story. The focaliser is Parimal Kaneria. The writer of the story does not hesitate in exposing the hypocrisy of Indian middle class society. The marriage of convenience is juxtaposed against the marriage of love. Rina leaves her ailing husband and son, as the rest of life may become a difficult struggle for her. Educated Urmil does not hesitate to divorce her exploitative husband and marries handicapped Niyogi, impressed by the latter's sincerity and perseverance. Indian arranged marriage glorified in our culture is exposed by the writer as two relative strangers are expected to live together the rest of their lives under the expectation that they will develop a loving relationship over time. When due to incompatibilities of temperament their marriages fail, man looks for love outside and often involves in sexual escapes with his heart still craving for love. While womenfolk confined to their homes develop self-effacing tendency. They underestimate their performance and capabilities at home and see the world in a way that puts them in negative light. Both Rina in this story and Manjula in *Love and Animality* fail to understand the delicate aspects of their simple yet blissful marital life and are loud-mouthed and arrogant.

Under the Lamp

This story is told by the narrator in the story. The focaliser is Karmaibai. This is the only story where the central character is woman. The writer presents the oppression of women not only with greater self-involvement but also with note of protest. In the story "Under the Lamp," Srivastava voices the plight of silenced and suppressed Dalit woman. The writer narrates the harrowing tale of a landlord's use of power and force to extinguish the flame of hope of a young widow whose sole aim of life is to bring up her son. The stories are marked by revolt and rebel towards the dark side of existing caste discrimination. In the male dominated and caste ridden society, dalit women suffer unimaginable subjugation. Their economic, political, social and cultural rights are violated. Here 'Dalit' term is used for those who have been broken and ground down by those high in social hierarchy. The story is a sensitive and vivid portrayal of a woman belonging to *lohar* community. The widow struggles to survive with dignity in a world that humiliates and subverts her every attempt at emancipation and progress. Traditionally working as *lohar* after her husband's untimely death the young woman is tortured and exploited by and sneered at by women of her own caste. Poverty, starvation and death are her constant companions in the daily struggle for survival. The spirit of endurance and courage is revealed through this story. The woman dreams a future of liberation through education for her son. The son is labeled illegitimate at his school and his mother addressed as mistress of *sabhapati*, the feudal lord of the village.

Spilled Milk

Spilled Milk is told by the omniscient narrator outside of the story. Focaliser is narrator himself. Here the narrator who does the focalising is also a character, Chhajjoo Ram, an internal textual element. Focalisation can be either external or internal to the story. External focalisation is felt to be close to the narrating agent, and its vehicle is therefore called 'narrator-focaliser' (Bal 37). Chhajjoo Ram in spite of being a crude and low caste poor youth is an altruist who puts all high castes and rich to shame when it comes to rescuing a child from being beaten up to pulp by her cruel step mother.

A Ruby of the Garbage

A Ruby of the Garbage is a story told by the child narrator with points of view of young rag pickers. The innocence and hard life of village boy is contrasted with the urban life of manipulations, crimes and deceit.

The English that the author uses is conditioned by cultural factors within the geographical bounds of India. The language becomes a vehicle to express culturally determined network of activities that are typically Indian, i.e. social stratification, caste system, societal faiths and beliefs. A close reading of these short stories makes one strongly aware that a certain type of ambivalence is to be found in their structure and that there is more to the written texts than just a series of narratives centered on various characters, both children and adults. The stories focus on love, marriage, family life and society from male perspective. They are noticeable for their freshness, irony, wit and satire, but most of all, for humanist concerns. The writer is disappointed at the lack of values in the society. Chhajjoo of *Spilled Milk* and Nirbhaya of *Terrorists in the Kitchen* are the only men who display effeminate behavior in Indian social and cultural context. For most men marriage and love are poles apart. While their wives manage their kitchens they seek love out of marital bond.

Our cultural ideology favors men, and the social institutions try to benefit men from the subordination of women, this has caused an imbalance and several malpractices have crept in. Changing laws and educating people against social prejudices would remedy gender discrimination, giving women equal opportunities with men to exercise individual choices in life. Masculinity theory argues that masculinity is socially constructed through performances and men construct their masculine identities through relationships with others. Men struggle to achieve hegemonic masculinity ideal and prove their masculinity by drinking heavily, sexual exploits, and mistreating the other sex. In this way they enhance their self-esteem. The purpose of this behavior is to solidify the men as a group and to identify women and others as outsiders. (Connell, 76-79) The stories aptly discuss how patriarchal societies have placed women and femininity in a subordinate position to men and masculinity, women having denied the rights to education, expression and mobility. These stories aim to correct erroneous assumptions about both women and men, and to imagine saner and more mature men and of women in the new age.

Works Cited

Bal, M. *Narratology. Introduction to the Theory of Narrative.* Translated by C. van Boheemen. 1st ed. Toronto; London: University of Toronto Press, 1985.

Barthes, R. *Image-Music-Text.* Translated by S. Heath; 1st ed. New York: Hill and Wang, 1977.

Chatman, S. "Story and Discourse" [introduction]. *Approaches to Media: A Reader.* Boyd-Barrett, O., Newbold, C. (eds.). 1st ed. London: Arnold, 1995.

Connell R.W. *The Social Organisation of Masculinity*, Masculinities University of California Press ed. II 2005.

Genette, Gérard, *Narrative Discourse Revisited*, trans. by Jane E. Lewin Ithaca, NY: Cornell University Press, 1989.

Srivastava, Ramesh K. *Under the Lamp*, Jalandhar, ABS Publication, 1993.

CHAPTER 17

Ramesh K. Srivastava's "Under the Lamp": A Study

Shipra G. Vashishtha

Ramesh K. Srivastava's "Under the Lamp" is a tragic tale of a rural woman Karmaibai who struggles for the survival of her son after getting widowed, suffers under the brutal thrashings of Sabhapati Bichitra Singh but unable to bear her torture and sexual exploitation any longer kills him with a *gandasa* and surrenders herself at the police station. It is a meticulously crafted short story with layers upon layers of symbolic implications. The very title of the story – "Under the Lamp" is the English translation of an Indian phrase which points out that there is always darkness under the lamp, implying thereby that those who are supposed to spread the light around conceal darkness behind, that the looks are deceptive and that there is a wide gulf between one's professions and actions.

Light and darkness have been traditional symbols which have been used internationally. Whereas light stands for hope, justice and happiness, darkness stands for despair, injustice and miseries. Nathaniel Hawthorne used the symbols of the light and the dark powerfully in his novel *The Scarlet Letter* in which, to use F. O. Matthiessen's words, "the light does not remain a dramatic property but becomes itself a central actor" (Matthiessen 103). Similarly, in "Under the Lamp," the lamp over the police station becomes a powerful symbol. The police station of Kaliana village is housed in a building having a lamp which lights all around but has darkness underneath, implying thereby that the police station which is meant to establish peace and security all around thrives with anti-social elements. It is through this police station that Bichitra Singh, the Sabhapati of Kaliana village, spreads out his tentacles all around and makes the life of Karmaibai miserable.

The initial use of the metaphor of light for Bichitra Singh refers to the general expectation about the Sabhapati in the village. Karmaibai collects cow dung at his place supposedly to remain "under the protective light of the Sabhapati" (*Under* 110) but in reality, he represents nothing other than darkness. That is why her father-in-law, being well-experienced, calls him "a crocodile" and "a cobra" which are not benevolent creatures but opposed to human peace and happiness. In contrast, in the new Head Constable Sinha's time, there was justice and fair play all around, and as such the same police station "became closely associated with the lamp on top of the building, throwing its light around, brightening many corners that had remained dark in the regimes of earlier police officers" (115). One dark spot that Karmaibai refers frequently to is the person of Bichitra Singh.

When Karmaibai goes to Head Constable Sinha to file an F.I.R. against the Sabhapati for the death of her son, he is surprised because all along he had the impression that the Sabhapati was "the lamp that guides not only Siddha, being her son, and you but other people of the village" whereas she associates him with "the darkness under such lamp" and then reveals that Bichitra Singh has been "the chief architect of her miseries" (119). For her, Siddha was "a ray of hope within me but it is all dark now" after his death. This wide-spread darkness symbolically comes before her because she has "no faith in the police, in judiciary or even in humanity (121). The *gandasa* in the story, like the lamp, too, comes out as a powerful symbol. It was "the traditional item of the family, passed on from generation to generation along with the belief that it would protect the family from all dangers" (108). Her father-in-law asks Karmaibai to keep "the ancestral *gandasa* as a token of your resolve to struggle in the world" (109). In accordance with the family tradition, she had worshipped it after her marriage. Her father-in-law has a sense of pride that his grandfather "had saved himself from a murderous assault by beheading the enemy" (108) with it. Since Karmaibai, the protective mother, is weak and so is her father-in-law because of his old age, it is the *gandasa* – a non-human agent – which is her source of strength and courage. When she gives away a small knife-cum-nail-cutter to Head Constable Sinha, she has at the back of her mind the use of *gandasa* against Bichitra Singh. Though it could save her neither from the Sabhapati's exploitation, nor her son Siddha from his death, yet in keeping with the weapon's past record, it saves the entire village and its people from Bichitra Singh's further exploitation when Karmaibai beheads him with the same weapon.

Bichitra Singh is virtually the Satanic ruler of Kaliana village and is synonymous with all round exploitation. He blocked all the three passages of light which might have given hope and happiness to Karmaibai: sabotaging her first engagement, challenging Fauladi to climb the highest branch of the mango tree which resulted in his death, and getting her son Siddha killed. His name literally means strange, exotic and peculiar, bereft of normal human traits of compassion and sympathy. He poses to be an altruist but is every inch an exploitative villain. Karmaibai knows that his words of sympathy for her are "words without spirit, hollow" (107). After her father-in-law's death, Bichitra Singh's hands were spread out over Siddha's head manifestly for protection but in reality they were "like the hood of a cobra but with the same hidden menace" (112).

Like that of Bichitra Singh, many other names are also meaningful. Karmaibai indicates a woman of *karma* – action. Though gifted with beauty unusual for a woman of *lohar* caste, she does not exploit any one. After her husband Fauladi's death, she begins to work at the blacksmith's smithy, learning the operation of leather bellows and of shaping various instruments with the sole aim of protecting and moulding the life of her son Siddha. When she finds out that Bichitra Singh had killed him, her last hope was gone. Eventually, she kills the Sabhapati and surrenders at the police station. Fauladi implies a man of steel so "tough" that he "had refused to budge from his stand" (105) of marrying Karmaibai against the wishes of Bichitra Singh and thereby earned the latter's enmity. The village people saw in Fauladi's passing away "the death of a healthy bull taken to be a model of the village" (106). Siddha is the colloquial form of the Hindi word *seedha* which means simple and direct. Being simplicity personified, Siddha cannot survive in a crooked world symbolised by Bichitra Singh and has to die.

Karmaibai is a powerful woman character who struggles relentlessly against several odds with a single-minded devotion for the advancement and security of her son Siddha. She works at the blacksmith's smithy, attempts to do menial job at the Sabhapati's house, makes small compromises, tackles her father-in-law psychologically, faces slanderous comments of the society and yet attempts to convince her son to disregard what others say or do in order to march forward on the path of progress. Unfortunately, all her attempts are thwarted by Sabhapati Bichitra Singh. Hence Lata Mishra considers the story "the harrowing tale of a landlord's use of power and force to extinguish the flame of hope of a young widow whose sole aim of life is to bring up her son" (Mishra 22). Usha Bande finds in Karmaibai "an unforgettable character" who, for the sake of her son, remains subdued but "becomes a fierce tigress and kills the source of her misery – Bichitra Singh" (Bande 143).

Though India is constitutionally a democratic country in which decisions are taken by the elected local bodies, in many villages, it is the tyranny of the so-called elected Sabhapati which operates there. The blacksmith's smithy and the character of Karmaibai have been taken from real life. Srivastava writes in his autobiography: "Occasionally I would go to the blacksmith's shop to see how the iron tools and agriculture implements are shaped or sharpened. It was here that I minutely observed the blacksmith's smithy and the working of the leather bellows" (*Autobiography* 139).

Questions have often been raised about Indian writer's competence to do creative writing in English without giving a sense of laboured exercise. Srivastava has been a prolific writer, having to his credit two novels – *Neema* (1984) and *Coils of the Serpent* (2011), and six collections of short stories, not to say of 12 critical books in English. In this story, as in his novels, Srivastava has shown his perfect command over the language. One finds poetic touches at many places in depicting the feelings of Karmaibai. Since Srivastava portrays here the picture of rural life, he understands the nuances of speech used by the rural people. It is not quite uncommon for the rural people to use *double entendre,* satire and irony in their speech. *Webster's New World Dictionary* defines *double entendre* as "a term with two meanings, especially when one of them has a risquè or indecorous connotation" (1970). While working at the house of Bichitra Singh, Karmaibai complains about the ditches in the ground of the stable, but he converts the simple statement into obscene one by talking of "filling" all the ditches with the implication of having sex with her. Looking at her breasts, he further tells her that "the right proportion of elevations and depressions causes attraction" (110). It was clear that he was talking of her breasts; after understanding his implication, she covers them with the fringe of her saree. Similarly, old women in the countryside are often jealous of young beautiful women and make no secret of it by their sly comments. They leave no opportunity of hitting out at the young women. Thus while talking of the plouging of Karmaibai's agricultural field by the Sahbhapati, one old woman makes use of *double entendre*, saying, "He is Sabhapati – the husband, the manager of the entire village and when your *pati* – husband – is dead, he has to take care of you and your land" and again "Such men sow the seeds but claim no share in the harvest" (112-113), implying thereby that if Karmaibai happened to have sex with the Sabhapati, he would claim no share in case she became pregnant. Karmaibai understood everything and in her anger would have killed the woman with her *gandasa* but had to bear everything for the sake of her son.

There are similes, metaphors, idioms and sayings often used by the village people which Srivastava used in his story. In an interview with Atma Ram, Srivastava confesses that his style is influenced by his mother tongue in the sense that he had been hearing proverbs, sayings and idiomatic expressions in his village since his childhood and considers it "inauthentic not to give the typical flavour of certain type of characters who are known to speak in a particular way" (Ram 21). He also told M. L. Mehta that he used "idioms, phrases, sayings, proverbs, epithets, words and expressions of the vernacular in their original forms and in literal or metaphorical translations" (Mehta 178). The dead body of Fauladi was like "the death of a healthy bull" while he was compared to "a young horse yet to be tamed." Karmaibai's first action at the smithy was as important "as the seed of a banyan tree;" she was asked to "avoid enmity with a crocodile if you are to live in a pond" and never to "wound a cobra if you can't kill him" (111). She was further advised to "avoid the front of the master and the back of a horse." The hands of Bichitra Singh were on Siddha "like the hood of a cobra, and with the same hidden menace" (112). Both Karmaibai and Siddha find that "there is always darkness under the lamp." Bichitra Singh tells Head Constable Sinha that Karmaibai "is one person who does not let a fly sit on the nose" (116). Besides, the use of Indian words in English, such as, *gandasa, huzoor, bindi, darogaji, ghee,* etc. also gives authenticity to the writer being Indian and further knowing well the rural nuances of language which he beautifully renders into English.

By using the first person narrative in the story, Srivastava liberally allows Karmaibai to articulate her inner struggle between the safety of her son, on the one hand, and the exploitation of her by Bichitra Singh, on the other. At the same time, she uses her discretion in not bothering her father-in-law about her sexual exploitation because in his old age the revelation would have made him worried while he could have done nothing against the Sabhapati. It is with the use of first person narrative that Srivastava builds up suspense before the Head Constable Sinha about the absence of the Sabhapati and reveals it only at the end by disclosing that he was murdered by her. The detailed portrayal of hopes and fears of Karmaibai has been so well done that it is hard to believe that it is done by a male writer. The first person narrative has been Srivastava's favourite narrative technique. Not only many of his short stories but his novel *Neema* has been written in the first person narrative, the latter minutely depicting the inner struggle of a woman married to an impotent husband.

The structure of the story is superb. Y. Joy in an interview with Ramesh K. Srivastava praised "an impeccable sense of form" in his stories and wondered whether it was "a conscious effort or spontaneous outcome" to which Srivastava replied: "Search for form is usually a conscious effort; it can rarely be spontaneous" (Joy 377). The story "Under the Lamp" begins at the end when Karmaibai is in jail and then gradually through flashbacks she chronicles the tale of her woe in episodes one after the other. The beginning is so attractive that it makes the reader go on with the remaining story so as to find out what makes her go willingly to the gallows and why has she no faith in any public institution, including judiciary. Two things that bind the story and carry it to the end are: the overriding concern of Karmaibai as a mother for the well-being of her son Siddha and her rising antagonism against the Sabhapati Bichitra Singh's exploitation of her. The two strands of the story go hand in hand in a parallel way up to the end and it is there that the story reaches to a climax with the deaths of both Siddha and Bichitra Singh. The reader holds his breath in suspense in finding out the reason behind Karmaibai's presence at the police station and her periodic refrain about Bichitra Singh: "He may not come." In the whole story the suspense has been built up meticulously.

In his interview with Atma Ram, Srivastava defined a good short story as "a frozen moment of life revealed through a sequence of words. It must be short, readable and meaningful" (Ram 22). Most of Srivastava's stories are short and effective. With the use of wit and humour, irony and suspense, he arouses the curiosity of the reader who does not rest till he has reached the end of it. That is why K. V. Chacko, while reviewing one of Srivastava's anthologies of short stories, calls him "a gifted writer of short stories who knows the tricks of his trade with an interesting narrative style, nearly impeccable language and appropriate technique to deliver into the reader's lap as a short story" (Chacko 1984). Srivastava's "Under the Lamp" is a classically written tale with all parts neatly woven together without leaving any loose end.

Works Cited

Bande, Usha. "Loving Vignettes – Mother in R. K. Srivastava's Short Stories." *Mother Figure in Indian English Fiction* (Ed.). Usha Bande. Jalandhar: ABS Publications, 1997. 142-147.

Chacko, K. V. Book Review of Srivastava's *Love and Animality: Stories. Hitavada,* Nagpur (9 September 1984).

Joy, Y. "Ramesh K. Srivastava in Conversation with Y. Joy." *The Critical Endeavour.* Vol. XIX (January 2013). 375-392.

Matthiessen, F. O. *American Renaissance.* New York: Oxford University Press, 1968.

Mehta, M. L. "An Interview with Ramesh K. Srivastava." *The Critical Endeavour.* Vol. VIII (December 2002), 15-18.

Mishra, Lata. "Narrative as Discourse: A Study of Ramesh K. Srivastava's *Under the Lamp: Stories." Virtuoso: A Refereed Transnational Bi-Annual Journal of Language and Literature in English.* Vol. II, No. 2 (February 2013): 17-24.

Ram, Atma. "R. K. Srivastava." *Interviews with Indian Writers in English* (Ed.), Atma Ram. Calcutta: Writers Workshop, 1992. 14-24.

Srivastava, Ramesh K. *My Father's Bad Boy: An Autobiography.* New Delhi: Authorspress, 2017.

.... "Under the Lamp" in *Under the Lamp: Stories.* Jalandhar. ABS Publications, 1993. 105-121.

Webster's New World Dictionary of the American Language. New York: The World Publishing Company, 1968.

CHAPTER 18

Conflict and Resolution: A Study of Srivastava's *A Christmas Gift and Other Stories*

Leela Kanal

Different kinds of short stories make it difficult to give a universal definition regarding this literary genre leading to a belief that a good story is that which does well rather than what it is supposed to do. Most of 20th Century writers recognise the short story as a distinctive form which can dramatize a moment of revelation, significantly affecting and altering a character's life permanently. The brief format of this genre can project the narrowness of life's possibilities as well as express the violent aspects of life. The deliberateness of its aim can convey all or some of this through the apparent casualness of a snapshot.

All works of literature, including the short story, are at their nuclear levels, a dramatisation of life's little ironies. Whatever the subject, the aim is to pull the reader along towards a single moment when he finds impressed on his mind an effect identical to the one preconceived by the writer. Ramesh K. Srivastava in his *A Christmas Gift and Other Stories* has vividly portrayed ordinary people, their happiness and sorrows, trials and tribulations. In his seminal essay on the genre of the short story, Srivastava strongly avers that the short story is "a frozen moment of life, carrying in it the seeds of perennial truths" (*Read* 99). He emphasises the necessity of keeping the reader in mind while composing stories:

> A highly complex and unintelligible story may tease and please an intelligent reader by his sense of discovering something not easily decipherable but confuses an average reader. . . . Hence unconsciously or consciously, the writer is and must be influenced and his stories molded by the type of readers available for him (*Read* 99-100).

Comparing him with Thomas Hardy, Atma Ram Sharma comments that, like Hardy, Srivastava also is deeply affected by the "elemental simplicity of the village folk" (73).

The human situation, in its essence, remains eternally conditioned by contingency and tragedy. Srivastava has successfully captured many complex facets of life as led by the common man both in urban and rural areas of India. The stories may be broadly categorised as based on caste, class and gender, many of them having over-lapping themes. Srivastava's *A Christmas Gift* is a collection of 28 stories published earlier both in popular magazines as well as in literary journals. In its Preface, he confesses that although he has published two novels earlier – *Neema* (1984) and *Coils of the Serpent* (2011) – he feels "much at home in writing short stories" (*A Christmas* 9). Aware of the decreasing interest in reading short stories among literary readers, he reassures the readers in advance of finding "an abundance of irony and satire, sharp wit and rollicking humour to show the vast gulf that exists between appearance and reality" (*A Christmas* 10).

The first feature that the discerning reader notices about the collection is the thematic consistency of the stories and the gradual evolving of the narratives from despair and disappointment towards self-discovery often ending with a positive conclusion. All the stories deal with crises in the lives of the protagonists and the unfolding of subsequent events that turn around the vicissitudes in their lives, bringing about a sense of justice, where there was none earlier. They are narratives of struggle, of conflict, and of eventual survival.

One of his favourite themes, bearing again a close resemblance to those of Thomas Hardy, is the ubiquitous presence of superstition and illogical religious beliefs in the lives of the average Indians, which he fictionalises in several stories in this collection. Revelations and exposures emerge with the gradual unraveling of the truth behind the hypocritical facades. The very first story "Maharshi Satyanand" explores the reality behind the false fronts of fake sadhus and the profound effect they manage to have on the gullible public who end up obsessing over them, represented by the protagonist Sheela. She was prepared to renounce her husband and son in order to join the Maharshi's *ashram* till her husband investigated about him only to find him to be Ranga, the dacoit, who carried a hefty sum over his head but was masquerading as the Maharshi. "Ganga Ma" is another story that examines the superstitious beliefs prevailing among the day-today lives of people, where even a mere leak in the underground water-pipeline that has sprung up in the centre of a road is perceived as an incarnation of Ganga Ma. Such blind beliefs can also have life-threatening consequences, when the sick child is forcibly given a dip during Makar Sankranti in the freezing cold pool caused by the leak, leading to his tragic death. Srivastava contrasts this illogical behavior where the fear of God or Shanischar Devta is given priority over modern medicines, and where illiterate or semi-literate people are exploited by the fraudulent priests.

Invariably, the endings of all the stories in this collection lead the protagonists from darkness to light and from conflict to resolution. There are stories dealing with complexes, such as, the short height of Garima in "A Short Work" or a dark complexion of Shyamali in "An Ugly Duckling" that further explore the various prejudices and bias towards physical appearance that underlie our social attitudes. Both these stories triumphantly lead their chief protagonists – Garima and Shyamali respectively – to a positive conclusion when the persons surrounding them awaken to their innate talents and strengths. Garima, despite her short height, excels in martial arts, kills a reward-carrying dacoit and claims an honour. Shyamali, as a neglected dark-complexioned daughter, quietly donates her one kidney to save her mother's life and wins the latter's love.

Then we have narratives revolving around varying hues that symbolise marital relations. "A Stray Mongrel," "Confession," "Masks and Men," and "The Prodigal Returns" – all deal with the fluctuations that characterise these relations, ranging from the negative consequences of infertility and infidelity to sacrifices resulting from mutual adoration and devotion. "A Stray Mongrel" has as its protagonist Mangal who is ridiculed, both at home by his spiteful wife as well as in the bureaucratic, corrupt environment of his workplace. It is a story of an unequal marriage leading to the deep humiliation of the husband who is ultimately driven to leaving his wife Shashi, and this demeaning marriage. Much against his wishes and due to his education, Mangal is persuaded by Shashi's father into this mismatched relationship. He ruefully states that: "Even at that time I had objected to the marriage because the rich and the poor are like acacia and banana – two trees that cannot co-exist peacefully" (69-70).

"Cooperative Colony" is undoubtedly the most comprehensive tale in this collection. It attempts to present a cross-section of the multi-dimensional society of our country in order to reveal the cowardice, hypocrisy and self-centeredness rampant in our country, albeit doing so in a witty and humorous manner. The eponymous colony which has been "placed on the tourist map of the city" is meant to be a model for "ideal colonies throughout the states... in order to foster the spirit of cooperation among people" (40). The narrative gives an amusing picture of the real faces of people as against the phony facades projected, especially since the colony was ironically "built mainly for the weaker sections of the society, but to make it run smoothly, people of various professions who believed in cooperation and mutual help were also included" (38).Through this story Srivastava takes a dispassionate jab at the events exposing the myth of the cooperative colony. The tragic fate of Garib Das who had pinned his hopes on this colony for salvation is a consequence of this hypocrisy accentuated in the unread letter of this doomed man:

> When I heard of the Cooperative Colony, I was very happy because . . . it appeared to be the best solution – with a doctor and a lawyer and a businessman and who-not to help you. . . I have a great desire to live in the colony . . . if I die before I have a thous and rupees . . . my money should go to the welfare of the residents of the Cooperative Colony (52).

H.L. Sharma considers the character of Garib Das as symbolic of "the pathetic condition of millions of poor Indians who make futile attempts of acquiring a house" (1990: 19) whereas for Manisha Sharma the story is "a harsh commentary on the people of the world who have become absolutely devoid of human values" (2014: 198).

"Lasting Victory" and "Straw in the Eye" continue with the thematic content of this collection but have for their background college dynamics. They describe different kinds of bullying ubiquitous in these institutes of higher education, but both develop their narratives towards a positive conclusion in keeping with the general temper of the tales. The former explores the experiences of a young pretty female lecturer Vimala Tiwari, the problems she faces, and her success in gaining victory through sheer integrity and gumption. "Straw in the Eye" is about Professor Kimloo and his attempt to tame the unruly and disrespectful student Rola. The irony of this story lies in the success that the sweeper of the college has in cutting Rola down to size. Tongue firmly in cheek, Professor Kimloo admits, by way of conclusion, that "the sweeper had proved to be a better teacher and even a better administrator" (96).

"New Generation" and "A Matter of Pride" explore the nuances of gender issues, and the changes visibly evolving in the status of women from pre-independence days to present times. Jyotsna and Narayani, the central characters in these two stories, represent the gradual evolution in attitudes of women from pre-independence society to a few decades later (the wearing of bell-bottoms dates it to the seventies). Narayani in "A Matter of Pride" represents the change already occurring in the decades preceding Independence in the realm of education of girls. The story traces the journey of Narayani from being the first girl of her village to receive schooling, thanks to her liberal and forward-looking father, to her successfully founding and running a school in her village against all odds, and finally being appointed the head of the village panchayat. The tale ends with her modestly admitting to herself that "a total of my humble activities could well be regarded a matter of pride."(194). "New Generation" takes us about three decades post-Independence when the emergence of the new woman was a palpable presence. It outlines the courage and no-nonsense attitude of modern women in Jyotsna who declares that she is not ashamed of belonging to the new generation and goes on to add: "Puritanical and orthodox people are out of place these days" (174). Wanting justice to be done to the wronged Deepika, she withdraws from her formally concluded marriage and proudly exclaims:

> "I belong to the new generation . . . For me taking seven rounds of the fire, chanting of a few mantras, and exchanging of garlands do not matter . . . . What matters most to me are not rituals or ceremonies but that people are not deceived and exploited" (180).

This theme is again picked up in "Cross Connections" – extending it further to include the travails of arranged marriages and the evils of the dowry system which continue to be the blight of our culture. "Rescuers," "A Goddess in Hell," "Untold Story" and "Blessings of the Cursed" explore some of the multi-dimensional personalities of women. "Rescuers" deals with the grim revenge of a girl Neeru who is a knife-thrower in a circus and is victimized and sexually exploited by a priest, particularly by one who had earlier ironically reassured her that "I too believe in the religion of humanity" (157), thus exposing the real faces behind the masks of supposedly venerated persons. "A Goddess in Hell" narrates the selfless sacrifice of a mother who is prepared to go to any lengths to protect her son who, she believes, is a boon of Shiva. The 'Hell' of the title connotes the crime-infested slums of Dharavi in Mumbai residing in which is a challenge in itself. "Untold Story" unfolds the life of a pretty washer-woman Sundari and the manner in which her life intermittently entwines with the lives of the narrator Udai and of his wife Mona. Sundari is a strong character, who, along with her simplicity and integrity, manages to survive the buffetings of life. In spite of an alcoholic husband, she succeeds in rearing her son well and puts him through medical school, who then marries a physician. When she returns to again work for Udai and Mona in a different city, their surprise at this intriguing turn of events, leads them to speculate on her 'untold story.' The reasons for her withdrawal from her son's life could range from a desire not to be an embarrassment to them or "their taunts or even their downright expulsion of her" (239).

"Savagery," "Road to Prosperity" and "Seeds of Democracy" touch different aspects of rural India, fluctuating from casteism – the permanent blemish of our society – to the thwarting of development plans and politicizing of such plans, and to planting the seeds of democracy in the prejudice-riddled ethos of rustic life. Without exception, all three stories meander through obstacles but eventually lead to triumphant conclusions. "Enigmatic Pleasures," "From Frying Pan," "For the Life of a Cow" are stand-alone stories but retain the general positive temper of this collection. All of them navigate through the different facets of the experiential world of both, urban and rural society. They explore, albeit in differing ways, the vicissitudes and conflicts present in the lives of the protagonists. All three, in different ways, maintain the theme, central to this interesting collection of stories: conflicting circumstances and dismal vicissitudes gradually evolve into a denouement which is not only positive, but also uphold the triumph of human nature.

"Savagery" touches the rampant caste conflicts in rural communities, through the clash between Rajputs, represented by Bhola Singh, and the lower castes represented by Kanna of the Rawat tribe. The subtle turnaround at the end of the story is in keeping with the style followed by Srivastava who always has an ironic twist in his narratives. Mahipal Das in "Road to Prosperity" and Parbhua in "Seeds of Democracy" succeed in their endeavours in spite of the multiple odds against their attempts to bring about much-needed change in their respective villages. "Enigmatic Pleasures" is about an "odd father-son relationship" (228). Rohit

Bhattacharya, an affluent advocate, and his son Saurabh, astonishingly an auto-rickshaw driver have differences of opinion regarding caste and un-touchability, which leads to Saurabh moving out of his father's home in order to be able to live peacefully with his wife. Neglect in upbringing and rigidity regarding caste are the themes that this narrative is concerned with. The story, redolent with its feudal prejudices, explores the dynamics of caste and the ugly presence of untouchability in our country. "For the Life of a Cow" upholds the integrity and honesty of the pujari Ganga Das, who, by marrying the poor Gauri, protects her from dishonor. The much-maligned pujari is vindicated at the end of the story when his honourable intentions are revealed. This tale emphasizes the occasional necessity of telling white lies if it can save the life of a cow. The pujari pragmatically was wont to state that "truth is the greatest virtue of life, but if a lie saves the life of a cow, it is not sinful" (273).

The title story "A Christmas Gift," which is also the centre-piece of this volume, is a poignant tale of a childless couple, Ankit and Suchitra, and their attempts to help their maid with the rearing of her pretty daughter Saloni. This story deconstructs the ambivalence of the dreams of teenage children who want to be able to have it all, but who are devoid of the sense of responsibility. The story explores the microcosmic existence of a hapless, beautiful girl from the lower strata of society, within the macrocosm of modern Indian society, with its televised projection of the 'good life' and 'love marriages,' beyond the realm of reason and good sense. It is a subaltern tale of grandiose visions leading to abjectness, abandonment, and a horrible death. The tragic and misled Saloni becomes Santa Claus for the childless couple, when she leaves her new born baby at their doorstep as a Christmas gift before throwing herself on the railway tracks before a running train. She thus fulfills the promise made by her to gift them a painting of a baby as soon as she learns to paint. Following the convention of a Srivastava story, it ends with Saloni giving a real baby, which is the ironical twist in the tale. The story also reveals the well-intentioned gestures of educated, liberal, middle-class employers.

"Century" and "Friendship, Love and Marriage" reflect a cross-cultural experience and sense of alienation experienced by immigrant Indian students, while studying in American universities. "Friendship" is a humorous story of Maharaja Kumar Chaturvedi and his encounter with Loveleen and her mother Patsy. The name 'Maharaja' creates a misconception in the minds of the American women who start believing him to be a true-blue maharaja. The story explores the general delusions and fallacies that people living in the West have towards India and the way Indians live. The avaricious nature of the two women is unveiled when they realise that he does not belong to a royal family and that 'Maharaja' is merely his name. Chaturvedi muses: "What had gone wrong? Why did Loveleen change her phone number . . . Were all her claims of love and marriage false, pegged on to his misunderstood kingship?" (116) "Century" superbly foregrounds the intense feeling of loneliness and alienation that Indian students experience when living in a foreign country, which is enhanced by the limitations of language which further hamper interconnecting with the local inhabitants of the host country. The story begins with Mohan's "overpowering sense of loneliness against which [he] had been forewarned in India." Language barriers add to this isolation and he finds it easier for him "to give a long lecture or to participate in a literary discussion, but difficult to indulge in simple, ordinary conversation where rules of grammar are conveniently forgotten" (53). The character of Jasbir is exactly opposite to that of Mohan, because of the facile manner in which he has adapted to the life in the U.S. Jasbir's easy morals are a contrast to the shy, studious ways of Mohan. Jasbir playfully advises him: "America is a land to enjoy, my boy! You have your whole life to study. . . ." (54) The difference in both attitudes typify the two extremes in behavior of visiting Indians in the U.S. – the moral turpitude and the compunctions towards moral laxity. The story beautifully encapsulates this dilemma that migrant students face in an alien land.

Reading this book is like oscillating between hope and despair, dark shadows and bright sunshine, mirth and sorrow, problems and solutions. There is a kaleidoscopic spectrum of identities, characters, emotions and relationships. The protagonists disclose the entire gamut of aspirations and limitations of various configurations of types – students, persons of various castes, pujaris and priests, artistes and artists, sex-workers, college teachers, and the simple village folk. Srivastava exhibits dexterity in weaving his tales around these characters. The progressive movement of the stories from despondency to cheerfulness, from despair to hope for mankind in general, reveals to the discerning reader that there is no right way to do wrong things, while posing questions that we need to ask ourselves. Through these stories, Srivastava unveils the ruthless exploitation of the weak and the helpless, as also various lacunae and inhuman mindset of Indian society. The wit and humour that he employs in the process soften the barbs and gibes he shoots out throughout the pages of this endearing volume. The themes of his short stories reflect the sentiments of Mahashweta Devi's words:

> I think a creative writer should have a social conscience. . . . The reason and inspiration for my writing are those people who are exploited and used... For me, the endless source of ingredients for writing is in these amazingly noble, suffering human beings. Why should I look for my material elsewhere, once I have started knowing them? (qtd. by Chatterjee 173).

Srivastava has good familiarity of life led in both rural and urban regions, encompassing the myriad shades of their milieu and experience, while being firmly grounded in social realism. Smita Das, commenting on this familiarity with both worlds, states that:

> Since early impressions remain deeply imprinted on his mind, the village life and city life are often compared and contrasted – their men and manners, their faiths and attitudes, their joys and sufferings and no less their fast-changing relations. (39).

The stories cut across multiple cross-sections of our society, weaving tales around the protagonists who are captured at some decisive moments or turning points in their lives. These situations are mostly low-key crises, but they help the characters to meditate on their lives or introspect, and to emerge stronger, perhaps leading to self-discovery. They are narratives of survival in spite of many predicaments they have to overcome. Tradition and modernity intersect, male and female viewpoints clash and coalesce, adversity and courage battle it out, virtues and vicissitudes of society meet head on, the feudal and the progressive come to grips – each and all these post a new dynamism that encapsulates the psyche and the experience of our nation.

Works Cited

Chatterjee, M.N. "Review of Three Sides of Life: Short Stories by Bengali Women Writers," *Indian Literature – Sahitya Akademi's Bi-monthly Journal.* (March-April 2008), 173.

Das, Smita. (Ed.). *Ramesh K. Srivastava: Man and his Work.* New Delhi. Authorspress, 2016.

Sharma, Atma Ram. "R. K. Srivastava: A Writer of Simple Ways," *Indian Poetry and Fiction in English*. Delhi: Bahri Publications, 1991, 71-72.

Sharma, H.L. Review of Ramesh K. Srivastava's *Cooperative Colony: Stories*. *Punjab Journal of English Studies*.5 (1990).118-120.

Sharma, Manisha. "Irony, Humour and Satire in Ramesh K. Srivastava's 'Cooperative Colony," *Indian Scholar: An International Multidisciplinary Research e-journal*. Vol. I, Issue II (December 2014), 195-199.

Srivastava, Ramesh K. *A Christmas Gift and Other Stories*. New Delhi. Authorspress. 2015.

………. "My Idea of a Short Story," *Read, Write and Teach: Essays on Learning to Live Together*. New Delhi: Authorspress, 2014, 99-104.

CHAPTER 19

Empowerment of Women in Ramesh K. Srivastava's *A Christmas Gift and Other Stories*

Smita Das

Women's empowerment, the most talked about issue in the present world, is meant to give equal opportunities to women and to make them confident enough to claim equal rights in social, economic, political and local matters. The tradition of patriarchy, which has given men the superior place, has always been the root cause of subjugation of women. The term "empowerment" has been widely used in different connotations. An empowered person is one who not only experiences self-confidence and self-worth but also is able to critically analyse his or her social and political conditions prevailing around him and then to exercise control over decisions that affect his or her life. Robert Adams defines empowerment as "the capacity of individuals, groups and/or communities to take control of their circumstances, exercise power and achieve their own goals, and the process by which, individually and collectively, they are able to help themselves and others to maximize the quality of their lives" (xvi).

The empowerment is not a magic wand that can transform any woman into an Amazon or a Rani of Jhansi but arouses within each one a feeling of self-empowerment, of self-respect and courage, and makes her resist the male-dominated customs and traditions. It removes too from within them a feeling of helplessness, a feeling that they are fated to be slaves subservient to men. To do menial jobs, to be merely male-driven sheep with no power to raise their heads or to take their independent decisions – this has been a long-standing patriarchal tradition.

Several movements in the American and European countries in the last century and even earlier have gradually brought a sense of realisation about the empowerment of women. Numerous books and papers have been published on the subject all over the world creating much awareness among the people about it. For Elaine Showalter, "John Stuart Mill was one of the first and most eloquent spokesmen for the theory that the subjection of women is akin to other oppressive political systems, such as slavery and feudalism and that marriage is a legal bondage that a woman is forced to seek because her society has systematically deprived her of any attractive and dignified alternative" (3).

While the western women adapt themselves easily to social changes, the Indian women are very slow and consequently their empowerment too is correspondingly delayed. Giving a revolutionary prescription for the empowerment of Indian women, Srivastava, in his essay "Why Colleges for Women?" recommends the abolition of women's colleges so that in co-educational institutions, they could easily select their life-partners, adding that "while Western women are coming forward with the liberation movement, shedding their bra and membrane – symbols of traditional restrictions – Indian women continue to waver between the traditional and modern ideas" (*Read* 98). Even as he advocates such changes in his essays and lectures, he is opposed to the idea of direct propagation of such ideas through his short stories and novels. However, such views can be hinted at by vivid portrayal of social evils, as he tells in his interview with Mehta, in order "to stir up the dormant conscience of the individual and the society" (170). This has been done well both by Indian writers in regional languages as well as Indian writers in English. Mulk Raj Anand's *Gauri,* Anita Desai's *Cry, the Peacock,* Kamala Das's *My Story* and Arundhati Roy's *The God of Small Things,* among others, depict the labour pains of the suffering women struggling for liberation and empowerment. Ramesh K. Srivastava's *A Christmas Gift and Other Stories* has a large number of short stories which show that women are actively asserting their rights for equality in all walks of life. Such women may not be all empowered to revolutionise the entire race but they do struggle for their rights and oppose being subjected to men.

In the early works of Srivastava, one finds women who were victimized by various powers. The protagonist of his novel *Neema* (1986) suffered under her parents who wished her to remain submissive and subordinated in line with traditional norms. For Jayanti Sharma, Neema's "life is ruined by rigid and inflexible social system" (140). In "Love and Animality," Mrs. Chaddha feels proud of being beaten by her husband – a "he man." In "Hospitality," Surinder, Parkash's wife, readily becomes a puppet in giving sexual favours for promotion of her husband's business.

In the late 1960s, Srivastava had seen the women's liberation movement in the U.S.A. He must have noticed the reverberations of global change in India too where many women were participating actively in political and social movements. During his stay in Amritsar, he was impressed by Smt. Laxmi Kanta Chawla who single-handedly fought against the suppression of women. In the later works of Srivastava, one finds a number of women who take up cudgels against repressive social practices.

Such women for convenience's sake can be placed in three categories – Crusaders, Activists and Resistors. By crusader, I do not really mean a woman who campaigns vigorously for the sake of women's cause extensively, but who comes out of her narrow grooves of customs and traditions in order to champion the women's cause. In "New Generation," Jyotsna behaves like a domineering male, snatches the plate of her lover Yadavendra, asks him to bring one more for her, begins to get married by going seven times around the sacred fire and garlanding each other. While they were being declared husband and wife, Deepika, with a little baby in her arms, claimed that Yadavendra had married her earlier and that the child belongs to him. After listening to Deepika's story, Jyotsna went against her own marriage, saying, "I belong to the new generation. For me, taking seven rounds of the fire, chanting of a few mantras, and exchanging garlands do not matter. I am still under the *mandap* and the marriage is not yet consummated. What matters most to me are not rituals or ceremonies but that people are not deceived and exploited" (*A Christmas* 179-180). She forced Yadvendra to own Deepika with her child by re-marrying her under that very *mandap*. It is here that people witness with fascination "this inexplicable lady of the new generation who had done with extraordinary vigor what many would not have been able even to utter" (180). Similarly, in "Cross-Connections," Romila is a known crusader in solving matrimonial and dowry cases of others. The problem arises when the dowry problem ironically affects her own marriage. Pankaj Kishore, with whom her marriage was fixed on his demand of a Santro car, suddenly asks for an expensive Honda City car failing which he threatens to marry not Romila, but her younger sister Pratha. When Romila is pressurised to garland Pankaj, she displays her boldness by declining the Honda City car, and even a Santro car to him and to agree only for a brand new auto-rickshaw.

Whereas the two preceding stories deal with marriage and dowry problems, "A Matter of Pride" unveils the story of Narayani and her father Ramanand, who relentlessly carry out their crusade against the widespread superstition that "if a girl was given education, she would become a widow, making her a permanent liability for the family and even for the village" (186). Being a headstrong crusader, Ramanand does not pay any heed to the people's advice against education of girls, and opens a Girls' Primary School in the village. With the passage of time, the people begin to accept her and her school's importance. After her retirement as the Headmistress, she was made the Head of the village *panchayat*. Bhure Lal commends her empowerment by pointing out that they had discouraged Narayani in her childhood from going to school but "she has proved all of us wrong, because she is not a liability but the best asset of the village" (193-194). Leela Kanal feels that the central characters like Jyotsna and Narayani "represent the gradual evolution in attitudes of women from pre-independence society to a few decades later" (116). The story "Lasting Victory" was inspired by the courageous act of Dr Sita Sharma of Medical College, Amritsar, who had jumped into the bus to save it from being burnt by students. Vimla Tiwari, a lecturer in a predominantly men's college, saves the public property when she jumps into the bus which Gurmel was attempting to burn, shouting, "If you are determined to burn the bus, burn it along with me" (*A Christmas* 146).

In the second category, there are women characters who are not so bold as to champion women's cause in defiance of the wishes of a large number of people but who do show up their courage in asserting their opinions, in choosing their own path independently and in winning general applause and appreciation. Initially, they grapple with adverse circumstances but later on take up a bold stand. Garima in "A Short Work" begins to have inferiority complex because of her short height, but with a strong will power attempts to overcome it by undertaking physical exercises, by excelling over others in studies and by learning shooting and karate. Since some of these activities traditionally fall in the domain of boys, she is derided and discouraged by her father. Garima succeeds in pacifying him by citing the examples of Goddess Durga and Maharani Laxmibai. Once some dacoits raid her house, place an AK-47 rifle on the chest of her father-in-law Thakur Karan Singh and take possession of his hidden jewelry and silver coins. After the dacoits begin to move forward with the booty, Garima picks up the machine gun, which was kept hidden as a secret weapon, and fires from it a volley of shots, killing all the three dacoits on the spot. By her exemplary act of bravery, she wins the heart of her father-in-law who says, "By saving my life and honor as well as our ancestral wealth, you have proved by your valor that it is not the size of a person but the spirit within that matters." (271). The District Collector honors her in a public function by giving her a cheque of one lakh rupees and a gold-lettered plaque with words: "But the shortest works are the best" (272). Karmaibai of "Under the Lamp" is a widow of blacksmith caste who unwillingly bears the exploitation in order to safeguard her son's future. When Bichitra Singh gets her son killed in a fake encounter, Karmaibai becomes like Goddess Kali. Having no further hopes or fears about her son, she becomes, what Usha Bande calls, "a fierce tigress" (146) and takes on the much-feared author of her miseries – Bichitra Singh – by killing him with a *gandasa.* Lata Mishra praises Karmaibai who "struggles to survive with dignity in a world that humiliates and subverts her every attempt for emancipation and progress" (22). Shyamali in "An Ugly Duckling" bears a coal-black complexion which makes her parents hate her so much that they wanted to throw her into a gutter. While good things are given to her fair-complexioned brother Shwetamukhi, she is always cursed and scolded for her skin colour. By concentrating on her studies, she earns praise from both teachers and students. The climax comes when she sets an example of her nobility by quietly donating her kidney and saving her mother's life. In "Masks and Men," Madhurima burns the cheque given by Dhanik Lal which was in excess of the price of painting on coming to realisation that "The price of these paintings has gone up because you have seen my beauty" (*A Christmas* 172).

The women in the third category can be called Resistors. A resistor is an electric device which gives resistance to the passage of an electric current. Here it has been applied to those women who make their humble contribution to the women's cause by resisting their exploitation in various ways. This too is no less creditable achievement in a society where majority of women still dance to the whims of their male members. Neeru, in "Rescuers," tactfully resists the efforts of three young men in kidnapping her on a motorbike and saves herself from them by approaching Father Joseph Sault. To her utter disbelief, when she finds herself raped by her saviour Father Sault, she feels that "the whole world was inhabited by wolves, some in their original, and some in sheep's skin" (160). When the Father blindfolds her eyes and asks her to hit the target with the knives on hearing the sound alone, she put all her energy into the knives, hurled them one by one which were deeply embedded in the Father's neck. Saloni, in "A Christmas Gift," serves as a maid in Suchitra's house. Against the wishes of her mother and the society, she not only falls in love with a boy named Man Mauji, a pick-pocket, but elopes with him. After becoming pregnant, she is abandoned by him. Unlike the girls of middle and high classes of society who cannot rise against the parents or the society, Saloni defies all of them. Pratima, in "A Goddess in Hell," is a great resistor. Living in the slum area of Dharawi which is rampant with illegal activities, she continues to work honestly despite the fact that she remains hard-pressed for money. All the neighbours persuade and pressurise her to move with the current and to indulge in shady activities, but she resists all temptations, holding the banner of honesty high. As a devoted mother, she bears the punishment of life imprisonment for a crime of murdering a girl which was accidentally committed by her son. Mithua of "From Frying Pan," stoically endures the torture inflicted by a strong muscular man named Darshana. Though she bears all the torture, she does not reconcile to her situation. Despite her forced starvation, repeated beatings and torture which make the lower parts of her body senseless and paralysed, she keeps her desire for liberation alive within her and finally escapes from the place by dragging herself to board a bus which leads her to liberation – literally and metaphorically.

The above categorisation of women is by no means watertight. Some traits of these women overlap so much that some of them from one group can conveniently claim a place in the other two categories. What is creditable here is that Ramesh K. Srivastava, though himself a male writer, has sensitively experienced and then highlighted the pathetic and miserable plight of these women and by portraying them in his writings has aroused the conscience of his readers. By mere portrayal of these women, Srivastava has brought them from darkness of oblivion and anonymity to the broad day light of the people.

Works Cited

Adams, Robert. *Empowerment, Participation and Social Work*. New York: Palgrave Macmillan, 2008, p. xvi.

Bande, Usha. "Loving Vignettes – Mother in R. K. Srivastava's Short Stories," *Mother-Figures in Indian English Fiction*. (Ed.) Usha Bande. Jalandhar: ABS Publications, 1997. 142-147.

Kanal, Leela. Review of Ramesh K. Srivastava's *A Christmas Gift and Other Stories*. *Cenacle: A Peer-Reviewed Annual Journal of English Literature and Language*. Vol. I. No. 6 (January-December 2016), 112-119.

Mehta, M. L. "An Interview with Ramesh K. Srivastava," *The Critical Endeavour*. Vol. VIII (December 2002), 167-179.

Mishra, Lata. "Narrative as Discourse: A Study of Ramesh K. Srivastava's *Under the Lamp*." *Virtuoso: A Refereed Transnational Bi-Annual Journal of Language and Literature in English*. Vol. II, No. 2 (February 2013), 17-24.

Sharma, Jayanti. "Neema – A Victim of Society," *Victim-Consciousness in Indian English Novel*. Ed. Usha Bande. Jalandhar: ABS Publications, 1997. 134-140.

Showalter, Elaine (Ed). *Women's Liberation and Literature*. New York: Harcourt Brace Jovanovich, 1971.

Srivastava, Ramesh K. *A Christmas Gift and Other Stories*. New Delhi: Authorspress, 2015.

.... "Why Colleges for Women?" *Read, Write and Teach: Essays on Learning to Live Together*. New Delhi: Authorspress, 2014. 96-98.

CHAPTER 20

Freedom of Women in K. S. Duggal's "Butterfly" and Ramesh K. Srivastava's "The Prodigal Returns."

Priyanka Agrawal and *Sadhana Agrawal*

A writer of short stories portraying society is bound to write about women, their pains and pleasures, their struggles and achievements. Kartar Singh Duggal, the Punjabi litterateur, and Ramesh K Srivastava, the Indian English writer from Bundelkhand, have chosen women as one of their primary subjects.

In his short stories, Ramesh K Srivastava focuses on showing the pains of women and how they are treated badly in what he considers to be a misogynic, male-dominated, patriarchal India. Smita Das considers his novel *Neema* "a chronicle of dreams and disillusionments of a rural girl" (Das 20). Kartar Singh Duggal, on the other hand, chooses to portray women in all their colors and forms "refraining from making judgment calls either from the point of view of tradition or modernity" (Ramana 77).

In the short story "Butterfly," Kartar Singh Duggal shows various facets of women while depicting the real society without compromising the artistic quality. The subject matter concerns a few minutes spent during a musical concert played in a small city. The story is set in an unnamed Indian city which is small enough for most of its important citizens to familiarise with each other. This familiarity and proximity bore the citizens as they happen to bump into each other on all possible occasions whether they celebrate or mourn, play or study, work or recreate. In such an atmosphesre, a town gets oppressive in no time, especially if there is no spiritual core in it. However, a musical drama is to take place in the town and everyone gets excited. Finally, the night arrives and the narrator goes to the venue along with his wife. The narrator's wife Mrs. Ram is the protagonist and becomes the centre of attraction in contrast to her husband Mr. Ram who is a tiring professor.

The story is artistically divided into two narratives which are connected in time and place but more so in meaning. The drama, soon to be enacted on the stage, is about a butterfly. It starts with the egg of a butterfly getting hatched by the heat of the sun and then the caterpillar emerges from it. Gradually the narrative progresses and the caterpillar goes from one leaf to another until it becomes a butterfly which starts drinking nectar of different flowers. Being true to its nature, it does not stop at any one flower for a long duration and is never satisfied with just one flower; it keeps hopping from flower to flower.

The story progresses in two parallel narratives. One narrative describes the scene on the stage and the activities of the butterfly (carried out by an actor) and in the other, the real-time activities of Mrs. Ram are being narrated. The reader soon realises that there is a stark similarity between both the creatures.

Though Mrs. Ram is quite attractive, she is excessively fond of putting on a lot of make-up, wears revealing clothes and craves to be the centre of attraction by chirpily chatting with all the important males in the room. Her husband happens to be a boring professor in a university who has hardly any interest outside his books. Though his salary has increased, it has left no impact on him. On the other hand, for Mrs. Ram, the promotion of her husband becomes a heady wine. She goes on a buying spree, purchasing expensive saris and other clothes for herself. She wears an extremely thin, see-through georgette sari, indulging in cheap vulgarity, making herself the centre of attraction for others.

Believing in exhibitionism, Mrs. Ram goes from one man to another and chats so intimately with many of them that she forgets the common decencies of public discourse and public behavior. She forgets that she is a married woman and that the men she is talking to, may not be interested just in the cheap contents of her talks, but in having sexual relationship with her.

Nevertheless, disregarding others' negative opinions about her amorous activities, she persistently goes on flirting from one important person to another, and establishing relationship with them. The narrator, whose wife remarks snidely about Mrs. Ram, correctly conjectures every time where she would go next. In establishing parallelism in the story, the movements of the butterfly are synchronised with those of Mrs. Ram. Whereas Mrs. Ram enjoys the game of flirting with men one by one, the butterfly goes from one flower to another drinking their nectar. Far from being satisfied with one flower, it constantly and impatiently keeps buzzing over different flowers one by one. Mrs. Ram also goes from one person to another. It is here that in Duggal's story, Mrs. Ram and the butterfly become one so much so that Mrs. Ram is called a butterfly. At last, the butterfly is over-satiated with the nectar and so is Mrs. Ram with men. Nevertheless, they do not wish to let go the opportunity of trying something new. The natures and characters of both the butterfly and Mrs. Ram are thus laid bare.

The best part of the story is that Duggal seems to be merely holding a movie camera before Mrs. Ram and the butterfly without commenting on them. It is obvious that the writer does not endorse the behaviour of both of them but he confines himself to present the world in all its colors, focusing the lens both on Mrs. Ram and the butterfly without pronouncing any judgment over them.

Ramesh K Srivastava considers a short story to be "a powerful and effective means of portraying prismatic reality of our time" (*Read* 101). He seems to be more interested in showing the miserable plight of women. Jayanti Sharma feels that in his novel *Neema* and some of his stories, Srivastava writes about "exploitation of women by men" (Sharma 135). However, in the story "The Prodigal Returns," he deviates from his usual motives and style a little and writes a story which is pleasantly surprising at the end. The story is about a marriage which breaks down temporarily because his wife Rupali commits a folly due to her error of judgment but reverts on the right track after correcting her course through genuine penance and repentance. It is a story in which Ramesh K Srivastava does not show the atrocities against women, as he had done in his earlier stories, but shows the restoration of familial harmony.

Rupali is a happily married woman with a loving husband, having two adorable kids but she falls a prey to the overtures of another man. Her kids Tanmaya and Shikha had a very loving relationship with her and both of them remember nostalgically how she devoted herself completely to the kids after sacrificing her own pleasure so that they have a comfortable life and a secure future. Her husband also had a loving relationship with Rupali and considered theirs a happy marriage.

The problem arose because Prafulla Kumar, her husband, was a college professor with limited means of income leading a quiet sedentary life which sometimes irked the ambitious Rupali who clamored for more and more. She yearned for adventure and excitement in her life, craving for a life of luxury. As Prafulla was too busy in his studies and books, another cliché that Srivastava is fond of, he introduces his wife to one of his friends Sanket Prakash, a Hindi professor, who happens to be romantic in nature and is equally fond of playing several magical tricks to enthrall the people around him. He manages to become the center of attraction wherever he goes and with his magic tricks and cheesy talks he manages to become a good friend of Rupali and her children. His praise of her was like that of "a salesman who knew how to present an ordinary item in dazzling colours to bewitch the eyes of the customer" (*A Christmas* 214).

At first Prafulla feels happy in his wife's happiness in the company of Sanket, but gradually things take such a shape that the latter aims for more than just camaraderie with Rupali. Using his knowledge of Hindi literature and poetry, he enthralls Rupali with Hindi couplets and poems, lightening the atmosphere at home and bringing much of variety, adventure, excitement and thrill for which Rupali had always thirsted. None suspects him at first that his game is to seduce her.

Deep within her, Rupali always wanted to become the center of attraction in her life. The praises that Sanket lavishes upon her become heady wine for her. She is enamored of Sanket's praises, bathing in the newfound romantic ecstasy in the words of accolades about her beauty which he lavished upon her. He praises her voice, arousing her singing ambitions and then her looks, fanning her dreams of becoming a model or even an actress in Mumbai. He calls her "a charming actress-like wife" (*A Christmas* 215)

Gradually their association turns into an affair as he begins to take Rupali out to movies. When the rumors of their activities reach Prafulla Kumar, he tries to make Rupali understand things, but the affair had gone on too far. Despite her husband's persuasion, she leaves him and her children for a mirage in Mumbai. Sanket ensnares her finally and gets her to elope with him.

Years pass when Rupali comes back again in their life. This time, Prafulla Kumar happens to be the Administrator of Valmiki Ashram Girls School in Amritsar in which a vacancy exists for a peon. Rupali is one of the applicants. Disillusioned thoroughly with the reality of Sanket and his rosy vision of her chances in Mumbai, she has come to realise her follies, thinking of a correctional course.

Quite repentant and submissive, Rupali is prepared to work as a peon in the school where her husband and son work. That way she would have the satisfaction of looking at them. Somewhat reluctant, Prafulla allows her to work and by her activities she wins everyone's heart. At the end of the story, she comes back to the household, making the family complete again.

This is a story of penance, repentance and self-realisation. Though in many of his stories, Srivastava has shown women to be victims of the society, in this story, Rupali's behavior shows that women can also commit blunders. However, the redeeming feature of the story is that she realises her mistakes and, at the same time, her family shows graciousness in accepting her back into the family fold, thus offering her redemption. Srivastava attempts to suggest here that it is human to commit mistakes, but forgiveness upon genuine repentance is close to being divine, and is helpful in bringing back the erring woman to the right path.

While Srivastava cannot help but judge women and society in this story, Duggal leaves the world as it is – good or bad. Mrs. Ram, unlike Rupali, does not repent for her behavior and Duggal does not pass even an implied note of judgment. He merely depicts the world as it is whereas Srivastava attempts to portray the world as it should be. The difference here is between what-it-is and what-it-should-be – reality and idealism.

Works Cited

Das, Smita. "A Critical Introduction," *Ramesh K. Srivastava: Man And His Work (A Collection of Critical Essays)*. Ed. Smita Das. New Delhi: Authors Press, 2015, pp. 15-71.

Ramana, Paramjit Singh. *Kartar Singh Duggal: A Reader*. Chandigarh: Pramod Prakashan, 1999.

Sharma, Jayanti. "Srivastava's *Neema:* A Victim of Society." *Victim-Consciousness in Indian English Novel*. Ed. Usha Bande. Jalandhar: ABS Publications, 1977, 134-140

Srivastava, Ramesh K. "My Idea of a Short Story," *Read, Write and Teach: Essays on Learning to Live Together*. New Delhi: Authors Press, 2014. pp. 99-104.

………. "The prodigal Returns," *A Christmas Gift and Other Stories*. New Delhi: Authorspress, 2015. pp. 212-221.

CHAPTER 21

Dream and Reality in Ramesh K. Srivastava's "Road Not Taken"

Gurdeep Tripathi

The title of Ramesh K. Srivastava's short story "Road Not Taken" has been taken from Robert Frost's poem of the same title and is pregnant with several ideas and interpretations. Naturally, many similarities exist between the themes of both the short story and the poem. In both of them, the discarded road symbolises the path which is not chosen in life. It also implies, though not stated, an inherent faith that the chosen path, though unusual and less frequently trodden, might lead to the fulfillment of a dream – a dream of being different, even superior to other average persons who go on the trodden path. David A. Sohn and Richard H. Tyre explain the dilemma of Robert Frost that between the two roads "the speaker chose the less used, less popular, more adventurous one" which had "determined his entire future" (Sohn and Tyre 712). Yvor Winters called such a traveler a "spiritual drifter" who makes no clear choices when confronted with moral and spiritual issues (Winters 61).

After reading the lines from Robert Frost's poem "And I took the road less traveled by/ and that has made all the difference" (Frost 223), Kushagra Mathur finds his plight not much different from that of Frost. He recalls how his father had insisted on becoming a Primary School teacher in his own village, which would have been the well-trodden path, but the circumstances had made him take a different road – more ambitious, seemingly inaccessible and the result was that he had landed in the U.S. which has been a dream place for most of the people in the world but which not many people succeed in attaining it.

When Robert Frost wrote of adopting a path "less traveled by others," it implied a deviation from the average choice. A new path involves hardships where the chances of success and failures are almost equal whereas in going over the path traveled mostly by others, there are very little chances of failures. In a rather implied way, the less traveled road implies the dream, the hope of the traveler that it might be more rewarding than the frequently-traveled one. Most geniuses in the world have been path-breakers who gambled for materialising their dreams in treading untrodden paths and who, more often than not, got successes in their lives. If Frost earned a good reputation in the world, it is because he had trodden the path which was different from others. Kushagra Mathur ventured to take the path of higher education in the U.S. in which he made significant contribution to research in the field of Mathematics which he had hoped to apply to the outer space. Consequently, in the lives of both Robert Frost and Kushagra Mathur, the selection of unusual road had "made all the difference" in their lives and careers.

Smita Das writes that "many of Srivastava's short stories are based on real incidents, characters and situations" (Das 30). This statement is quite true of the present story in which incidents, characters and situations are broadly modeled on reality, as disclosed to me by the author himself. The story is based on the real life of Vashishtha Narayan Singh, an Indian mathematician from Basantpur village of Bhojpur district in Bihar for whom the rules of Patna University were amended to enable him to take the complete B.Sc. examination in one year. After reaching the U.S., Vashishtha Narayan had received his Ph.D. degree from the University of California at Berkeley (USA). This is what happens in the present story. Kushagra Mathur hailed from Nariari village in U.P. He exhibited his genius by appearing in complete B.Sc. examination and was admitted to the University of Massachusetts at Boston in the U.S. which provided him a fertile ground for the fulfillment of his dream through the flowering of his genius, though somewhat oblivious to the harsh realities of life that lurked behind the corner.

Even if Kushagra Mathur makes no explicit statement of his dreams, the story unambiguously points to his wishes, which were fanned by his college teachers as well as by Dr Johnson of the University of Massachusetts. Kushagra did succeed to a very large extent in the concretisation of his as well as his teachers' dreams and in putting the name of his small village on the international map. This is evident from the newspaper reports on his return to India which gave catching headlines like "A village boy conquers America" or "Kushagra's achievements justify his name" (*Road* 98).

By his genius and expertise in Mathematics, Kushagra Mathur could make his "utopian vision" (83) a reality. That is the reason that upon reaching the U.S., he could not believe that his dream had turned into reality and had to take the support of his physical existence when "he touched his head, pinched his skin, shook his hands and stamped his feet only to realise that it was not a dream but a reality" (83).

When a man attempts to realise his dream, he faces two kinds of people – facilitators and detractors. It was a sheer luck of Kushagra Mathur that he initially found a good facilitator in his mentor Dr Eknath Ranade – an excellent teacher of Mathematics – whose one word in praise of Kushagra had virtually changed his life. In the U.S., Professor Harold Johnson was another facilitator who took Kushagra to the U.S. and saved his time there by getting the waiver of certain mandatory courses "in order not to waste a genius's time in these requirements" (87) though at a later stage, he indirectly becomes a detractor by publishing Kushagra's research paper in his own name. Principal Abhyankar helped him in saving his two years by arranging three distinguished professors from Allahabad University who asked him the most difficult questions from the entire syllabi of three classes but which Kushagra solved "with complete ease as if he were on a familiar path" (88). What more sign of genius can there be than that the untrodden path seems "familiar" to him! It was in these tests that the experts found in him "a second Ramanujan in embryo" (88). The Vice-Chancellor got the rules of Allahabad University amended thereby saving his two years. Dr Harold Johnson personally visited India for Kushagra Mathur. It was in his presence that Dr Ranade told Kushagra's father that his son had "to abandon this rural dusty road" for "the road to the U.S.A."(90) – a rare opportunity.

Along with Kushagra Mathur, there are other characters too whose dreams have been depicted in the story. Dr Eknath Ranade, a minor yet pivotal character, had dreamt of seeing his disciple Kushagra's name in the international arena. After successfully getting the study period of Kushagra shortened in India, he secured the help of his professor Dr Harold Johnson in the U.S. and persuaded Kushagra's father to let his son go to the U..S. with the "hope that he brings honour to the family, the village, the country and even the world" (90). His dream does get converted into reality when

Kushagra reaches the U.S. – "a place about which many students merely dream but cannot reach" (85), gets his Ph.D. and his research papers are published and get international recognition. However, like most dreams, it is short-lived because of Kushagra's emotional upheaval which turns into his paranoid schizophrenia. For the treatment of this disease, the nursing home keeps him in captivity because its exorbitant bills could not be cleared by him. Here Dr Ranade fears the failure of his dream and helps in getting Kushagra released from the nursing home by arranging finances. Finally, when Kushagra was asked to apply to various IITs, where his dreams could still have been materialised, Kushagra said, "I would prefer not to take that road again" (106) and that shatters Dr Ranade's dream.

Jane, the daughter of Professor Johnson, also nurtured a dream of settling down in her married life with Kushagra. Initially, she was asked to make him feel at home in the U.S. but this concern grew into a prospect of her marriage with him. Kushagra, on the other hand, had considered Jane as his sister – a grown-up Priya, her American substitute. Besides, he also knew that Jane would not be able to adjust in India. To checkmate her marriage with him, he got married to Akrati Kulshreshtha which shatters the dream of both Dr Johnson and his daughter Jane.

There are smaller dreams of two minor characters – Dhairya Kumar and Akrati Kulshreshtha. The former dreams of going to the U.S. on some grant or fellowship, and pressurises Kushagra through his wife Priya to arrange for it. He even thrashes and tortures her but it could not be materialised into reality. Akriti Kulshreshtha, after her marriage with Kushagra, had the dream of staying away from his parents in India and to accompany him to go to the U.S. When it did not materialise into reality and her dream appeared to be shattered, she served a legal notice of divorce by leveling false charges against him which brought him a lot of ill name.

Kushagra's father also had a dream of seeing his son as a school teacher in a local Primary School. Being a simple-minded person confined to a village, he could not have dreamt of a bigger dream than that. Incidentally, he is the only person who got his dream fulfilled even though through a circuitous route. In reality, he got much more than he had dreamt, as towards the end of the story, Kushagra does become a local primary school teacher but after getting academic recognition in India and abroad.

The form of this short story meets Srivastava's own concept of composition, as he opines, like Edgar Allan Poe, that a short story must be "a classic in miniature with precision-made parts and singleness of effect" (*Read* 101). Looking at the failures of almost all the characters in realising their dreams, the story is indeed a woven maze of dreams, reveries and visions ultimately meeting reality. Neeta Maini had found that some of Srivastava's short stories "present a kaleidoscopic view of life, revealing too the gulf that lies between appearance and reality, what appears to be and is" (Maini 186). This is precisely what happens with the dreams of most characters which can be considered realised only up to a point, not wholly, and certainly not for a longer period – but this is life! It is universal truth that life does not offer everything in totality; the world of dreams and hopes, of how-it-should-be is always poles apart from what-it-is. From the beginning to the end, the story deals with the perennial theme of dream and reality in a very interesting way, and the secret of holding the reader's interest lies in Srivastava's own confessional statement he made in his interview with M. L. Mehta, that "humour and irony make my writings fairly interesting and readable" (Mehta 171). Srivastava's "Road Not Taken" is indeed an artistic conglomeration of perennial truths concerning prismatic dreams and pallid realities well-woven to create a fascinating illusion of life.

Works Cited

Das, Smita. "Introduction," *Ramesh K. Srivastava: Man and his Work,* Ed. by Smita Das. Authors Press, 2016, pp. 15-71.

Frost, Robert. "The Road Not Taken," *A Pocket Book of Robert Frost's Poems.* Ed. by Louis Untermeyer. Washington Square Press, 1963, p. 223.

Maini, Neeta. "R. K. Srivastava," *Studies in Contemporary Indian-English Short Story: A Collection of Critical Essays,* Edited by A. N. Dwivedi. B. R. Publishing Corporation, 1991, pp. 185-197.

Mehta, M. L. "An Interview with Ramesh K. Srivastava," *The Critical Endeavour,* Vol. VIII, December 2002, pp. 169-179.

Sohn, David A. and Richard H. Tyre. *Frost: The Poet and his Poetry.* Bantam Books, 1969.

Srivastava, Ramesh K. "My Idea of a Short Story," *Read, Write and Teach: Essays on Learning to Live Together.* Authors Press, 2014, pp. 99-104.

.... "Road Not Taken," *Road Not Taken and Other Stories.* Authors Press, 2018, pp. 83-106.

Winters, Yvor. "Robert Frost: or, the Spiritual Drifter as Poet," *Robert Frost: A Collection of Critical Essays,* Edited by James M. Cox.: Prentice-Hall, Inc., 1962, pp. 58-62.

CHAPTER 22

Love and Exploitation in Ramesh K. Srivastava's *Road Not Taken and Other Stories*

Gurdeep Tripathi

The story telling is Srivastava's forte, characterised by simple yet fascinating plot, true-to-life characters, economy of words and sublime narration – all of which give sustained pleasure to the readers. One seems to be taking a joyful ride in the wonderland of his themes of love, exploitation and many more which give its rider an introduction to a whole new world of the writer. Occasionally, even readers identify themselves with the characters. The day-to-day incidents of common life find a creative focus in his stories. Srivastava deals with everyday situations faced by an average person in the rural or urban India, on one hand, and the American scenario, on the other, with consummate ease giving his own stint of first-hand experience of living a considerable amount of time in all these places. He had tasted life in the Indian countryside when he was young, thereafter did teaching jobs in the urban areas and also spent a substantial part of his life in the U.S., making him adept with the cultural background of all these places, and hence he is able to portray rural, urban and foreign life with perfect ease. With his dexterity, Srivastava weaves his themes and characters in such a way that they leave a permanent mark on the mind and heart of his readers.

Edgar Allen Poe considered "unity of effect" of the greatest importance in a short story and once he has chosen it, "he then invents such incidents – he then combines such events as may best aid him in establishing this preconceived effect" (Poe 174). It appears that Srivastava has taken this prescription to his heart and fashions his short stories accordingly. In his essay "My Idea of a Short Story," he goes on to elaborate the singleness of effect which "depends largely on the end of the story which, like that of a play, must have a resolution or a sting so as to leave an unambiguous impact on the reader" (*Read* 101). Neeta Maini writes that Srivastava "has exploited the *genre,* not as a by-product of novel writing but as an independent *genre* to depict various experiences of life." She further goes on to say that highlighting various facets of life, his "stories present a kaleidoscopic view of life, revealing too the gulf that lies between appearance and reality, what appears to be and is" (Maini 186).

Srivastava's stories are woven around such characters one comes across in daily life. He himself puts it in his essay "My Idea of a Short Story," by pointing out the need for realistic incidents and characters in a story so that "the story competes with the very life itself' (*Read* 104). Smita Das points out that for Srivastava, "a short story is not a sort of museum to parade unusual and exotic characters and situations, but something portraying hitherto unexplored ideas hinting at the universal truths of life" (Das 28). Srivastava deals effortlessly with the whole gamut of human experience, including man-woman relationship, orthodox and superstitious people, criminals and revenge seekers, love and exploitation, and human dreams and aspirations, among others. In the present paper, I propose to confine myself to the themes of love and exploitation in their various manifestations in some of his stories.

Srivastava's short story "The Silver Lining" perfectly blends the theme of love, deception, exploitation, crime, revenge, dreams and aspirations. The female protagonist Shravasti is cheated in love by Shahid Ahmad. He "with his persuasive words and helpful attitude made [her] fall in love with him" (Road 29) and persuaded her to accompany him along with her money and jewellery. Innocent as she was, Shravasti failed to understand his true motives. As a cheat and hypocrite, Shahid robbed her of everything, including all her money and jewellery, leaving her completely desolate and shattered in Bombay.

A studious and diligent girl, Shravasti aspired to become an IAS or IPS officer so that she could bring about some improvement in the method of administration in order to help the rural people but now all her dreams were shattered and she was left to become a criminal. A beautiful girl with high aspirations in life, she had landed up eventually to become a hardcore professional pickpocket after months of severe and harsh training. The only dream that she nurtures now is to take revenge on Shahid. She along with an accomplice succeeds in taking revenge by trapping and getting him arrested. The story has amalgamation of love, exploitation and revenge intertwined adroitly by Srivastava's adept handling of the details.

His "A Dumb Show of Lovers" is the story of "dumb" lovers in the sense that Harsha and Ajay looked at each other with love but failed to communicate it in words. After the death of her mother, she brought up the infant brother Banti by becoming his "sister and mother both" (*Road* 134). Rather than being rewarded for her sacrifice, Harsha is cheated by her younger sister Taruna and her fiancé Ajay by being both vocal and selfish, and in doing so she shattered the elder sister's happiness by ditching her. Her father characterised Harsha as "a simple dumb cow" and Yogeshwar Chaturvedi called her "a Satyugi girl" for taking care of the entire family after her mother's death "the same way as her mother would have done" (137). For Harsha's absence of being vocal and communicative with her lover, her friend Madhurima called her "not only simple but simpleton" (139). In not articulating her love openly and in staying away from him in shyness, Harsha "had burnt her own citadel" (140).

Love can be a great driving force to inspire people to make sacrifice for their loved ones in the same way as Harsha had done for her entire family on the death of her mother. On the contrary, the love between Taruna and Ajay was full of selfishness and hypocrisy which had driven Harsha and her father to despondency. These human emotions have very well been captured in the story by Srivastava, since he is adept in tapping the right chord of human emotions.

Srivastava's "Together We Live" is a story mainly of intimate love and friendship between two friends – Jai Kiran Upadhyaya and Pravendra Prajapati whose motto was: "Together we live and together we die." Their love and friendship for each other was so intimate that people felt as if "god had made them for each other" (157). The story has another kind of love too – between Jai Kiran Upadhyaya and his wife Chandra Kanti who "could not live without each other" (161). Pravendra Prajapati, despite being a friend of Jai Kiran, had an evil eye on his friend's beautiful wife Chandra Kanti. He exploited Jai Kiran's absence from the town by molesting her. Since Chandra Kanti had taken a decision that in case anybody ever attempted to molest her, she would either kill him or herself. Unable to check or harm Prajapati, she committed suicide after leaving a detailed note behind, stating the reason. Jai Kiran had so much love for his wife that without her he could not imagine his life and took poison but at the same time, he also poisoned Pravendra with an ironical remark: "To continue our friendship, both of us are going to die together" (164).

His "Agony and Ecstasy" deals with two kinds of love: the real love of Kunwar Pal for his long-lost-now-found daughter Shreya and the one-sided love of Rohtas Lal for her. Shreya is Kunwar Pal's daughter and for her, he not only gave all the money he had but also his own life by taking upon himself the crime which could have resulted in the death punishment for her husband. The other sort of love of Rohtas Lal for Shreya is one-sided and can be better called "infatuation." Rohtas Lal is a road side Romeo who had a huge crush on Shreya and wanted her husband Vijay Kiran to divorce her so that he could marry her. In the absence of divorce, he then "threatened to take her forcibly away after killing" Vinay Kiran (177). When Kunwar Pal's repeated attempts failed to bring Rohtas Lal on the sane path, on the former's advice, Vinay Kiran shot Rohtas Lal dead while trying to defend himself from his attack. When Kunwar Pal was accepting the blame of killing of the culprit on himself, Vinay Kumar suspected that he, like Rohtas Lal, could also be in love with Shreya, but Kunwar Pal clarified, "Yes. I am indeed in love with Sheya but not like Rohtas Lal. I am in love with her in the same way as a father loves his daughter" (182). Taking the blame of murder on himself, Kunwar Pal surrendered to the police in order to make her lead a peaceful life. Here Kunwar Pal's display of love for his long-lost daughter at the cost of his own life amounts to a great sacrifice which has aptly been dealt with by the writer.

Srivastava also deals with the issue of exploitation, particularly in villages very remote from the modern world which are still secluded from the rest of the world, making their inhabitants act like puppets in the hands of the people of dominant caste or class. Whereas the presence of love makes the world a heavenly place, the prevalence of exploitation sours everything, making the theme of exploitation well-intertwined with that of love. In the story "Silver Lining," Shahid Ahmad had transformed Shravasti's dream of becoming an IAS or IPS for serving the common people into a criminal through sheer exploitation by promising to help her in becoming an actress or a model but swindling all her jewelry and money so that she had no choice but to be a pickpocket. Of course, to seek revenge upon him, she too exploited the opportunity of his presence in the hotel by planting packets of brown sugar into his room and in getting him arrested. In "A Dumb Show of Lovers," Taruna exploits her elder sister by trapping her fiancé Ajay whose marriage with the latter was fixed many years back. In this case, Ajay too cannot be considered innocent because he too ditched the elder sister for the younger one. In "Together We Live," though Jai Kiran Upadhyaya and Pravendra Parajapati were intimate friends, the latter exploited the friendship by raping his wife which results in the deaths of the victim as well as of both friends.

The entire story of "Lucky Rope" deals with the issue of "unbridled" exploitation of the underprivileged by the landlord Bhunaresh Singh, a self-declared Raja of his village through his money, power and goons. Lusty as he was, he had "sex with any woman worker when and where he wanted" (62). Any woman of his choice had to spend with him as many nights as he wanted and whenever he pleased. It is therefore quite natural that in the story different epithets have been used for him, such as, "woolf," "devil," "quintal-weighing woolf," "demon," "an incarnation of Ravan," "the sexy bear" and "Bhasmasur" (61-70). Bhanwari Bai, the female protagonist, had been suffering for whole life, right from the day of her marriage at fourteen to the present when she is forty four. Now that her own son is married to Hulli – young and beautiful –, Bhunaresh Singh had her as his companion for some nights. She is the new victim of his exploitation. Hulli knew well that she had to do something in order to free herself from the perpetual shackles of the landlord. She too exploited his weakness and made him drink liquor excessively to take revenge and to safeguard her future by eliminating him. The room of Bhunaresh Singh in which he was sleeping was made to explode in such a way by a piece of rope that it seemed to be an accident out of which she came out clean, thereby saving herself and other women of the village from his exploitation. Binod Mishra points out that Srivastava "uses concepts and myths from the ancient times" and goes on to point out how in the story Hulli, "a diminutive localised form of the name Holika literally burns and kills the local tyrant landowner in his own mansion" (Mishra 432). Prabha Shankar Dwivedi feels that "though the woman suffers torture and exploitation, she emerges victorious" (Dwivedi 285).

Srivastava is a master of the art of storytelling that comes so naturally to him. His stories testify well that he has seen life himself not from the sky, but from the bare earth, rubbing shoulders with common people, listening to their woes and miseries and chronicling them in an interesting way. Leela Kanal writes that Srivastava "has a keen eye for detail and sees life the compassionate blend of hope and trust" (Kanal 130). Srivastava's stories are verbal portryals of the Indian people in all their diversities.

Works Cited

Das, Smita (Ed). "A Critical Introduction," *Ramesh K.Srivastava: Man and his Work: A Collection of Critical Essays.* New Delhi: Authors Press, 2016, 15-71.

Dwivedi, Prabha Shankar. Book Review of *Road Not Taken and Other Stories. The Recognition of Ramesh K. Srivastava: A Collection of Book Reviews on his Creative Writing,* edited by Shipra G. Vashishtha. New Delhi: Authors Press, 2020,.282-288.

Kanal, Leela. Book Review of *Road Not Taken and Other Stories. Writers, Editors, Critics: An International Biannual Journal of English Language and Literature.* Vol. VIII, No. 1 (March 2018), 128-130.

Maini, Neeta. "R. K. Srivastava," *Studies in Contemporary Indian English Short Story: A Collection of Critical Essays,* edited by A. N. Dwivedi. Delhi: B. R. Publishing Corporation, 1991, 185-197.

Mishra, Binod. Review of *Road Not Taken and Other Stories. The Indian Journal of English Studies.* Vol. LV (January 2018), 431-434.

Poe, Edgar Allen. "*Twice-Told Tales* by Nathaniel Hawthorne: A Review," *American Literature Survey,* Vol. II, edited by Milton S. Stern. New York: The Viking Press, 1969. 171-178.

Srivastava, Ramesh K. "My Idea of a Short Story," *Read, Write and Teach: Essays on Learning to Live Together.* New Delhi: Authors Press, 2014, 99-104.

.... *Road Not Taken and Other Stories.* New Delhi: Authors Press, 2018.

CHAPTER 23

An Interview with Ramesh K. Srivastava

Y. Joy

Note: (Ramesh K. Srivastava, Former Professor and Head, Department of English and Dean, Faculty of Languages, Guru Nanak Dev University, Amritsar (Punjab), and currently Professor of English, S. R. Group of Institutions, Jhansi (U.P.) has published two novels: *Neema* (1986) and *Coils of the Serpent* (2011) and five collections of short stories: *Love and Animality: Stories* (1985), *Cooperative Colony: Stories* (1985), *Masks and Men: Stories* (1986), *Games They Play and Other Stories* (1989) and *Under the Lamp: Stories* (1993). He has also published several critical books and articles in American Literature, English Literature and Indian Literature in English.)

Joy: "Wordsworth sees the smallest fragment in the world as wakeful and alert and twinkling with the life of the whole." This is true of a short story. Can this statement be compared to the definition of a short story? You have expressed almost the same views in your preface to your collection of short stories *Under the Lamp: Stories*. Have you got anything more to say about this?

Srivastava: As seconds, minutes and hours add up to form a day, a month and a year, small fragments of life, real in themselves, have their individual entities. They form parts of a larger canvas of life. A short story depicts such fragments of life I have talked about it in detail in the introduction to *Games They Play and Other Stories.* I give here a couple of lines: "A short story is a frozen moment of life, carrying in it the seeds of perennial truths. It reveals in a flash an image of hitherto unexplored aspects of life fleeing each moment before us. A good short story is like a supply of fresh air that makes the human life delightful, meaningful and no less healthy."

Joy: Do you agree with the view that a short story writer must confine himself to a single theme or tone?

Srivastava: If a short story is really short, a writer will have to confine to a single theme and tone. However, in order to make it readable, interesting and enjoyable, introduction of minor digressions, anecdotes, wit, irony and humour may be desirable.

Joy: "It is said that photography in the form of cinema is closely allied to short story." Will you please explain the relevance of the statement in relation to the definition of a short story?

Srivastava: The statement can be justified in a limited sense that the photography in a cinema represents external reality. A short story, on the contrary, presents both external and internal reality. Dreams and disappoints, happiness and sorrow, feelings and sentiments, thoughts and views, fancy and imagination can be well-represented only in short story, not in photography.

Joy: It is often said of a good short story writer, "What he writes is the expression of his personality and manifestation of his instincts, his emotions, his intuitions and his experience" Does this statement agree with the definition of a short story?

Srivastava: Every work of art is an expression of the writer's personality and so is the short story. It is also a manifestation of his instincts, emotions and experience in a broad sense in which they are not limited to his personal life but to the whole world which he internalises and to which he responds both subjectively and objectively.

Joy: "The short story is concerned with the world as it is, not as it should be; it has rhythmical and unified plot and it is less limited by convention in its handling of point of view." (T. E. Apter, *Fantasy Literature: An*

Approach to Reality. Bloomington: Indiana University Press, 1982). Will you please make a comment on this statement?

Srivastava: I do not quite agree with T. E. Apter's statement that a short story "is concerned with the world as it is, not as it should be." When a short story writer selects an incident, a character or a situation for presentation, he also thinks of how it would best appeal to the readers. If in the process of depicting a dark tunnel, he turns a hint of how to come out of it, there is nothing wrong as long as the hints do not turn into obtrusive solutions, and a short story does not become a part of propaganda.

Joy: "A short story may be as factual as what happened to its author yesterday." (Kenneth Payson Kempton, *The Short Story*. Cambridge: Harvard University press, 1964). If I say this is true of your short stories, Will you agree?

Srivastava: Yes, it is true of my short stories. A writer holds a mirror to reality – or factuality – and it comes out in the form of a short story. If the characters and their dialogues momentarily transport the reader to the real world – alive and kicking – he has succeeded in his mission.

Joy: It seems that you experiment with a wide variety of approaches to the form of short stories. Will you please relate the impact of each approach of communicating the theme effectively?

Srivastava: That would be rather difficult. In an earlier question, you had compared art of photography to that of a short story. A photographer, at a given moment, selects a particular angle from which to take a photograph which appeals to him. He cannot lay down rules for it, even if some broad guidelines can always be given. My first task was to make a short story most effective. Characters, dialogues, situations, narrative techniques – all contributed towards this effect.

Joy: In almost all your short stories, you express an impeccable sense of form. Is it really a conscious effort of a craftsman or a spontaneous outcome?

Srivastava: Search for form is usually a conscious effect; it can rarely be spontaneous. Wordsworth who considered poetry as spontaneous overflow of powerful feelings labored hard to make his language simple enough so as to give a semblance of spontaneity.

Joy: "Good fiction is aesthetically valid." Will you please make a comment on this?

Srivastava: One must not forget that a short story is a form of art. It is one of many literary genres. Unless it is aesthetically valid, it would not be acceptable as a work of art. Clumsiness in art is an unpardonable sin. A piece of art must be chiseled and polished till it is aesthetically perfect and so must a short story.

Joy: The anecdote is, in fact, the greatest tempter of the writer of stories. How far this statement is applicable to your short stories? Realism is only a veil and shadow of reality. Do you agree?

Srivastava: An anecdote is a seed from which a short story grows. As the writer ponders over it, the seed germinates, small leaflets unfurl themselves and it becomes a small plant in which the reality of the tree is hidden. In a good short story, the reality is not so much on surface as it is in between the lines. A perceptive creative reader can discover many layers of deeper reality in a short story whereas an ordinary reader can remain confined to its surface enjoyment. I hope it answers your queries.

Joy: Will you please tell me about the great masters of the art of short story who had exercised considerable influence in shaping your career?

Srivastava: It is difficult to enumerate which writers have influenced me. In the beginning, when I was writing my short stories in Hindi during 1955-57, I was charmed by Munshi Prem Chand – a Hindi novelist and a short story writer – who had a considerable influence on me. As I studied English, American and

World Literature in English Translation (including Indian), I had many writers from whom I might have learnt something or other. Edgar Allan Poe, Nathaniel Hawthorne, Henry James, Ernest Hemingway, Thomas Hardy, Charles Dickens, D. H. Lawrence, O. Henry, Alberto Moravia, Guatave Flaubert, Franz Kafka, Raja Rao, Kamala Markandaya, Mulk Raj Anand, R. K. Narayan, Manohar Malgonkar, Arun Joshi – I could go on and on. But I cannot precisely point out which writer has influenced me in what way in the same manner as one cannot tell which part of the body or temperament carries the stamp of which of the parents or grandparents.

Joy: The relationship between man and nature is one of your principal concerns. Has it been primarily moulded by your deep awareness of the traditional culture of India?

Srivastava: May be, but I have not consciously thought of it.

Joy: The short story in India is said to be both ancient and modern. It is ancient because it was born before literature itself. It is modern because in its present form, it derives mainly from new conditions and social urges. Indian short story has its earliest examples in the Vedas and the Upanishads. What in your view are the forces that shaped the modern short story in Indian English writing?

Srivastava: Before asking the question, you have already given the answer. Yes, you are right in saying that the Indian short story is a product of the ancient and the modern. As a child, I was fascinated by the stories from the *Ramayana* and the *Mahabharata.* Later on, I was told of do's and don'ts of life through the stories from *Panchatantra.* As I grew up, I read all kinds of literature good or bad. Other writers had the same sort of background. Raja Rao, Mulk Raj Anand, Khushwant Singh, Arun Joshi, and Manohar Malgonkar's short stories can be considered the product of both the East and the West.

Joy: As a writer your fictional world provides you with ample scope for portraying life from the colonial to the contemporary world and even to the future. You are concerned mainly with the Indian context. Many of the contemporary writers go beyond the present context while you have confined yourself to the comparatively narrow world. What inspired you to do it?

Srivastava: A writer is often a product of the world he lives in. Day and in and day out, incidents of everyday life go into him and affect his psyche, his thoughts and his concerns. My three earlier visits to the U.S.A. and the fourth one which is continuing come to a total of no more than four years. For the rest of my life, I have stayed on in India and naturally got concerned with its people and problems. Some of my short stories collected in *Love and Animality: Stories, Cooperative Colony: Stories* and *Masks and Men: Stories* deal with the American life as well, but most of them are based on my experience in India – with Indians and their problems – in the past as well as in the present.

Joy: Your short stories reveal that you are a sensitive observer of life. The short stories are capable of stirring the depths of our emotional life through the human material. This I feel is the magic touch of your art. May I know your views on this?

Srivastava: Sensitivity is essential for any creative artist without which external incidents would not have any effect on him. A writer's mind is like the mythological Kshirsagar holding numerous things within it. Some of them remain deep in it while others are at somewhat at shallower level. You have to churn the Kshirsagar – ocean of the mind – in order to get the precious material.

Joy: Manjeri Iswaran who has made a pioneering contribution to Indian English short story is said to have made a remarkable study of women in their different relationships to the society. It is also observed that the characterisation of women is an outstanding feature of his art and genius. After having made a thorough reading of his short stories, the reader feels that what has been said about Iswaran is true of you as a short story writer. If the statement is true what inspired you to deal with women in such a way? Have you been influenced by post-colonial feminist writings?

Srivastava: Unfortunately, I have not read any short story by Manjeri Iswaran. If at all I depicted women in several forms, I must have seen them in real life. Of course, they are usually modified with imagination

Joy: Some of your short stories are sprinkled with melancholic tones which make the stories memorable.

Srivastava: Happiness and sorrow are two sides of life. If there is the tone of melancholy in some of the short stories, there is fun and laughter in others.

Joy: Tone is inseparable from style; style is inseparable from the meaning which it forms. How can the tone, style and meaning be made a unified whole?

Srivastava: They are a unified whole and inseparable. It is only the viewpoint from which you look that it matters.

Joy: It is said that tone is the attitude of the author towards what is being presented. Thus how can your attitude towards your characters be justified?

Srivastava: Your question is not clear. I don't know what you mean by my attitude towards my characters. Unless you give a particular example from my short stories, it cannot be explained.

Joy: The tone of a short story is the 'voice' in which it is conveyed and the attitude that voice expresses. What are the major tones in your stories? Plot is a writer's arrangement of events that will express his attitude towards the human condition. I feel this statement is true of your stories. Have you got anything to say more about this?

Srivastava: It is not for me to point out how many tones are there in my short stories; rather, it is for you to find them out. I try to give a realistic portrayal and the tone usually takes care of itself.

Joy: Landscape alone is not creative of atmosphere; anything created imaginatively is creative of atmosphere. Atmosphere is subsidiary to mood in your story. Is it an accepted principle?

Srivastava: It is true that landscape alone cannot create atmosphere; rather, many things contribute to it. I agree that the atmosphere is subsidiary to mood because one creates atmosphere in order to give a particular effect or occasionally depending on what mood /intention has motivated it.

Joy: Atmosphere no less than tone must be appropriate to the general intention or the main impulse of the story. A short story that is a work of art has but a single intention, one total meaning, and one composite theme. Will you comment?

Srivastava: Yes. When a writer writes a short story, he aims at a unity of effect. He creates then an appropriate atmosphere and tone for it. Naturally, the short story thus created has one meaning. Nevertheless, if the short story is good enough, it transcends to become universal and can have many implied meanings as well.

Joy: You give a sympathetic revelation of Indian life with which you are familiar in its many aspects. "The most obvious element shared by all good fiction, whatever form that fiction may take, is intellectual honesty." This is a statement by John Gardiner and Lennis Dulap in their *Introduction to the Forms of Fiction* (New York, 1962). Despite having a rich experience abroad you haven't made any effort to depict them in your stories. How will you explain it?

Srivastava: I give a sympathetic revelation of Indian life because, as you say, I am familiar with it. I have spent over 60 years in India. In contrast, my total period spent outside India would come to less than four years. You can decide for yourself how "rich" it might have been. Though my longest stay in the U.S.A. – over three years – was when I was working for my Ph.D. degree. Even at that time, I had stayed there in a rather insulated atmosphere of a university dormitory. Whatever I experienced and observed in the U.S.A. has been depicted in some of my short stories collected in *Love and Animality: Stories*, *Cooperative Colony: Stories* and *Masks and Men: Stories.* During my subsequent visits to the U.S.A. in 1984-85, 2003 and now in 2006-07, the period of each visit did not exceed four months at a time. If I had written more about American characters or incidents without being wholly well versed with the American life, that would have been a good example of intellectual dishonesty and falsification of real life…

Joy: You seem to have modified the facts with varying amounts of imagined experience, characters, scene and action. What observations do you make on this?

Srivastava: One cannot write a short story or a novel without modifying the facts with varying amounts of imagined experience, characters, scenes and action. One can write a newspaper report without modification, but for a short story to be effective, characters, incidents, dialogues, situations are bound to be modified. A successful short story depends primarily on the totality of effect it has on the reader. Other things mainly contribute to it.

Joy: "Unerring ear for the right word in the right place which can neither be translated nor transposed" is the essential style of a perfect short story. I feel that this is true of your literary endeavors. What have you got to say about it?

Srivastava: It is for you to decide and say whether my short stories have right words at right places or not. A writer does his best to do so in order to bring verisimilitude in the short story whether he has adequately succeeded in his attempts or not is for the readers to decide.

Joy: Going through your words, I could perceive your language simple, lucid, effective without being deliberate or laboured. I think this may be the cause of your stories being very popular with the readers

Srivastava: Since I always kept my readers in view, I did make an attempt to make my language simple, lucid and effective. Yes, it could be one of the reasons for their popularity.

Joy: The language of short story is as important though not as explored as that of poetry, because the short story is compared to a lyric. What is your opinion about this?

Srivastava: A short story is a lyric in prose when it comes to having a single theme, a single effect and a single tone. If the language of a short story remains unexplored, the only reason, in my view, could be that their readability is more important. If one chisels and polishes the language of the short story, and makes it poetic, the theme and the totality of effect could become secondary to the language and its readability could be adversely affected.

Joy: "Unlike the scientific language of observation and report, the language of fictional literature is a total language. It employs such devices as rhythm, metaphor, image, symbol, plot, character, setting, and point of view to convey feelings and express ideas that will appeal to the whole man – to his senses emotions, imagination and intellect." (R.F Dietrich, Reiger H. Sundell, *The Art of Fiction*. New York: Holt, Rinehart and Winston, 1978, introduction, page 4). What have you got to say about this?

Srivastava: I agree with the observation of R. F. Dietrich and others about the totality of the fictional language as opposed to the scientific language. The scientific language is a means of conveying factual details as they happen to be. On the other hand, all the devices, such as, rhythm, metaphor, image, symbol, plot, character, setting and point of view are used in a fictional language to make them appeal to the whole man. What it implies is that the short story is not a mere narration of an event, but a medium of communicating in totality what a writer has in his mind – a vision of deeper reality of life, its universality, his point of view, the characters which best appealed to him, the fragments of life which have deeply touched him, through the use of rhythm, metaphors, images and symbols so that the appeal of the short story is to the whole man – all his senses and faculties. However, all of them may not be used in the same story. Much will depend on the plot and character as also many other factors, or else it may drift into artificiality.

Joy: A short story is in fact a linguistic construct much in the manner as lyric is. Both the literary forms have marked aesthetic undercurrent. The mode of this construction, however, is bound to differ with respect to the writer's artistic intention. Do you agree?

Srivastava: Yes, I agree. I have already given my views on it in response to one of your earlier questions.

Joy: In lyric, the language is meant to communicate curves and contours of feelings, but with respect to short story, the lyric intention gets naturally displaced or replaced by the writer's sense or meaning of reality. Though the aesthetic motivation of language in both the genres differs, the aesthetic functions remain constant. Have you got more to say about this?

Srivastava: In a short story, the writer's sense or meaning of reality is uppermost. Not so in a lyric where a poet is more concerned with representation of a mood or a feeling aroused by a particular object. Both of them aesthetically aim at a totality of effect.

Joy: In great short stories of the world, it is said, there is a total fusion of the author's technique with his vision. Will you please explain to me how this phenomenon has been successfully achieved in your major short stories?

Srivastava: A total fusion of the author's technique with vision makes a short story undoubtedly great. I tried to achieve it in some of my short stories. For example, the short story "Century" gives a total picture of an Indian student in the U.S.A. where he suffers from a terrible sense of alienation. To achieve this, I had to create in him a feeling of being uprooted and transplanted in a place where life, people, culture – everything is different. The feeling of alienation comes out very well when physical environment, psychic condition of the protagonist, with all his limitations and drawbacks, his muted desires and mounting frustrations are revealed in a language which runs smoothly and gives a visual representation of the inner sufferings. The magazine *Caravan,* (now renamed *Alive,* published by Delhi Press, New Delhi) had selected this short story as one of the ten best short stories during the preceding decade published in the magazine. Many more short stories could be cited as "Friendship, Love and Marriage," "Maharshi Satyanand," "The Human Thirst" and so on, but it is embarrassing for me to say so. You should find them out.

Joy: The fantastic circumstances can be viewed as an economically effective means of revealing characters, interest and emotions. What in your view is the purpose of using fantasy in short story?

Srivastava: As long as fantasy does not fall into the category of improbability, I see nothing wrong in making use of it in a short story in order to achieve its totality of effect. Sometimes fantasy can be used symbolically, as Henry James did in his short stories.

Joy: Everything about a character defines and contributes to the impact on the reader – looks, gestures, attire, social class, words spoken, views held, motives revealed, deeds done or not done. What were the major influences on you to bring about the art of characterisation perfect?

Srivastava: I cannot particularly point out to any major influence on me regarding characterisation. When a character is being presented in a short story, his or her image comes on my mental screen in a three-dimensional form – both inside and outside. Then I speculate and evaluate him or her and decide what traits, gestures, words and other things are to be represented and in which manner. One equips a character for the short story as a traditional Indian-bride-to-be is made presentable before her prospective selectors from every point of view – her complexion, her eyes, her ears, her saree, and even the way she walks and glances around.

Joy: Compression and suggestion working together creates the point of illumination and that in a nutshell is what the short story is all about. Does this statement apply to your stories?

Srivastava: Compression and suggestion are excellent devices which through hints reveal a great deal. However, these things are used much more in those short stories which are read usually by intelligent readers. Common readers of short stories in magazines do not bother to ponder over them. They are like average Hindi movie viewers who have a good time for three hours in a theatre and then forget about the whole thing. Nevertheless, I have used occasionally the devices of compression, suggestion and symbols in short stories like "Friendship, Love and Marriage," "The Handicapped," "Seeds of Democracy," "The Drowning Man," "Terrorists in the Kitchen" and so on, though I do not know how effective they have been. My purpose in most of my short stories has been two-fold: the short story should be interesting to the common reader but to an intelligent one, it may yield many additional hints and suggestions depending upon his capacity and patience in churning it.

Joy: Will you please give the details of the art of the relationship between the story teller, the story and the reader?

Srivastava: The relationship between the writer, the short story and the reader is the same as among the potter, the pot and the buyer, even though the mediums are different. A writer creates a short story which is meant to be read, but while doing so he performs his work to the best of his ability, putting his soul into it, as it were. He makes it so perfect that it becomes the reader's story and he cries out, "I, too, had thought of it but I could not have expressed it so well."

Joy: The substance of the thought of many outstanding short stories remains poetical. The short story has been compared to a lyric. Can it be true of a prose narrative?

Srivastava: Why not? Lyrics and short stories have been written on love, hate, revenge, friendship, etc. It is only the treatment which can make all the difference. Anita Desai shows the incompatibility of man-woman relationship between Gautama and Maya in her novel *Cry, the Peacock* and it reads like sheer poetry. Similar examples can be found in parts in D. H. Lawrence's novel *Lady Chatterley's Lover,* Gustave Flaubert's *Madame Bovary* and Arundhati Roy's *The God of Small Things.* Of course, on the small canvas of a short story, it calls upon the writer's best creative powers.

Joy: The pictures of the great masters of the short stories are said to be vivid and their imagination highly inspired. Will you please comment on this?

Srivastava: The statement is quite true. Rabindranath Tagore's "Kabuliwallah," Mulk Raj Anand's "The Lost Child," O'Henry's "The last Leaf" and "The Gift of Magi." Ernest Hemingway's "A Short Happy Life of Francis Macomber," Munshi Prem Chand's "Chess Players" – one can give a long list of short stories which portray vividly and are examples of highly inspired short stories.

Joy: Your fictional world retains the spirit of Indian culture and also its contact with the western culture with all its diversities and complexities. This world is rich and complex in variety, but at the same time endued with an underlying sense of stability and continuity. What have you got to say more about this?

Srivastava: Since most short stories have Indian culture as their bases, occasional wanderings provide a variety, a change but only to come back to the Indian culture, like a homing pigeon. The ultimate satisfaction is in one's own culture. In "The Human Thirst," the narrator and the truant cow represent this phenomenon. After initial wanderings and set-backs, they come back to their roots disillusioned with their wanderings. In "Love and Animality," Mrs. Chaddha comes ultimately as a devoted wife who would not like to hear of her husband's criticism beyond a point. In "A Drowning Man," the narrator, despite his American experience, remains attached to the Indian culture, which provides both stability and continuity.

Joy: Guy de Maupassant sought to make his stories dramatic.He was prepared to do away with probability to achieve dramatic effect. Is there any such experience in any of your stories?

Srivastava: In my short story "Confession," probability has been sacrificed for dramatic effects. The short story has many dramatic elements of twists, turns and suspense in it. The reader enjoys a series of shocks and surprises. A theatre group in Cuttack (Orissa) took my permission not only to dramatise it on the stage but to make a film on it. Similarly, in "Rescuers," "A Drowning Man," "Terrorists in the Kitchen" probability took a back seat for dramatic effects. But this is for readers, not for me to point out.

Joy: Effective dialogue sounds the way people talk, for dialogue is interaction while the author has to face the most difficult situation of putting an alien tongue into the mouth of his characters whose culture and linguistic background differ widely. How can he compensate for one?

Srivastava: Once a writer begins to write in any language, the characters and their dialogues begin to flow naturally in that very language. If a writer has a command over a particular language, the difficulties are not insurmountable. Occasionally, some expressions in a native language, such as, an idiomatic expression, a saying, a proverb, do pose some problems but a way could always be found as has been done by Raja Rao in *Kanthapura.* Some short stories of mine dealing particularly with rural characters like "The Living Doll," "Seeds of Democracy," "Confession," "Road to Prosperity," did momentarily create problems but with good translations they were managed. The same thing I did in my novel *Neema* which deals with rural life and characters. I had to roll the rural dialogues in my mind to see that they appeared real.

Joy: An exact balance between realistic details and delicate suggestiveness which a short story demands have been achieved in some of your best short stories. Will you please comment on this aspect of the short story?

Srivastava: In my short story "Friendship, Love and Marriage," the realistic details are given about the ways of adopting "friendship" in which neither Maharaja Kumar Chaturvedi nor Loveleen are motivated with a genuine desire for friendship. Both say and do things which are not genuine. The suggestiveness is given by the symbol of the image of Shiva which is thrown in a garbage can by Loveleen implying thereby that selfishness, and not genuine love, was behind her friendship. It is also there when Chaturvedi and Loveleen talk about their possible marriage, there is red traffic light and he had to apply brakes to his car. The image of Venus that Chaturbedi was given by Loveleen had fallen down and was broken. He also threw it in the garbage can. Shiva and Venus represent the East and the West which fail to bring Chaturvedi and Loveleen together and become irrelevant objects. The American girl's knowledge of India actually shows only her ignorance of the country. In "A Drowning Man," the metaphor of drowning has been used for Shyam who himself wanted an Indian virgin but was going ahead flirting with Amelia, Jamie and Cathy and when the Indian girl Sarala tells him that she was also playing the same game in India without being aware of the fact that it was something bad. Shyam's hopes and dreams are shattered and he becomes a drowning man literally when the water-bed develops a leak and metaphorically when his hopes are completely dashed. In "Terrorists in the Kitchen," cats have been found to be more human than the terrorists. Their activities are humanistic whereas those of terrorists are animalistic. In "Cooperative

Colony," everyone poses to be cooperative though the end shows everyone to be otherwise.

Joy: Chekhov once said "medicine is my lawful wife and literature is only my mistress." Have you got any such things to relate about your career as a short story writer?

Srivastava: Without going into the question of medicine and literature, I can say that the more a writer comes into contact with human beings – men, women and children – the more his works ring with reality. It differs from person to person as to who comes as medicine and who as literature, but each one has a contribution to make in the enrichment of a short story. A writer's mind is like the hard disk of a computer in which all sorts of things are recorded but which can be recalled at any given moment.

Joy: It is seen that after Manjeri Iswaran, you are the only Indian English writer who rose to fame only by attempting at short story writing as the most favourable art form. What have you got to say about this?

Srivastava: In response to one of your questions, I have already told you that I have not read Manjari Iswaran's short stories. As far as your words "You are the only Indian English writer who rose to fame by attempting at short story writing as the most favorable art form," I can humbly say that I cannot rightly claim this honor. There are writers like R. K. Narayan, Raja Rao, Khushwant Singh, Ruskin Bond and many more who have better claim to this honour.

Joy: It is often found that creative artists are poor critics and great critics are poor creative artists. In your case you have attained more or less equal attainment in both the faculties. What made you to make this unique achievement? You may have definitely to say more about both the faculties.

Srivastava: To some extent, you are right that, at least in India, creative writers have not been found to be good critics and vice versa. Not so in English and American

Literature. In British Literature, we have William Wordsworth, Samuel Taylor Coleridge, Matthew Arnold, T. S. Eliot and E. M. Forster whereas in American Literature, we have Edgar Allan Poe, Nathaniel Hawthorne, Henry James and many more. Basically, my soul is in creative writing in the composition of which I find real pleasure. Critical writing is a professional necessity which gives me bread and butter. It is so shocking and illogical that creative writing in India is not considered respectable. A university teacher who writes short stories is ridiculed among his colleagues as a "teller of *kisse-kahani*" (tales and short stories) but if the same teacher writes anything critical on others' short stories, novels and poems, he is considered a respectable person endowed with a critical faculty. In most American universities, creative writing programs are operated either independently or as parts of Departments of English Language and Literature. Serious students who have creative talents are encouraged to take up courses in creative writing – fiction or poetry from the very first year of their university education, whereas on maturity, they are encouraged to work towards Master's or Ph.D. degrees in creative writing – usually poetry or fiction. In addition, they also take up courses in critical studies. The result is that good students develop both creative and critical faculties. Not so in India. Here only one or two universities have started creative writing programs but they are yet to attain respectability.

CHAPTER 24

Looking Behind His Short Stories: An Interview with Ramesh K. Srivastava

Smita Das

[Ramesh K. Srivastava has been a Professor of English at Guru Nanak Dev University, Amritsar; Bundelkhand University, Jhansi and now S. R. Group of Institutions, Ambabai, Jhansi (U.P.). He was awarded Fulbright and Senior Fulbright Fellowships for advanced studies in the U.S.A. With a Ph.D. degree from the University of Utah, Salt Lake City, Utah (U.S.A.), he has published about 21 books of critical and creative writing in English, including two novels – *Neema* and *Coils of the Serpent* as well as six collections of short stories titled *Love and Animality, Cooperative Colony, Masks and Men, Under the Lamp, Games They Play* and *A Christmas Gift and Other Stories.*]

Das: I have gone through all your novels, short stories, essays and interviews. Besides, I have also gone through all the critical articles and book reviews which have been published on your creative writing. I still have numerous queries which arise probably from my anxiety to find out what went into the background of some of these memorable short stories. The queries are mostly about your motivation, sources of your characters, incidents and dialogues and the degree of realism in them. But before I take up these queries, first of all let me ask you: what in your opinion is a good short story?

Srivastava: I am happy that you have taken so much interest in my creative writing, particularly in my short stories. Since you have already read my interviews, I wish to remind you that this question I have answered many times, particularly in my interview with Dr Atma Ram in which I had pointed out that "a good short story is a frozen moment of life revealed through a sequence of words. It must be short, readable and meaningful." In one of my essays titled "My Idea of a Short Story," I have given a detailed idea of my short story. There is no point in repeating my views again.

Das: What is your basic motivation behind writing novels and short stories?

Srivastava: This question too has been answered many times. In my interview with Dr M. L. Mehta, I had pointed out that "Creative writing is definitely an expression of one's irrepressible urges. Through it, I try to fictionalise my experiences – real, vicarious and even imaginary." I stand by this statement.

Das: When I read a short story of yours, I fail to figure out how much of it has been based on reality and how much from your fertile imagination. To what extent, do you modify your characters, incidents or action of the stories?

Srivastava: Your failure to segregate reality from imagination in my stories is indirectly a compliment to my creativity because each story must appear real and probable. However, for the satisfaction of your curiosity, I may add here that quite a few of my characters and incidents have been modeled on persons I have met or observed in real life but not in their entirety. A trait in one character or an aspect of another character must have been taken from real life but they have been fused with additional details from my imagination. They have been modified in order to make the stories effective so that the totality of effect on the reader is the greatest. The questions which haunt your mind cannot be answered categorically because each work of art is a unique creation of its own kind and is different from others. Hence, unless you name a specific situation, incident, character or dialogue, I cannot precisely answer your question.

Das: Let me take your first story "The Living Doll." We have two fascinating but contrasting characters – Kashi and Darua. Are they real? Did you meet them in real life?

Srivastava: Kashi and Darua along with their names have been taken from real life. Both of them worked as agricultural laborers for us for many years in my village Banpur. Kashi was dumb-witted whereas Darua was sharp. Kashi was healthy and muscular whereas Darua was intelligent but physically weak. When my first short story was published in India, I was in the U.S.A. I showed the published short story to my professor Dr William Mulder and he thought that I had imitated two characters Lennie and George from John Steinbeck's novel *Of Mice and Men.* I don't blame him because these characters are identical to Kashi and Darua, but I did not have Steinbeck's characters in mind at all. The character of Karni, wife of Darua, is completely from my imagination and has some base in real life only to the extent that I saw – and still see – many such women among laborers in my village and elsewhere.

Das: Is it true that the story "A Drowning Man" has been transformed from a joke heard all over the world, of course, with some variations?

Srivastava: To some extent, yes. The story has been transformed from a joke which is also prevalent in India. The fact is that I had seen many Indians in the U.S. going around with American girls for fun but thinking of marrying simple girls in India for obvious reasons because they are likely to be simple and pure. The coloring and the details are from my observation of life in the U.S. so that the story appears realistic.

Das: In "Century," the minute details about Mohan's suffering from an acute sense of alienation and his unfulfilled sexual adventure somehow give the impression that they are autobiographical. What are your comments?

Srivastava: You are not the first person to have such an impression. Since the story is written in the first person narrative, my colleagues at Guru Nanak Dev University, Amritsar scandalised me by interpreting it as an account of my personal experiences. Let me clarify it: a writer has two kinds of experiences – direct and vicarious. I had personal experiences of alienation, particularly after leaving my wife and very small sons in India. Hence Mohan's suffering from acute sense of alienation is really what most students, including I personally experienced in the U.S. The feeling of loneliness is occasionally so poignant that one often gets addicted to liquor, drugs, sex and so on. With my wife and children in India, I did not want to have intimate relationship with American girls, fearing problems and complications. As far as minute depiction of Mohan's unfulfilled sexual venture is concerned, I came across many of my friends who narrated minutely their exploits in this area and that too with a sense of pride. Jasbir's character is modeled on a real Indian student in the Engineering Department of the same university.

Das: In "Ganga Ma," you have written about many women and children who mistook the flow of water from the underground pipe burst as the miraculous appearance of the Ganga Ma. Is such a thing possible in the 20th century India?

Srivastava: The story is based on a wide-spread English newspaper report published from Chandigarh in which a couple of ladies and children had died due to exposure from cold because they had taken a dip in the cold water from the underground pipe burst, mistaking it for Ganga Ma, on the occasion of Makar Sankranti even when it was freezing cold.

Das: The story "Lasting Victory" seems to highlight the plight of women in a predominantly men's college. Does it have a base in reality?

Srivastava: The story is based on a real incident in Medical College, Amritsar in which Dr Sita Sharma, a lady doctor, had taken the risk of boarding the public bus which the medical students had hijacked over the campus and had threatened to burn it. After a surprise move of suddenly boarding the bus, Dr Sita Sharma had told the students clearly that they would have to burn the bus along with her and that she would not get down from the bus unless they abandon the idea of burning it. The students had to abandon the idea. Her heroic act was reported in most newspapers of the Punjab state. Of course, other episodes and details are from my imagination.

Das: In "Rescuers," you have shown four male characters belonging to different religions – Hindu, Muslim, Sikh and Christian. Does the story not look like a parable rather than a realistic one?

Srivastava: The story is based on a real incident. One of my friends Mr. Jawahar Singh Dhaka had witnessed it in Amritsar on an evening when he was going for a walk. He had seen three boys forcibly lifting a school-going girl, making her forcibly sit on the pillion of their motorbike, while the girl went on pathetically crying for help. Mr Dhaka was deeply disturbed in not being able to help the miserable teenager because, by being alone and unarmed, he could not have done anything to help her. This was the reality. I converted it into a story which, as you say, looks like a parable. My purpose in making them belonging to different religions was to point out that human beings are basically the same everywhere and religions become incidental in the matter.

Das: It appears that in this story, you have sacrificed probability for the dramatic effect.

Srivastava: Guy de Maupassant was prepared to sacrifice probability for the sake of dramatic effect in his stories. In this story, as also in "The Confession," probability has certainly taken a back seat. There are many dramatic elements of twists, turns and suspense. The reader enjoys shocks and surprises even if they appear to be improbable. A theatre group in Cuttack not only dramatised "The Confession" successfully but also converted it into a regional movie. In "Rescuers," Neeru dramatically brings an anti-climax by hitting Father Sault with her knives and converts the victimizer into a victim and vice versa.

Das: In "The Handicapped," you have touched a very controversial and burning problem for jobs. In many cases, the reservations of jobs certainly appear quite illogical. Any particular incident which inspired you to write this story?

Srivastava: There is no particular incident but I firmly believe that the irrational way in which reservation for various categories has been done pained a very large number of people, particularly those who are capable but are not being given a chance to work because of the reservation system. To give the job of a typist to a person whose both hands were chopped off is the height of irrationality in this reservation system.

Das: Two short stories "Cooperative Colony" and "Seeds of Democracy" point out, among other things, to the unprincipled politics prevalent in our country. Did you have any particular incident in mind which inspired you to write them?

Srivastava: I was born under the British colonial rule and grew up in the politically independent India. Contrasting the two regimes, my father and other people of the village openly discussed and confessed that the British regime in administration was much better than the one by corrupt and unprincipled politicians of independent India. As I became mature, I too noticed the duplicity of these corrupt politicians who announced rosy visions and tempting schemes for the poor people but which in reality turned out to be clever moves for winning elections, grabbing power and making money. I also noticed a gradual decline in moral values, administration, education, and so on which I have portrayed with wit and humour in "Cooperative Colony." Having observed the real democratic practices in the U.S.A., I found in India only loud-mouthed professions of democratic principles but no real democracy has been existent, as has been portrayed in "Seeds of Democracy." I have also written this fact in my essays titled "An Essentially Democratic Country," "Democracy in India: Secular or

Seculiar," "Unanimity" and many other essays in this connection.

Das: Your short story "A Known Witness" points out to the corruption in banks. Did you experience it yourself?

Srivastava: Yes. I did observe it in banks, post offices and telegraph departments which at one time enjoyed the reputation for honesty. I complained in writing against such incidents. What I have pointed out in the story is a tip of the iceberg whereas corruption is rampant in every department of the country.

Das: I have a feeling that "An Ugly Duckling" has been inspired by Anderson's story. Is it true?

Srivastava: A writer cannot always precisely point out the sources of his inspiration. I had read these western tales at various levels and cannot deny being inspired by some of them.

Das: In Hans Christian Anderson's story, it is "THE Ugly Duckling" whereas in your story, it is "An Ugly Duckling." Any reason for using the indefinite article in your story?

Srivastava: Anderson uses the definite article before ugly duckling, probably because he might be pointing out to one definite case. In my story, I wanted to make Shyamali a representative of all such female – and even male – characters who are looked down upon because of various drawbacks in their personalities, such as, complexion, caste, facial features, height, weight, etc. The same idea I have used in "A Short Work" where Garima is looked down upon because of her short height but wins everyone's heart because of her courageous feats.

Das: Your "Untold Story" is quite a pathetic account of washerwoman Sundari and her sacrifice for her son. Is she modeled on some real person?

Srivastava: Some traits of Sundari are from our present washerwoman who is very cool headed. One day, Mrs. Srivastava and I, feeling pity over her miserable plight because of her husband's habit of drinking, tried to blame him, but she, being a devoted wife, coolly justified her husband's occasional drinks because of his hard work in such an old age. This was the seed out of which the whole story grew. Since I have been in Rewa and Gwalior cities, those locations have been taken for the story.

Das: I suspect that "A Matter of Pride" could be associated with your village, as it depicts the rural situation with superstitious beliefs about education of girls. What do you say?

Srivastava: The story is largely about my eldest Bua – Ram Kunwar – whose education was criticised by the village people even after she had become a widow within a year of her marriage. But my grandfather had vision and he started a girls' school in our own house in the village in opposition to the village people who had strong superstitious belief that an educated girl becomes a widow and hence strongly resisted their daughters from joining the school. Gradually, they came round. Her familial and moral activities at home and in the village are still remembered.

Das: It appears from some very short stories that you have over compressed them whereas in others you are happily elaborate in giving minute details. Any reason?

Srivastava: There are two kinds of stories. There has been no restriction on the use of number of words in the short stories meant for popular magazines as long as the story happened to be interesting. For publication in literary journals, there is a fixed limit of words within which I have to fit in my short story even if it appears rather cramped. One cannot help in the matter. To give some examples: "Century," "A Drowning Man" and "Friendship, Love and Marriage" are fairly long as they were published in Indian popular magazines whereas "An Ugly Duckling," "A Short Work" and "A Matter of Pride," among others, have been published in literary journals and as such no detailed characterisation or element of humour could be introduced in them.

Select Bibliography

Primary Sources

Creative Writing

Love and Animality: Stories. Calcutta: Writers Workshop, 1984.

Cooperative Colony: Stories. Calcutta: Writers Workshop, 1985.

Neema (a novel in English). Calcutta: Writers Workshop, 1986; republished as *Neema: A Village Girl.* New Delhi: Authorspress, 2019.

Masks and Men: Stories. Calcutta: Writers Workshop, 1986.

Games They Play and Other Stories. New Delhi: Prestige Books, 1989.

Under the Lamp: Stories. Jalandhar: ABS Publications, 1993.

Coils of the Serpent (a novel). New Delhi: Authorspress, 2011.

Read, Write and Teach: Essays on Learning to Live Together. New Delhi: Authorspress, 2014.

A Christmas Gift and Other Stories. New Delhi: Authorspress, 2015.

My Father's Bad Boy: An Autobiography. New Delhi: Authorspress, 2017.

Road Not Taken and Other Stories. New Delhi: Authorspress, 2018.

A Man of Gold and Other Stories. New Delhi: Authorspress, 2022.

Critical Writing

Determinism in Hemingway. Amritsar: Guru Nanak Dev University, 1975 (monograph).

Hemingway and his For Whom the Bell Tolls. Amritsar: Guru Nanak Dev University, 1980.

Perspectives on Bhabani Bhattacharya (Edited). Ghaziabad: Vimal Prakashan, 1982.

Thoreau's *Walden* (with an Introduction and annotations). New Delhi: Oxford University Press, 1983.

Perspectives on Anita Desai (Edited). Ghaziabad: Vimal Prakashan, 1984.

Six Indian Novelists in English.. Amritsar: Guru Nanak Dev University, 1987.

Colonial Consciousness in Black American, African and Indian Fiction in English (Edited). Jalandhar: ABS Publications, 1991.

Critical Studies in English and American Literature. Jalandhar: ABS Publications, 1993.

Symbolism in Indian Fiction in English (Edited). Jalandhar: ABS Publications, 1997.

The Novels of Kamala Markandaya: A Critical Study. Amritsar: Guru Nanak Dev University, 1998.

Ten Indian English Writers. Jalandhar: ABS Publications, 2005.

Wit and Humour in Indian English Literature (Edited). Jalandhar: ABS Publications, 2008.

Interviews

Das, Smita. "A Good Short Story is a Frozen Moment of Life Revealed through a Sequence of Words: An Interview with Ramesh K. Srivastava." *Illuminati: A Transnational Refereed Journal of Literature, Language and Culture Studies*. Vol. VII (2016-17), pp. 18-24.

Joy, Y. "Ramesh K. Srivastava in Conversation with Y. Joy." *The Critical Endeavour,* Vol. XIX (January 2013), pp. 203-227.

Mehta, M. L. "Interview with Ramesh K. Srivastava." *The Critical Endeavour,* Vol. VIII (December 2002), pp. 167-179.

Ram, Atma. "Ramesh K. Srivastava," *Interviews with Indians Writing in English* (Ed). Atma Ram. Calcutta: Writers Workshop, 1992, pp. 14-24.

Secondary Sources

Critical Book

Das, Smita (Ed.). *Ramesh K. Srivastava: Man and His Work*. New Delhi: Authorspress, 2016.

Vashishtha, Shipra G. (Ed). *The Recognition of Ramesh K. Srivastava: A Collection of Book Reviews on his Creative Writing*. New Delhi: Authorspress, 2020

Critical Articles

Agrawal, Priyanka and Sadhana Agrawal. "Freedom of Women in K. S. Duggal's 'Butterfly' and Ramesh K. Srivastava's 'The Prodigal Returns.'" *Chronicle of Humanities and Cultural Studies,* Vol. IV, No. 1 (January 2018), 36-38.

.... "Sufferings of Women in Ramesh K. Srivastava's Short Stories," *New Man International Journal of Multidisciplinary Studies,* Vol. VI, Issue 8 (August 2019), 53-56.

Bande, Usha. "Loving Vignettes – Mother Figure in R. K. Srivastava's Short Stories." *Mother Figure in Indian English Fiction* (Ed). Usha Bande. Jalandhar: ABS Publications, 1997, pp.142-147.

Das, Smita. "Authenticity of Rural Life in Chinua Achebe, Kamala Markandaya and Ramesh K. Srivastava." *International Journal of Multicultural Literature*. Vol. VII. No. 2 (July 2017), pp. 85-92.

........, "Empowerment of Women in Ramesh K. Srivastava's *A Christmas Gift and Other Stories." International Journal of Multicultural Literature.* Vol. VII, No. 1 (January 2017), pp. 89-95.

.... "Human-Animal Relationship in Ramesh K. Srivastava's Short Stories," *Writers Editors Critics: An International Biannual Refereed Journal of English Language and Literature.* Vol. VIII, No. 1 (March 2018), 118-123.

.... "Imagery in Ramesh K. Srivastava's *Neema." MIT International Journal of English Language* & *Literature.* Vol. I. No. 2. (August 2014), pp. 72-77.

.... "Loss of Identity of Chandan Mohan in Srivastava's *Coils of the Serpent." MIT International Journal of English Language and Literature,* Vol. III, No. 1 (January 2016), pp. 60-65.

.... "Making Essays Palatable: An Analysis of Ramesh K. Srivastava's Views and Expressions in *Read, Write and Teach: Essays on Learning to Live Together." Illuminati: A Transnational Refereed Journal of Literature, Language and Culture Studies.* Vol. VI (January-December 2015-16), pp. 122-130.

.... "Najama as Serpent in Ramesh K. Srivastava's *Coils of the Serpent." International Journal on Multicultural Literature.* Vol. III, No. 1 (January 2013), pp.131-138.

.... "Pangs of Lacerated Psyche – An Analysis of Ramesh K. Srivastava's *My Father's Bad Boy: An Autobiography." Writers, Editors, Critics: An International Biannual Journal of English Language and Literature.* Vol. VII, No. 2 (September 2017), pp. 46-52.

.... "Ramesh K. Srivastava's 'Games They Play': A Study," *Illuminati: A Transnational Refereed Journal of Literature, Language and Culture Studies.* Vol. IV (2013-14), pp. 105-110.

.... "Suppression and Revolt in Ramesh K. Srivastava's Short Stories," *Writers Editors Critics: An International Biannual Refereed Journal of English Language and Literature,* Vol. VIII, No. 2 (September 2018), 43-49.

.... "Theory and Practice of Ramesh K. Srivastava's Short Story," *MIT International Journal of English Language and Literature.* Vol. III, No. 2 (January 2016), pp. 30-35.

Jha, Pashupati. "Truly a Professor's Novel: Ramesh Srivastava's *Coils of the Serpent.*" *The Indian Journal of English Studies.* Vol. XLIX (2012), pp. 241-246.

Kanal, Leela. "Conflict and Resolution: A Study of Srivastava's *A Christmas Gift and Other Stories.*" *Illuminati: A Transnational Journal of Literature, Language and Culture Studies.* Vol. VII (2016-17), 138-146.

.... "East-West Encounter in Ramesh K. Srivastava's Short Stories," *International Journal on Multicultural Literature,* Vol. XI, No. 1 (January 2021), 37-43.

Maini, Neeta. "R. K. Srivastava," *Studies in Contemporary Indian-English Short Story: A Collection of Critical Essays,* Ed. A. N. Dwivedi. Delhi: B. R. Publishing Corporation. 1991, pp. 185-197.

Mishra, Lata. "Literary Representation of Community, Culture and Ideology: A Study of Ramesh K. Srivastava's *Coils of the Serpent.*" *Writers, Editors, Critics: An International Biannual Refereed Journal of English Language and Literature.* Vol. III, No. 2 (September 2013), pp. 41-47.

.........."Narrative as Discourse: A Study of Ramesh K. Srivastava's Under the Lamp: Stories." *Virtuoso: A Refereed Transnational Bi-Annual Journal of Language and Literature in English.* Vol. II, No. 2 (February 2013), pp. 17-24.

.... "Silence, Wound and Choice: Disciplining of the Female Body in Srivastava's *Neema.*" *Poetcrit: An International Refereed Bi-annual Journal of Literary Criticism and Contemporary Poetry.* Vol. XXVI, No. 2 (July 2013), pp. 77-82.

Purwar, Alka Rani. "Indian Sensibility: A Reading of Ramesh K. Srivastava's *Coils of the Serpent." Nativism: Indian English Fiction* (Ed.) J. P. Singh. New Delhi: Radha Publications, 2014, pp. 49-55.

Ram, Atma and R. K. Dhawan, "Contemporary Indian Short Story" in Ramesh K. Srivastava's *Games They Play and Other Stories.* New Delhi: Prestige Books, 1989, pp. 13-18.

Ram, Atma. "R. K. Srivastava: A Writer of Simple Ways." *Indian Poetry and Fiction in English.* New Delhi: Bahri Publications, 1991, pp. 71-73.

.... "Ramesh K. Srivastava," *Interviews with Indian Writers in English* (Ed.) Atma Ram. Calcutta: Writers Workshop, 1992, pp. 14-24.

Sethi, Vijay Mohan and Satnam Kaur, "The White and the Brown: Colonial Encounter in the Short Stories of Khushwant Singh and Ramesh K. Srivastava." *Colonial Consciousness in Black American, African and Indian Fiction in English.* (Ed). Ramesh K. Srivastava. Jalandhar: ABS Publications, 1991, pp. 199-212.

Sharma, Barinder K. "Human Follies, Curses and Punishments in Ramesh K Srivastava's *Coils of the Serpent." The Aesthetica* (2012), pp. 40-50.

.... "Ramesh K. Srivastava's 'Century': A Study," *Poetcrit: An International Biannual Refereed Journal of literary Criticism and Contemporary Poetry.* Vol. XXXIV, No. 1 (January-June 2021), 54-58.

.... "Symbolism in Ramesh K. Srivastava's *Cooperative Colony: Stories* and *Masks and Men: Stories.*" *International Journal on Multicultural Literature.* Vol. XI, No. 1 (January 2021), 44-49.

.........."Symbolism in Ramesh K. Srivastava's *Neema,*" *Symbolism in Indian Fiction in English* (Ed.) Ramesh K. Srivastava. Jalandhar: ABS Publications, 1997, pp. 211-220.

.........."Tragic Realities of Human Ambitions in Ramesh K. Srivastava's *Coils of the Serpent." Pragati's English Journal.* Vol. XI. No. 2 (December 2011), pp. 1-8.

Sharma, Jayanti. "Neema – A Victim of Society," *Victim Consciousness in Indian-English Novel.* Ed. Usha Bande. Jalandhar: ABS Publications, 1997, pp.134-140.

Sharma, Manisha. "Irony, Humour and Satire in Ramesh K. Srivastava's 'Cooperative Colony,'" *Indian Scholar: An International Multidisciplinary Research e-Journal.* Vol. I, Issue II (December 2014), pp. 195-199.

Srivastava, Swati. "Wit and Humour in the Works of Ramesh K. Srivastava." *Stars Behind the Clouds: Unexplored Indian Writers in English* (Ed.). Syed Mashkoor Ali. Jaipur: Surabhi Publications, 2004. pp. 89-106.

Tewari, Anil Kumar, "Psychodynamics of Power Discourse in Srivastava's *Games They Play*," *Panjab Journal of English Studies*, Vol. VII. (1992), pp. 45-53.

Tripathi, Gurdeep. "Dream and Reality in Ramesh K. Srivastava's 'Road Not Taken,'" *International Journal on Multicultural Literature,* Vol. IX, No. 2 (July 2019), 80-85.

.... "Love and Exploitation in Ramesh K. Srivastava's *Road Not Taken and Other Stories.*" *Writers Editors Critics: An International Refereed Biannual Journal of English Language and Literature.* Vol. X (March and September 2020), 35-41.

Vashishtha, Shipra G., "Masks and Masqueraders in Ramesh K. Srivastava's Short Stories," *International Journal of Multicultural Literature.* Vol. VIII, No. 1 (January 2018), pp. 92-98.

.... "Ramesh K. Srivastava's 'Under the Lamp': A Study," *Writers, Editors, Critics: An International Biannual Journal of English Language and Literature.* Vol. VII, No. 1 (March 2017), pp. 48-54.

Notes on the Editor and Contributors

1. **Barinder K. Sharma** is Associate Professor in the Department of English, Baring Union Christian College, Batala (Gurdaspur), Punjab. He is a researcher, critic and book reviewer who has published about 40 research articles and book reviews in national and international journals. During his academic career of three decades, he has presented research papers in a large number of national and international seminars and conferences.
2. **Priyanka Agrawal** completed her research work and has been awarded a Ph.D. degree by Jiwaji University, Gwalior (M.P.) on "Socio-Cultural Issues in the Fictional Writing of Ramesh K. Srivastava and Kartar Singh Duggal: A Critical Study." She has also published some research papers in national journals.
3. **Sadhana Agrawal** is Professor and Head, Department of English, Government Maharani Laxmi Bai Autonomous College, Gwalior (M.P.). She has published her research papers in many national and international journals.
4. **Usha Bande** till recently Fellow, Indian Institute of Advanced Study, Shimla and also Visiting Professor at Vishwa Bharati University, Shanti Niketan (West Bengal), was on the faculty of English in Government College for Women, Shimla. She retired as the Principal, Government College, Arki (H.P.). She has a dozen books and numerous research papers to her credit. She completed a major U.G.C. project on the Indian Short Stories in 1998. Besides academic writing, Dr Bande is fond of journalistic and creative writing.
5. **Smita Das** is the former Assistant Professor of English, S. R. Group of Institutions, Ambabai, Jhansi (U.P.). Besides being the editor of the book *Ramesh K. Srivastava – Man and his Work: A Collection of Critical Essays,* she has published many critical articles and research papers in national and international journals.

6. **Y. Joy** is Lecturer in English, Mahatma Gandhi University, Research Centre in English, C.M.S. College, Kottayam (Kerala). He was awarded a Ph.D. degree on "The Short Stories of Ramesh K. Srivastava" by Mahatma Gandhi University, Kottayam (Kerala).
7. **Leela Kanal** is retired Associate Professor and Head, Department of English, Bundelkhand College, Jhansi (U.P.). Besides authoring a book *Temporality and Turmoil, Ernest Hemingway: A Study of Revolt and Affirmation in His Novels,* she has published a number of research papers and book reviews in many national and international journals.
8. **Neeta Maini** (R. Dhawan) has been Assistant Professor of English, B.B.K. D.A.V. College for Women, Amritsar (Punjab).
9. **Lata Mishra** is the editor of *Labyrinth: An International Refereed Journal of Post-modern Studies.* She also edits *World Journal of Gender and Literature (WJGL)* published by Authors Press, New Delhi. She has been teaching English Literature at Kamla Raja Girls Postgraduate Autonomous College, Gwalior (M.P.) since 1994. Besides authoring six books, she has published more than 45 research papers in various international and national journals.
10. **Atma Ram** academician, educationalist and writer, taught English Literature and Language for over three decades in H.P. University, Shimla and other government colleges. He occupied various administrative posts, such as, College Principal, Joint Director Colleges, Director of Education and Education Advisor. He published over three dozen books and guided several Ph.D. and M.Phil scholars. He lives at Sat Sadan, Sessions Road, Kotwali Bazar, Dharmasala (H.P.).
11. **Manisha Sharma** has a Ph.D. degree on "Diasporic Sensibility in the Novels of Bharati Mukherjee and Jhumpa Lahiri." She teaches in the Department of English, Bundelkhand University, Jhansi (U.P.)
12. **Ramesh K. Srivastava** is Professor of English at S. R. Group of Institutions, Ambabai, Jhansi (U.P.). Earlier to it, he was Professor and Head, Department of English and Dean, Faculty of Languages, Guru Nanak Dev University, Amritsar (Punjab). He also remained the Director, Institute of Languages, Bundelkhand College, Jhansi (U.P.). He got his Ph.D. degree from the University of Utah, Salt Lake City, Utah (U.S.A.) in 1972. He was

awarded a prestigious Fulbright (U.S. Government) Fellowship in 1969, the University of Utah Graduate Research Fellowship (U.S.A.) in 1970-72, Senior Fulbright (U.S. Government) Fellowship in 1984-85 and the University Grants Commission Emeritus Fellowship in 2003-05. He is a novelist, an essayist and a short story writer. He has published 24 books in English, including two novels *Neema: A Village Girl, Coils of the Serpent* and an autobiography *My Father's Bad Boy.*

13. **Swati Srivastava** worked as Lecturer in English, Institute of Languages, Bundelkhand University, Jhansi (U.P.)
14. **Gurdeep Tripathi** is Lecturer in English, Bundelkhand University, Jhansi (U.P.). She attended many seminars and conferences. She has also published research papers and book reviews in various national and international journals.
15. **Shipra G. Vashishtha** is Coordinator, Department of English, Bundelkhand University, Jhansi (U.P.). She edited a book *The Recognition of Ramesh K. Srivastava: A Collection of Book Reviews on his Creative Writing.* She has also published a number of research papers and book reviews in national and international journals.

Index